SVEN TÀ

editor

Ethnicity and Nation Building in the Nordic World

HURST & COMPANY, LONDON

This work has been sponsored by the Joint Committee of the
Nordic Research Councils for the Humanities.
Linguistic Coordinator: Richard Fisher
Translators: Jasmine Aimaq, Roy Dunford, Richard Fisher,
Ilja Wechselmann
Maps: Tomas Tägil
Editorial Assistant: Kerstin Nyström

First published in the United Kingdom by
C. Hurst & Co. (Publishers) Ltd.,
38 King Street, London WC2E 8JT
© Sven Tägil, 1995
All rights reserved.
Printed in Hong Kong

ISBNs
1-85065-216-3 (cased)
1-85065-239-2 (pbk)

CONTENTS

NOTES ON THE CO-AUTHORS

HANS JACOB DEBES, born 1940, Professor at Fróðskaparsetur Føroya, Tórshavn. Ph.D 1984, University of Iceland, with dissertation *Nú er tann stundin … Tjóðskaparrørsla og sjálvstýrispolitikkur til 1906* (1982), on nationalism and independence movements in the Faroe Islands in the 19th century.

MAX ENGMAN, born 1945, Ph.D 1983. Professor of history at the Åbo Academy, editor of *Historisk Tidskrift för Finland*. Publications include *St. Petersburg och Finland: Migration och influens 1703-1917* (1983), *Kaksoiskotka ja Leijona* (1992), and *Mannen i kolboxen: John Reed och Finland* (1979, with Jerker A. Eriksson). Has edited *Ethnic Identity in Urban Europe* (1992), and *Finland: People, Nation, State* (1989, with David Kirby).

GUNNAR KARLSSON, born 1939, Professor of Icelandic History at the University of Iceland, Reykjavík. Ph.D 1978. Has studied Iceland's political history in the 19th century and the High Middle Ages as well as theoretical questions, and has published a number of history textbooks.

AXEL KJÆR SØRENSEN, born 1937, lecturer at the University of Aarhus. Has specialized in the history of Greenland. Publications include *Grønlandsk nationalisme* (1979).

EINAR NIEMI, born 1943, M.A with major in History, Oslo, 1972. County Curator in Finnmark and Professor of History at the University of Tromsø. Has published *Oppbrudd og tilpassing* (1977), *Den finske fare* (with Knut E. Eriksen, 1981), and *Vadsøs historie* (1983).

viii   *Notes on the Co-Authors*

LORENZ RERUP, born 1928, in Flensburg, educated at the University of Copenhagen, Professor of Modern History at Roskilde University Centre. Has focused on researching the history of Denmark and Southern Jutland in the 19th and 20th centuries, and the nationality problem.

HARALD RUNBLOM, born 1939, Associate Professor of History at the University of Uppsala. Doctoral dissertation: *Svenska företag i Latinamerika* (1971). Director of the Emigration Research Project, Uppsala, Head of the Centre for Multiethnic Research, Uppsala.

HELGE SALVESEN, born 1947, Chief Librarian at the University Library at Tromsø, and Professor of History at the University of Tromsø. Has focused on settlement history in early times, Sami history and methodic/theoretical problems as well as historiography. Ph.D 1983 with dissertation *Fire forskningsfaser i studiet av bosetning og bruksmåter i det gamle bondesamfunn*.

SVEN TÄGIL, born 1930, Professor of Empirical Conflict Research at the Council for Research in the Humanities and Social Sciences. Ph.D 1962, University of Lund, with dissertation *Valdemar Atterdag och Europa*. Other publications include *Deutschland und die deutsche Minderheit in Nordschleswig* (1970), *Studying Boundary Conflicts* (ed.) (1977), *Regions in Upheaval (ed.) (1984)*.

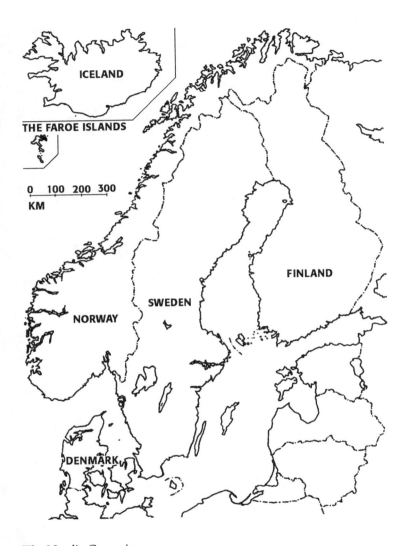

The Nordic Countries

INTRODUCTION

Sven Tägil

Throughout history, people have organized themselves into groups in order to optimize the realization of their common interests. Originally, the elementary requirements for survival were of prime importance; subsequently, the focus shifted to the possibilities of self-realization within the framework of a common culture and mode of communication.

Over the course of time, there has emerged a sense of solidarity which has stressed the importance of shared experiences, and endowed them with special significance. Emphasis has been placed on a presumed common heritage, even though such a presumption has often become shrouded in the mists of the mythical past. What we have done, actually, is to share mutual historical experiences; we have developed life styles, manners and customs that we perceive as the fundamental components of our common identity. One crucial prerequisite for the continuing existence of such a society—one based on identity—is that everyone should have access to a common language.

The evolution of such identities is a dynamic process, and the changes occur so slowly that they cannot be observed by the individual member of society. This implies, at the same time, that the degree of continuity is remarkably high. A sense of solidarity, once acquired, is difficult to expunge, and to effect changes in such an identity by means of external force is practically impossible.

Although the basic features of such identity processes may appear similar in different cultures and in different temporal contexts, it is nevertheless clear that both forms and contents vary dramatically. Even the earliest high cultures recorded in history have emerged from populations who have lived together and developed social

1

structures anchored in specific geographical areas. "History" has often been apprehended as the story of a people, and in this context, "people" has referred to a sizeable group of human beings who have had certain biological features in common, or at least a sense of a common origin, and who have been perceived both by themselves and by those around them as comprising some kind of cultural community.

Issues involving ethnicity and nation building have also had great relevance in the part of northern Europe customarily designated as the Nordic region. There are five independent states in this region today—Denmark including the autonomous Faroe Islands and Greenland, Finland including the autonomous Åland Islands, and Iceland, Norway and Sweden. In addition to the sovereign states and autonomous regions, there are also several different nations, ethnic groups, cultures, languages and regional identities. In the international context, the relations among the various states, peoples and groups in the Nordic region are regarded as exemplarily peaceful, displaying many shared values and interests. Indeed, against the background of all the national and ethnic antagonisms characterizing contemporary international developments, such a positive image of the Nordic region is by and large correct.

Today's relations, however, are the result of a long historical process which has by no means always been peaceful and unproblematic. The method of resolving conflicts between states and peoples, and the problems of coexistence among ethnic majorities and minorities, is also based on unique historical experiences. With this background in mind, it is interesting to investigate both what distinguishes the ethno-national development in the Nordic region, and whether there may be some Nordic model for the resolution of interethnic conflicts.

In a continental perspective, the history of the Nordic peoples is peripheral. The Nordic region has been an outlying area which contributed to the cultural development of Europe only at a relatively late stage. The earliest known societies in the region were clans based on common descent, that is to say biological kinship. During the Viking period and the early Middle Ages (800–1200), more permanent structures of government organized on a territorial basis gradually emerged. During the Nordic High Middle Ages, the clan societies developed into state societies. The territorial division manifested in the earliest Nordic state formations was derived from the settlement structures of prehistoric times, but in many cases it proved possible to adjust it to meet the needs of the growing state at a later stage.

This pattern of territorial organization applied in principle to all the main areas of settlement in the Nordic region. Just as we can distinguish a number of ethnic groups, each linked to a definite geographical area, we can also distinguish different provinces or "historical regions", each with its own institutions and identities.

The first states in the Nordic region—Denmark, Norway and Sweden—emerged in the 10th and 11th centuries. Ethnically and culturally, all three were closely related, but this did not prevent political and military confrontation between them.

In the North Atlantic, nation building also began early on Iceland, based on a culture that can be described as West Nordic.

The struggle for hegemony in the Nordic region had different outcomes at different times, but for a long time Denmark was the economically and militarily strongest state in the region, while Norway became increasingly weaker, being united first with Sweden for a time (1319–1355) and then, from the late Middle Ages, with Denmark. The model of a Nordic union embracing all three states was also tried, but it was clear by the end of the Middle Ages that the Swedes preferred a national kingdom of their own to a union with Denmark-Norway.

During the following centuries there was a struggle for hegemony in the Nordic region between Denmark and Sweden. In their heyday as regional great powers, both states were constructed by and around national élites, but these did not represent closed cultures. On the contrary, in many respects they were dependent

on immigration from abroad. These immigrants naturally influenced the domestic, national cultures in many ways, but they
were also gradually absorbed into those cultures in a slow process of
assimilation.

In this way certain sectors and classes of society were internationalized, but the great majority of the population in the Nordic countries remained homogeneous and relatively unaffected by immigration. Both Denmark and Sweden were, however, multi-ethnic societies with several regional cultures, which often diverged from the
center in language or dialect. For example, the Baltic empire controlled by Sweden during her period as a great power included areas inhabited by Swedes, Danes, Norwegians, Finns, Lapps or Sami, Ingrians, Estonians, Latvians and Germans.

The weakness of national identity is demonstrated by the many
border changes which occurred in connection with the constant
wars between the Nordic states, and by the changes in nationality
which followed. The territorial transfers that proved definite included three provinces conquered by Sweden from Norway—Bo-
huslän, Härjedalen and Jämtland. In the middle of the 17th century
Sweden also conquered the entire eastern part of the Danish kingdom—the provinces of Scania, Blekinge and Halland.

In the 19th century the nationalist ideology and the idea of the
national state reached the Nordic peoples, and—as on the European
continent—the political consequences were considerable. In the
Nordic region, as elsewhere, the nationality principle had both divisive and integrative effects, but the divise effects had preponde-
rance for the former.

The most immediate consequences for the Nordic region were
Norway's becoming an independent state in 1905 through the dissolution of the Swedish-Norwegian union, the strengthening of
Denmark's character as a national state through the loss of the predominantly German-speaking duchies of Schleswig and Holstein in
1864 and Finland's breakaway from Russia in 1917.

When the King of Denmark ceded Norway to Sweden in 1814,

the three Norwegian possessions in the North Atlantic were not included. Instead Iceland, the Faroe Islands and Greenland became parts of the Danish monarchy. Of the three ethno-territorial groups, the Icelanders were the first to start a process of national liberation, which was achieved in stages: limited self-government in 1874; autonomy in 1904; independence in a personal union with Denmark in 1918; and, finally, the independent Republic of Iceland in 1944, after a plebiscite.

In several respects, the preconditions for ethnic identification on the Faroe Islands were similar to those on Iceland. Like the Icelanders, the Faroese had a distinct territory of their own, a common spoken language, cultural awareness and an indigenous class of officials. After the middle of the 19th century, ethnic consciousness began to be strengthened on the Faroes, but opinions were divided over the form of self-government. The home rule law, which is valid today, did not emerge until 1948.

In comparison with national developments on Iceland and on the Faroes, Greenland followed for a long time the opposite course. As late as 1950, when Denmark initiated an extensive program of modernization in Greenlandic society, there were no protests from the Greenlanders, even though this program in reality involved far-reaching measures of cultural Danicization. In 1979 Greenland obtained autonomy within the Danish kingdom.

The nationalistic wave of the 19th century also influenced Danish-German relations by bringing the Schleswig-Holstein question to a head. The boundary of 1864, after Denmark's military defeat by Prussia and Austria, left a substantial Danish minority in northern Schleswig. The state boundary of 1920, which emerged after Germany's defeat in the First World War and after a plebiscite imposed by the victors, was an attempt to create a stable political frontier, but dissatisfied groups were left on both sides, and it was only in the period after the Second World War that the previously open or latent tension gave way to more conciliatory attitudes.

In 1917 Finland emerged as an independent state after having been part of the Swedish realm until 1809, and later a grand duchy within the Russian empire. The process of Finnish liberation did not affect only the relations with Russia. It also had internal cultural and ethno-national dimensions in that it affected relations between the Finnish and the Swedish-speaking parts of the population. The majority of the population were Finnish-speaking, while Swedish was the mother tongue of much of the rural population on the south and western coasts and on the Åland Islands. The Finnish state was based on the two nationalities and the two languages. Only the Åland Islands differ from the rest of the country through constituting a monolingual Swedish-speaking administrative area, as a result of a decision by the League of Nations in 1921.

In the Nordic region, ethnic identity has served as an important basis for nation building. The nationalist ideology has mainly had a differentiating effect: the Scandinavianist currents of the 19th century did not survive the confrontation with political reality. Both Denmark and Sweden became more ethnically homogeneous. After the disappearance of her Baltic empire, the successful Swedification of the provinces conquered from Denmark-Norway, the loss of the Finnish parts of the kingdom, and after the dissolution of the union with Norway, Sweden was more of a nation-state than ever before. Denmark followed the same pattern. The boundary of 1920 in Schleswig, the cession of Norway in 1814 and the various attempts to regulate relations with Denmark's North Atlantic territories all had the effect of strengthening Danish identity as a Danish nation-state.

Ethno-territorial nationalism was able to triumph in both Iceland and Norway through the achievement of independent statehood. The emergence of independent Finland can be seen as a victory for the same forces, but with the qualification that in this case the state was sustained by two ethnic groups with an equal right of domicile. In other Nordic areas, where independent statehood could not be regarded as a viable solution—Greenland and the Faroes—or where the state affiliation had been determined by international agreement—the Åland Islands—various forms of autonomy were achieved.

Finally, the Nordic region also contains ethnic minorities which do not present demands for political control of their territories—the Finnish-speaking Kvens in northern Norway, the Torne valley Finns of Sweden, and the Lapps (or Sami in their own terminology), who occupy an extensive area in the northern parts of Finland, Norway and Sweden.

In the course of time, there has also been large-scale immigration into the Nordic region. Germans, Walloons, Dutch, Scots and many others came and were rather quickly assimilated into the surrounding majority culture. In recent decades, refugees and labour immigrants have strongly influenced the ethnic picture, particularly in Sweden and Denmark.

In an international comparison, the societies of the Nordic region have been described as being characterized by a relatively small degree of interethnic tension. Historically, this harmonious description is not entirely accurate. The image of a homogeneous, peaceful Nordic region deserves a new, unified examination, in which the focus should be on the relationships between state and nation, between ethnicity and territory, and between ethnic majorities and minorities. That is indeed the purpose of this book, which attempts both to analyze the specific Nordic model of ethnic relationships and to place it in a wider context, both theoretically and empirically.

PART ONE

ETHNIC AND NATIONAL MINORITIES IN THE NORDIC NATION-BUILDING PROCESS: THEORETICAL AND CONCEPTUAL PREMISES

Sven Tägil

States have long been the central actors in the historical development of the international system. Each state consists of both territory and people, and the majority of a country's inhabitants have an affinity with both their fellow countrymen and the particular territory which they inhabit. They possess a specific national identity, a common history and to a large extent a shared culture, and live in a community of communication. Such is the ideal state and nation model as it has been portrayed for approximately the past 200 years. According to the 19th century notion of nationalism, the national principle, the boundaries of the state should coincide with those of the nation, and the state and nation thus represent one organic whole.[1]

Yet ideal and reality are two different matters, and the national principle has indeed proved difficult to uphold in practice. There are thousands of distinctive groups around the world which, although they may possess an individual culture, specific symbol systems and

---

[1] A standard work in the field is Seton-Watson: *Nations and States*. A good overview is provided in Williams: "The Question of National Congruence", pp. 229–265. For various aspects of the functions of boundaries, see Tägil et al.: *Studying Boundary Conflicts*, particularly the Appendix, pp. 150 ff.

often also a specific language, have never had the opportunity to establish their own states. Many groups have not even had such a desire. Furthermore, of the some 180 states presently represented in the UN General Assembly, only a handful live up to the criteria of consisting of only one ethnic group and of constituting a single, homogeneous cultural entity. The overwhelming majority of states are made up of different groups with specific ethnic identities and cultural particularities.

However, the concepts state and nation are in no way static. States have come into existence, functioned and been eradicated throughout the course of history, often in connection with wars and international upheavals, but also as a result of other processes, such as older eras' dynastic policies. Nations are likewise subject to change through slow-moving processes. Cultures may subside, they may be modified, or they may appear in new forms. In a long-term historical perspective, both state and nation building appear more as the result of structural factors or by chance than as the consequence of consciously operating actors. Only in modern times has it become possible to influence nation building more actively, particularly since the development of a nationalist ideology,[2] although contemporary international events offer ample proof that this is in no way a problem-free process.

National identities generally developed slowly and unnoticeably, and individuals and groups who could identify with their particular state organization existed already in Antiquity's Europe. Such an organization could be embodied in a city and its surrounding countryside which would be tangible for its citizens, such as Athens for the Athenians, or it could be complex and less palpable, as the Roman Empire must have been for the Romans. A cultural community developed within the given group and territory in both cases and espe-

---

[2] See, for instance, Breuilly: *Nationalism and the State*. A good overview of theoretical aspects of nation building is provided by Taylor: *Political Geography, World Economy, Nation-State and Loyalty*, pp. 95–140.

cially prominently in the case of the Greek city-states,[3] yet one can hardly speak of any widespread popular national sentiment throughout the larger territories during this time. The ordinary population's loyalty was most likely limited to the immediate environment and whomever held power at the time.

A series of territorial principalities arose in various parts of Europe following the dissolution of the Roman Empire and the dramatic upheavals correlated to the Germanic Invasions. The core of these units could, in certain cases, be linked to ancient tribal divisions—i.e. the German tribal duchies—but the feudal structure seldom favored the rise of more solidly organized state entities. Loyalties were more commonly tied to the prince rather than to the state. State entities with both a solid territorial core, firmly established institutions and territorially bound loyalties did, however, appear towards the close of the Middle Ages.[4]

Several of Europe's presently existing states have a long, uninterrupted history which can be traced back to medieval times. The states in question may have come into existence through the actions of a dominant national élite, such as France,[5] or may be the result of the gathering of several national groups under one common state, such as Switzerland. The formation of such states was in many cases a reaction against the existing universal authorities, such as the Catholic church which demanded religious supremacy, or the Empire with its equivalent claim to secular superiority. Other states have a significantly shorter history of independence. The 19th century witnessed the rise of a nationalist ideology which had the potential to influence the development of national identities in various ways and

[3] Hammond: *City-State and World State in Greek and Roman Political Theory until Augustus;* Johansson: "Nationalitetsproblemens rötter: idéhistoriska aspekter".

[4] Cf. Strayer: *On the Medieval Origins of the Modern State;* Johansson: "Nationalitetsproblemens rötter", p. 4.

[5] Kirkland: "France"; Johansson: "Nationalitetsproblemens rötter", p. 4.

to implement them as bases in the state-building process, and it is
following this development that Europe's political map underwent
its most significant alterations.[6]

The national principle—substantiated by the political doctrine
of a nation's right to self-determination [7]— could in some cases have
a unifying effect, and ethnically related groups could thus be gathered under state entities such as Germany and Italy. In other cases,
the principle of national self-determination acted as a disintegrative
force and could thus lead to the dissolution of multinational states,
as was the case with the Habsburg Empire after World War I. Such
changes did not, however, take place without serious conflict, and
Europe's history from the time of the French Revolution to the two
World Wars provides a rich sample of the difficulties in applying the
national principle and of the shortcomings of the prevalent state
system.

The history of the Nordic states during the 19th and the beginning of the 20th century can be seen from the same perspective, as
nationalism had both unifying and divisive effects here as well. After
1864, the Danish state comprised groups and territories with diver-
gent identities on Iceland, the Faroe Islands and Greenland beside
the state dominating Danish people and culture. Simultaneously
Denmark experienced a boundary problem in Schleswig involving
national complications in relation to Germany. The dissolution of
the Swedish-Norwegian union in 1905 represented a triumph for
the nation-state model, although both Sweden and Norway continued to house peoples such as Sami/Lapps and Finns/Kvens whose
ethnic identities diverged from the majority population. Finland,
which gained complete independent statehood only following the
collapse of Czarist Russia, differed from the remaining Nordic

---

[6] See, for instance, Seton-Watson: *Nations and States;* Hobsbawm: *Nations and Nationalism.*

[7] See, for instance, Østerud: *Nasjonenes selvbestemmelsesrett.*

model by basing its national identity on two state dominating peoples, the Finnish and the Swedish.

From an international perspective, the Nordic countries have often been depicted as a homogeneous and stable area with exemplary interstate relations in modern times, and a strong solidarity in terms of values both among the Nordic peoples and internally between the ethnic majorities and minorities. Against this background, it would be of value to investigate whether this characterization of the Nordic ethno-cultural development is indeed correct, and if there exists a possible Nordic model for inter-ethnic relations and conflict resolution. Yet it is first necessary to highlight certain conceptual distinctions in order to correctly understand and analyze this development, all the more so since the terminology within the field is less than uniform and at times confusing.

The first point concerns the concepts "ethnic" and "national" and various constructions incorporating these terms.[8] Ethnic originates from the Greek *ethnos*, while national goes back to the Latin *natio;* the fundamental meaning in both cases is people, and the difference lies primarily in the employment of these terms. The term nation is often used by historians to designate a group of people who have formed—or strived to form—their own state on the basis of a common culture. When corresponding groups have for some reason failed to achieve statehood, they have instead been labeled nationalities. It becomes natural to employ the concept of nation in political contexts, and the size and stability of the group, its common institutions as well as the existence of politicizable issues and manifestations of will are then taken into account.

The crucial point in this context is the conceptual distinction between state and nation. A nation is a social group, while a state is a political, territorially demarcated unit. This difference is not always made in English-language texts since nation can refer to both people

---

[8] See, for instance, Kloss: *Grundfragen der Ethnopolitik im 20. Jahrhundert.* Compare also with Deutsch: *Nationalism and Social Communication.*

and state. The Nordic languages likewise suffer from semantical confusions. In everyday language, nationality is often used to determine state citizenship. A person with a Norwegian passport, for instance, can administratively be labelled a Norwegian national even if that person is ethnically a Sami.

In extra-political contexts, the term ethnic group has been employed to describe social groups with common descent, language and culture. Definitions can be based on both subjective and objective criteria, on both what the actors themselves perceive their specific qualities to be and on what the outside world can distinguish.[9] Ethnicity as a comprehensive term was launched within Anglo-Saxon Social Science and is a relatively recent invention. One problem is the lack of agreement within the academic world over what background variables should be determinant in defining ethnicity.[10] Both descent and culture do, however, figure in most definitions, which thus incorporate both inborn and acquired characteristics and proficiencies.[11] It is common for human beings to be born into a group with a cultural heritage which they later come to share and identify with. In individual cases, however, it is also possible to move into a group and become "acculturated". The context rather than the content determines if the term national or ethnic should be used.

These are theoretical considerations. In practice, there are diverging opinions within research concerning which criteria should be ascribed principal importance in determining whether any given

[9] Concerning the differences between subjective and objective criteria, see Murphy: *The Regional Dynamics of Language Differentiation in Belgium*, pp. 14 ff. Compare also with Enloe: *Ethnic Conflict and Political Development*.

[10] An overview of research on ethnicity and ethnic identity is available in Lange–Westin: *Etnisk diskriminering och social identitet*.

[11] An often used definition of ethnic group is the American sociologist Nathan Glazer's: "a social group which consciously shares some aspects of a common culture and is defined primarily by descent" (in Glazer and Moynihan (eds.): *Ethnicity. Theory and Experience*, p. 4.).

group should be labelled national or ethnic. In earlier literature, it was for instance common to consider the Sami population an ethnic minority, while the German minority in Denmark was designated a national minority. The Sami have thus been perceived as neutral in a Swedish national context, while the Germans could be loyal citizens yet with another national identity than the majority population. Yet the difference is less than crystal clear even in this example, and one must under all circumstances realize that the relationship may change over time. Ethno-nationalism is a dynamic concept. [12]

A fundamentally interesting discussion concerning the problem of ethnicity and nationality was conducted in the mid-1970s by the Danish historian Troels Fink and the German ethnologist Kai Detlev Sievers, where the former criticized Sievers' use of the ethnicity concept regarding the German minority in Northern Schleswig. Fink saw the criterion of descent as irrelevant in this context, since in the case of Schleswig it was solely a matter of disposition: German-minded or Danish-minded. There were hardly any notable outward differences. For Sievers, however, it was important to adhere to terminology provided by the behavioral sciences and to avoid terms which had connotations such as people, nation, or *Volkstum*.[13]

In order to understand ethno-national processes correctly, some further distinctions are necessary. First, it is important to keep apart the concepts identity and identification. Identity depicts a more fundamental condition, whereas identification implies a conscious acti-

[12] The term ethno-nationalism was launched by Connor: "The Politics of Ethno-Nationalism", pp. 1 ff. See also Smith: *The Ethnic Origins of Nations* concerning the connection between ethnicity and nationality.

[13] Sievers (ed.): *Beiträge zur Frage der ethnischen Identifikation des Bundes deutscher Nordschleswiger;* Fink: "Hjemmetyskernes identifikationsproblem"; Sievers: "Einige prinzipielle Bemerkungen zu Troels Finks Kritik...". For conceptual demarcations, see Elklit–Noack–Tonsgaard: "Nationalt tilhørsforhold i Nordslesvig", Chap. 2.

vation of the identity.[14] It is assumed that ethnic identity—based on qualities, proficiencies and attitudes which are shared by members of the group—should somehow be perceivable by the outside world. Purely biological traits represent the most prominent distinguishable attributes, yet it must here be emphasized that these features represent ethnic distinctions only if people wish to view them as such. Skin color is an example of an outward characteristic which is commonly considered to be relevant, whereas features such as eye color or hair color are not.[15]

In the present context, however, the most pertinent qualities are cultural rather than biological, although the notion of culture itself is vague. A workable definition of culture might be the following: "acquired patterns of thought and action (including the products thereof), based on values common to a group of people, where the members are or have been in contact with one another."[16] This definition takes into account both attitudes and behavior, and the qualification must be made that more than one criterion is generally required.

The foundations for ethnic identity are most often established by a combination of various cultural components: language, religion, customs, traditions, symbols, and history. Language often plays a key role, since it not only represents the basis for communication within the group but is independently of this also of high symbolic value.[17] Yet there are examples, also in the Nordic region, where the everyday spoken language and ethno-national identification do not absolutely coincide, as is the case in the Danish-German boundary area. The level of ethnic awareness can naturally be strengthened or weakened in any given individual, depending, among other things,

[14] Tägil (ed.): *Regions in Upheaval: Ethnic Conflict and Political Mobilization*, pp. 18 ff.

[15] See, for instance, Allardt–Starck: *Språkgränser och samhällsstruktur. Finlandssvenskarna i ett jämförande perspektiv*, p. 21.

[16] Johansson: *Kulturella beroenden. Sverige – världen – framtiden*, p. 13.

[17] Stokes: "Cognition and the Function of Nationalism".

on the degree of external pressure. Identification with a given group culture also presupposes the existence of other distinguishable identification objects. Furthermore, the prominence with which the cultural pattern manifests itself is significant, as is the cultural distance to other groups within the same society. Fredrik Barth has therefore interpreted ethnic identity precisely as a question of "borders".[18] A certain degree of contact is deemed necessary for any given individual to develop specific ethnic awareness.[19]

An increase in identification on the individual plane is of limited value, yet the potential to mobilize the group increases if many individuals embrace the same awareness. Differences between "us" and "them" are sharpened as group identification grows. The process need not necessarily lead to conflict with other groups of a different identity, since conflict will arise only where the question of identity has been politicized and the group perceives itself as one party in a relationship with a counterparty.[20]

The manner in which relations between ethnic majorities and minorities develop is both an interesting theme and an important question in the study of conflict theory and within the discipline of History. A primary observation is that general theories are of limited value in explaining ethnic conflict, at least in the long term perspective. Liberal theories concerning modernization and integration are based on the notion that historically inherited distinctions characterizing different groups gradually diminish in conjunction with the development of state identities. According to this interpretation, ethnic conflict represents a more primitive form of societal conflict which would eventually cease to exist.[21] Marxist schools of

[18] Barth (ed.): *Ethnic Groups and Boundaries.* For a critique of Barth see, for instance, van den Berge: "Ethnic Pluralism in Industrial Societies: A Special Case?", p. 242.

[19] The aspect of communication has primarily been emphasized by Karl Deutsch: *Nationalism and Social Communication.*

[20] Tägil (ed.): *Regions in Upheaval,* pp. 242 ff.

[21] See Lijphart: "Political Theories and the Explanation of Ethnic Con-

thought would in their turn argue that tensions among ethnic groups will decrease parallel to the leveling of conflict among social groups.[22] Empirical evidence contradicts the claims of both schools of thought. The Nordic experience in majority/minority relations could perhaps yield a fresh and interesting basis for a discussion of one of the central and most urgent issues at the heart of current international strife.

The Nordic countries comprise different types of ethnic and national minorities. The very term minority can be used to differentiate among both various categories and various structures.[23] The construction ethno-national minorities will here be employed to designate groups whose members are or have been consciously or unconsciously in a state of functional reciprocal connection. The terms minority and majority reveal a purely quantitative relationship in the specific Nordic context, although in recent years it has also become common to label underprivileged and oppressed groups as minorities even if they constitute the numerical majority, such as the black population in South Africa. The Finnish population in Finland before 1809 might fall under this category, since those of Finnish ethnicity outnumbered the politically dominant Swedish group.

It may in certain contexts be important to distinguish territorial minorities from immigrant minorities.[24] The former category has its identity bound to a given region where the group resides and often

flict in the Western World", pp. 47 ff. Compare with Hah and Martin: "Toward a Synthesis of Conflict and Integration Theories of Nationalism", pp. 361 ff.

[22] For the question of Marxism and nationalism, see, for instance, Hobsbawm: "Some Reflections on the Break-up of Britain", which gives a Marxist perspective of Marxism's trouble in dealing with ethnic problems.

[23] Kloss: *Grundfragen der Ethnopolitik*, p. 63.

[24] A good overview of research concerning ethno-regional problems is provided by Murphy: *The Regional Dynamics of Language Differentiation in Belgium*, pp. 14–40. For a definition of the concept of *region*, see Paasi: "The institutionalization of regions".

constitutes the majority, whereas the latter generally lacks such a territorial base and is dispersed among the country's population as a whole. Although local ghetto formations may certainly arise among immigrant minorities, the historically fostered territorial identity is usually absent. It is not uncommon for the so-called ethno-regional minorities, who have their identity linked to both ethnicity and territory, to pose a serious threat to the unity of the existing state. This is especially true of regions which have a historical claim to autonomy, such as Iceland before independence or the Faroe Islands today. On the other hand, it is more debatable whether a province such as Scania would likewise allow itself to be mobilized for ethnoregional purposes even after over 300 years of incorporation into the Swedish state and with extensive integration into the Swedish nation.

Mobilization occurs only after the question of ethnic identity has become politicized, and the situation becomes critical primarily in cases where the given ethnic group has come to perceive its position as threatened in some vital way and thus consciously reacts to this real or imagined threat. Politicization takes place against the background of various structural circumstances, be they social, economic, political, cultural or territorial. The two societal processes which provoke particularly forceful reactions from ethnic groups are centralization and discrimination. The ethnic minority often interprets the centralization of the state's political structure as a measure directed against the group's power and influence, although this need not always be the central authorities' actual intention.[25]

An ethnic group whose members perceive themselves as wronged by the majority can react to this by choosing among three principal strategies. The minority can choose to defer to and be loyal to the majority. Certain minorities live under external pressure of such a degree that the group's identity is weakened and the minority is gradually assimilated into the dominant group in terms of language

---

[25] Tägil (ed.): *Regions in Upheaval*, pp. 244 ff.

and culture. From a historical perspective, such a development is particularly likely to happen where the identification process is still rudimentarly and no politicization has thus as yet taken place. For other minorities, the reaction may entail a conscious drive to politicize the conflict and to various attempts at strengthening the group's infrastructure through improved education and internal communication, and through more efficient organization. All of these main strategies, which are theoretically known as "loyalty", "exit" and "voice",[26] are represented on the Nordic arena in some form. In certain cases, one and the same minority may pursue different strategies at different periods, as in Greenland.

Relations between ethno-national majorities and minorities certainly play an important role both in the nation-formation process and in the question of state allegiance. An increase in group identity can at times be followed by increased state allegiance, while in other cases, the same phenomenon may entail the group's questioning of the basis of the state community. There are several factors to account for such tendencies. A high level of integration within the ethnic minority group may, for example, render the development of a state identity more difficult. Conversely, a low level of integration within the group may facilitate the rise of a state identity, which is possible in cases where the nation-formation is inclusive, or in other words by definition compatible with both the majority's and the minority's interests. Finally, the state is most likely to be readily accepted by the minority if the degree of integration between the majority and the minority group is high.[27]

Today's Finland provides such an example, where the Finland-Swedish sector of the population is a numerical minority but is well integrated into the Finnish state. The consciously implemented inte-

[26] Hirschman: *Exit, Voice and Loyalty*, compare with Rokkan: "Entries, Voices, Exits: Towards a Possible Generalization of the Hirschman Model", pp. 39 ff.

[27] Tägil (ed.): *Regions in Upheaval*, particularly the closing chapter, "The Conditions for Ethno-Regional Conflict: Conclusions", pp. 240 ff.

gration of the boundary regions which Sweden conquered from Denmark in the 1600s into the dominant Swedish society is also a point of historical interest. The population in these areas seems to have fully accepted the Swedish state after a few generations. Conversely, the Faroe Islands provide an example of a minority characterized by high internal integration and relatively low integration with the majority in the Danish state as a whole, and one would thus expect the Faroese to less readily accept the Danish state.

The sense of national solidarity and the multitude of common interests shared by the inhabitants of a state are obvious ingredients in state allegiance. Against this background, it is essential to appreciate the dynamic nature of the nation-formation process, the existence of various bases for establishing identity, and the possibility that the process may be at different stages at different points in time. The relationship between the state and the nation also differs depending on the type of state in question, and it may therefore be important to pause here for a moment in order to reflect on the various existing patterns for state formation.

As has already been mentioned, the ideal model of the modern state—at least in a European context— is that it should comprise a single nation and coincide with the area which this nation inhabits.[28] If a single ethno-national group has succeeded in building a state, this organization is commonly labeled a nation-state. Iceland, which due to its ethnic and territorial homogeneity makes up a genuine nation state, is a rare example of the very few true nation states existing in the world community.[29] In the case of most nation states, a state entity has been built around one dominant ethno-national group, and whatever diverging interests may have existed had to subordinate themselves to the politics of the majority population. Both Sweden and Norway can be counted in as nation-states based on this expanded definition, even if both countries house older endogenous

[28] For a typology of states see Buzan: *People, States and Fear,* pp. 46 ff.
[29] See Mikesell: "The Myth of the Nation State", pp. 257 ff.

minorities within their borders and have in recent years accepted a significant number of immigrants from abroad, which is especially true of Sweden.

Another main type is represented by the so-called multi-nation state, where the state entity comprises two or more ethno-national groups, each of which is state dominating. Such states are often federative, but the level of integration can vary, as can the readiness to accept the legitimacy of the state. These types of states are most likely to function when the federative structure can base itself on a long historical claim and has been in existence prior to the development of ethno-national identification, as in the case of Switzerland.

Developments tend to be characterized by a higher degree of conflict in cases where federalization takes place in order to solve already existing ethno-regional problems. Belgium provides an example of the difficulties involved in creating an encompassing state identity in a country where historically developed, stable ethno-regional identities (the Flemish and the Walloon respectively) already exist. Finland can be employed in line with the Swiss model as an example of a state where it has been possible to join two separate ethno-national identities under one superordinated state identity, and where the question of inter-ethnic relations has been settled with relatively little conflict.[30]

A third type of state formation consists of the so-called state nation. The nation formation process is based upon both territorial and cultural grounds in such a state, and one can summarize the process by asserting that the state precedes and molds the nation which in its turn originally consists of several ethnic groups. This type of state formation is often represented by relatively young

[30] For a discussion on ethno-national development in Switzerland, Belgium and Finland, see Johansson: "Varieties of Conflict Development: Ethnic Relations and Societal Change in Belgium, Finland and Switzerland", pp. 44 ff.

states, primarily with a colonial background. The US embodies this type of nation where the state and the culture act as mobilizing factors and where various ethnic groups have subordinated themselves to a shared national ideology. One of the preconditions for such a solution has been that the various groups have neither made claims to, nor dominated, specific territories, but have instead coexisted along with numerous other groups. Ghetto formations have arisen at the local level, but the degree of integration at the federal level has been high. Concentrations of Spanish-speaking residents with weaker tendencies towards establishing a common, national American identity have developed in the South, and a significant portion of the native Indian population has also existed on the outskirts of the nation-building process.

An encompassing common identity covering the various ethnic groups can be a necessary condition for endowing newly built multi-ethnic states with legitimacy and functioning capability. Since it is in principle possible to influence identity, the state leadership in every multi-ethnic state of this kind must recognize the importance of consciously creating precisely such an identity. Yet the process is lengthy and stretches over at least a few generations even in successful cases, as can be seen in post-colonial Africa.

On the other hand, there are instances in which it has proven impossible to administrate such an encompassing identity in cases where it has not coincided with the genuine interests of the ethno-national group. It was, for example, not possible to create a superordinated Soviet identity in the multinational Soviet Union, not even in the case of the Russian population which constituted the majority in the Russian republic.

This third category of states, state nations, have not yet had any relevance to the Nordic context. The Nordic states have been described either as nation states or as multi-nation states. The recent influx of people immigrating from diverse cultures mainly to Sweden and Denmark has naturally altered the picture of strong ethnic homogeneity in the Nordic countries, as the immigrants have been dispersed among the majority population. The national identity may well change over time if present trends concerning immigration and refugees are reinforced. Against this background, it is relevant to concentrate not only on the historically developed territorial minorities, but also on more recent immigrated minorities and their significance in nation and state-formation.

In the foregoing discussion, we have suggested various ways in which the ethnic and national development in the Nordic countries can be seen as a process operating at different levels, namely intrastate, state, and suprastate. On the individual plane, this implies that each individual must take a stand on the region he or she inhabits, on the state which comprises the region and in certain cases also on relations outside of the particular state. Ethnic and national identities are similarly hierarchical.[31] One can, for instance, simultaneously be Scanian, Swedish, and Nordic without this leading to internal contradictions or conflict. Yet there are instances where this hierarchy does not apply, such as when individuals give priority to the interests of the given group or region over those of the common state. In this aspect as in so many others, the Nordic countries do not differ from other countries in a fundamental way. Yet the methods which are employed to resolve conflict and those which are used to shape identity may be particular to the Nordic experience and may be linked to the historical development of the countries in question. It is therefore important to analyze the Nordic area from a long-term historical perspective.

Modern research concerning nationalism (Ernest Gellner and others) has often linked the breakthrough of nationalism to the processes of modernization and industrialization and the consequent development of a national bourgeoisie. The nature of industrialized society allegedly called for a united, standardized culture, a common language and a basic educational level for the major portion of the

---

[31] See, for instance, Knight: "Identity and Territory: Geographical Perspectives on Nationalism and Regionalism", pp. 515 ff.

population. According to this view, the middle class was responsible for fostering nationalist ideology and shaping it into a mass movement with high political explosivity.[32]

Eric Hobsbawm has highlighted the rise of formal educational institutions which is said to have occurred hand in hand with the development of nationalist ideology.[33] Benedict Anderson has with somewhat exaggerated emphasis, attempted to depict nationalism as a consequence of mass literacy and the breakthrough of mass printing.[34] This general explanation cannot be taken for granted, although the importance of these elements as such must not be underestimated. The historical exceptions to the rule would be far too many, and the existence of proto-nationalism, a type of undeveloped and unarticulated nationalism[35], would need to be taken into consideration even in contexts which would provide support for the theory.

Part of the strength of 19th century nationalism lies in the fact that it could be coupled with various political ideologies and could thus act as a type of superideology with high mobilization potential. The notion of highlighting each people's uniqueness—the "Volksgeist"—has its intellectual roots in the Romantic era and was thus compatible with conservative ideology. The idea of accentuating popular sovereignty, a thought which developed during the French Revolution, expressed a radical, revolutionary idea. In its implementation, the notion of nationalism was employed mainly by liberal forces in Europe during the first half of the 19th century, yet was equated with conservatism towards the close of the century.[36]

Nationalism is undoubtedly compatible with a diversity of

[32] Gellner: *Nations and Nationalism.*

[33] Hobsbawm: *The Age of Capital.*

[34] Anderson: *Imagined Communities: Reflections on the Origin and Spread of Nationalism.*

[35] See, for instance, Hobsbawm: *Nations and Nationalism.* See also Armstrong: *Nations before Nationalism.*

[36] See Kohn: *The Idea of Nationalism*; Mommsen: *The Varieties of the Nation State in Modern History.*

aims [37] and appears in various guises at different times. Miroslav Hroch has distinguished three main phases in the general European development: In the first "intellectual" phase, the basis of the culture is developed—in terms of language, history, and common cultural traditions—upon the initiative of the intellectual middle class. In the next "agitatory" phase, politicization and mass mobilization occur, resulting in political mass movement in the third phase.[38] Anthony D. Smith has suggested a somewhat different temporal division for the process, which would then be characterized by an initial integrative phase, an ensuing disruptive phase, followed by an aggressive phase and closed with the final phase of global propagation after 1945.[39]

The question is whether this division may also be applied to the Nordic countries. An immediately apparent difference in this case would be that industrialization arrived later in the Nordic countries than in Great Britain and the continent, and that there was a considerable time lag between the first and last Nordic states to be industrialized.[40] It is thus already doubtful whether one should assign determinant importance to industrialization in the rise of nationalism in the Nordic case. A thorough analysis of each given Nordic state is warranted in order to determine whether the Nordic model follows a general European trend. Did the same integrative forces which united Germany and Italy on the continent find expression in pre-1864 "Scandinavianism"? Can the dissolution of the Swedish-Norwegian union in 1905 represent the close of a disruptive phase?

[37] For a typology of five main types of nationalism (State nationalism, Unification nationalism, Separation nationalism, Liberation nationalism and Renewal nationalism) see Orridge: "Varieties of Nationalism". Compare also Taylor: *Political Geography*, pp. 128 ff.

[38] Hroch: *Die Vorkämpfer der nationalen Bewegung bei den kleinen Völkern Europas*, p. 121.

[39] Smith: *Theories of Nationalism*, p. 186.

[40] See, for instance, Jörberg: *The Industrial Revolution in Scandinavia 1850–1914*.

How should one then assess Finland's attaining independence and the development of interethnic relations within that state, and in what manner should the national development pattern of the North Atlantic island world, which is included in the wider Nordic community, be understood?

There remains a multitude of questions to be dealt with concerning nations and interethnic relations in the Nordic countries. Contemporary problems provide one among many reasons to conduct a closer investigation, as ethno-regional conflict has become a significant current international issue which is proving obstinate to resolution. Slumbering ethnic identities in various corners of the globe have been awoken and politicized, and have resulted in separatist claims and demands which have in several cases challenged the existing state. Ethnic awareness has been heightened in original populations such as the Sami/Laplanders and Greenlanders through an increase in information, more efficient organization and internationalization of the issue. Due to a rise in immigration, majority populations have likewise become increasingly conscious of their own culture and individuality in a manner which would hardly be possible in a markedly monocultural society. The dramatic increase in ethnic mobilization during recent years is against all the predictions made by social science research, and represents an urgent research task joining historians and social scientists. Structural social science theories attempting to discern factors behind ethno-national conflict generally lie at such a high level of abstraction that their concrete application becomes problematic.[41] The practical solution would be to connect general domination theories to more specific theories such as those concerning center/periphery relations, as Galtung or André Frank have done with their imperialism theories, or as Wallerstein has done with his interpretation of the antagonism between elites in the center and elites in the peripheries.[42]

[41] Tägil (ed.): *Regions in Upheaval*, pp. 30 ff.
[42] Galtung: "A Structural Theory of Imperialism", p. 8; Frank: *Capital-*

A theory of particular interest for the Nordic case would be Hechter's interpretation of the development in Great Britain's peripheral zone, "the Celtic Fringe".[43] The theory of "internal colonialism" is constructed around the relationship between the center of the state (the "core area") and the peripheral regions which Hechter sees as a fundamental domination relationship between the developed and the underdeveloped world. The center holds the economic power and distributes the economic resources. Through the so-called "cultural division of labor", the distribution follows the cultural and ethnic demarcations between center and periphery to the periphery's disadvantage and thus tends to reaffirm these discrepancies. The theory can be viewed as a stuctural theory of domination reminiscent of Marxist theory, yet with the important qualification that ethnic identity rather than class represents the central and determinant element.

Hechter's theory leads us to questions concerning the relation between ethno-national and other societal conflicts, such as those of a religious nature. In cases where religious affiliation is a direct part of the ethnic identity, a differing creed held by the counterparty can present a formidable obstacle to mutual understanding. Ethnic and religious identification reinforce one another, which facilitates mobilization and increases the potential for conflict. The religious dimension does not play nearly as important a role in the development of conflict in the Nordic context as in many other parts of the world. Yet the language of worship itself may be pertinent to the identity question, as it was in the German-Danish border area.[44] The religious awakening which Laestadianism brought to the Kvens and

ism and Underdevelopment in Latin America; Wallerstein: *The Modern World System*, p. 363.

[43] Hechter: *Internal Colonialism*. A similar theory has been developed by Mughan: "Modernization and Regional Relative Deprivation". Critique against Hechter has been offered by e.g. Ragin: "Class, Status and Reactive Ethnic Cleavages".

[44] Gregersen: *Plattysk i Sønderjylland*.

the Sami also influenced the development of these groups' ident-ities.[45] Concerning the future, the religious homogeneity which characterizes the Nordic area may well decrease primarily as a result of immigration. In Sweden, for instance, the number of baptized Catholics has increased to c. 150,000 (1985), and the number of Muslims to c. 45,000 (1987),[46] yet it is as of yet impossible to specu-late on what implications this may have on the development of identity.

Finally, there can be no generally valid answer to the question of whether it is ethnic identity or class affiliation which decides an indi-vidual's position. Cases where the ethnic conflict fails to be subdued despite an increase in social parity testify to the weight of the ethnic dimension. Relative parity can, however, alleviate a cross-pressure situation between ethnic and class-based identification, by reducing the class factor in relation to the ethnic dimension which thus becomes more prominent.[47] Conversely, the development of an un-equal economic situation can undoubtedly reinforce ethnic identifi-cation. An ethnic group experiencing economic discrimination may compare itself to groups enjoying a relatively fortunate position and attribute this cleavage to ethnic discrimination.[48] On the other hand, there are few cases where regions which are economically exploited and poor in resources have embodied the foundations for ethno-na-tional mobilization.

Several of the aforementioned issues will be further developed and expanded on in the ensuing empirical presentation. The con-cepts which have been discussed here will be central points, namely, the relationships between majority and minority populations, be-tween state and nation, and between ethnicity and territory. The

---

[45] See Boreman: *Laestadianismen.*

[46] The numbers are obtained from Svanberg–Runblom: *Det mångkul-turella Sverige.*

[47] See, for instance, Tägil (ed.): *Regions in Upheaval*, pp. 251 ff.

[48] For "relative deprivation", see, for instance, Gurr: "A Causal Model of Civil Strife: A Comparative Analysis using New Indices".

Nordic area, characterized by its combination of high homogeneity in terms of basic values and patterns and extensive diversity in terms of specific forms and manifestations, will provide the general framework. For historians as for the world in which we live, ethno-national issues represent both a challenge and a fateful question.

LITERATURE

Allardt, Erik–Starck, Christian: *Språkgränser och samhällsstruktur. Finlandssvenskarna i ett jämförande perspektiv*, Stockholm 1981

Anderson, Benedict: *Imagined Communities: Reflections on the Origin and Spread of Nationalism*, London and New York 1986

Armstrong, John A.: *Nations before Nationalism*, Chapel Hill 1982

Barth, Fredrik (ed.): *Ethnic Groups and Boundaries. The Social Organization of Culture Difference*, Oslo 1969

Berge, Pierre van den: "Ethnic Pluralism in Industrial Societies: A Special Case?", *Ethnicity* 3, 1976

Boreman, P.: *Laestadianismen*, Stockholm 1953

Breuilly, J.: *Nationalism and the State*, Manchester 1982

Buzan, Barry: *People, States and Fear. The National Security Problem in International Relations*, Brighton 1983

Connor, Walker: "The Politics of Ethno-Nationalism", *Journal of International Affairs*, 27:1, 1973

Deutsch, Karl: *Nationalism and Social Communication*, Cambridge, Mass. 1966

Elklit, Jörgen–Noack, Johan Peter–Tonsgaard, Ole: "Nationalt tilhørsforhold i Nordslesvig", *Acta Jutlandica* 49, 1978

Enloe, Cynthia: *Ethnic Conflict and Political Development*, Boston 1973

Fink, Troels: "Hjemmetyskernes identifikationsproblem", *Sønderjysk Månedsskrift*, okt/nov 1975

Frank, André Gunder: *Capitalism and Underdevelopment in Latin America*, New York 1969

Galtung, Johan: "A Structural Theory of Imperialism", *Journal of Peace Research*, 8, 1971

Gellner, Ernest: *Nations and Nationalism*, Oxford 1983

30   Sven Tägil

Glazer, Nathan–Moynihan, Daniel P. (eds.): *Ethnicity. Theory and Experience*, Cambridge, Mass. 1975

Gregersen, H.V.: *Plattysk i Sønderjylland. En undersøgelse af fortyskningens historie indtil 1600-årene*, Odense 1974

Gurr, Ted: "A Causal Model of Civil Strife: A Comparative Analysis using New Indices", *American Political Science Review*, 62:4, 1968

Hah, Chong-Do–Martin, Jeffrey: "Toward a Synthesis of Conflict and Integration Theories of Nationalism", *World Politics* 27:3, 1975

Hammond, Mason: *City-State and World State in Greek and Roman Political Theory Until Augustus*, Cambridge, Mass. 1951

Hechter, Michael: *Internal Colonialism. The Celtic Fringe in British National Development 1586-1966*, Berkeley and Los Angeles 1975

Hirschman, Albert: *Exit, Voice and Loyalty*, Cambridge, Mass. 1970

Hobsbawm, Eric: *Nations and Nationalism*, 2nd edition, Cambridge 1992

Hobsbawm, Eric: "Some Reflections on the Break-up of Britain", *New Left Review* 105, 1977

Hobsbawm, Eric: *The Age of Capital*, Reading 1981

Hroch, Miroslav: *Die Vorkämpfer der nationalen Bewegung bei den kleinen Völkern Europas. Eine vergleichende Analyse zur gesellschaftlichen Schichtung der patriotischen Gruppen*, Praha 1968 (English edition 1985)

Johansson, Rune: *Kulturella beroenden. Sverige – världen – framtiden*, Stockholm and Lund 1976

Johansson, Rune: "Nationalitetsproblemens rötter: idéhistoriska aspekter", in Karlsson, Klas-Göran (ed.): *Östeuropa i förvandling. Nationalitetsproblem i Jugoslavien och Sovjetunionen*. (Aktuellt om historia, nr 1-2, 1990)

Johansson, Rune: "Varieties of Conflict Development: Ethnic Relations and Societal Change in Belgium, Finland and Switzerland", in Tägil, Sven (ed.): *Regions in Upheaval*, 1984

Jörberg, Lennart: *The Industrial Revolution in Scandinavia 1850-1914*, The Fontana Economic History of Europe IV:8, London 1970

Kirkland, Dorothy: "France", in Tipton, Leon (ed.): *Nationalism in the Middle Ages*, New York 1972

Kloss, Heinz: *Grundfragen der Ethnopolitik im 20. Jahrhundert*, Bad Godesberg 1969

Knight, David B.: "Identity and Territory: Geographical Perspectives on

Nationalism and Regionalism", *Annals of the Association of American Geographers* 72:4, 1982

Kohn, Hans: *The Idea of Nationalism: A Study in its Origins and Background*, New York 1946

Lange, Anders–Westin, Charles: *Etnisk diskriminering och social identitet. Forskningsöversikt och teoretisk analys*, Stockholm 1981

Lijphart, Arend: "Political Theories and the Explanation of Ethnic Conflict in the Western World: Falsified Predictions and Plausible Postdictions", in Esman, Milton (ed.): *Ethnic Conflict in the Western World*, Ithaca and London 1977

Mikesell, Marvin W.: "The Myth of the Nation State", *Journal of Geography* 82:6, 1983

Mommsen, Wolfgang: "The Varieties of The Nation State in Modern History", in Mann, Michael (ed.): *The Rise and Decline of the Nation State*, Blackwell 1990

Mughan, Anthony: "Modernization and Regional Relative Deprivation: Towards a Theory of Ethnic Conflict", in Sharpe, L.J. (ed.): *Decentralist Trends in Western Democracies*, London 1979

Murphy, Alexander B.: *The Regional Dynamics of Language Differentiation in Belgium*, Chicago 1988

Orridge, A.W.:"Varieties of Nationalism", in Tivey, Leonard (ed.): *The Nation-State: The Formation of Modern Politics*, Oxford 1981

Østerud, Øyvind: *Nasjonenes selvbestemmelsesrett. Søkelys på en politisk doktrine*, Oslo 1984

Paasi, Anssi: "The Institutionalization of Regions: a Theoretical Framework for Understanding the Emergence of Regions and the Constitution of Regional Identity", *Fennia* 164:1, 1986

Ragin, Charles: "Class, Status and Reactive Ethnic Cleavages: The Social Bases of Political Regionalism", *American Sociological Review*, 42:3, 1977

Rokkan, Stein: "Entries, Voices, Exits: Towards a Possible Generalization of the Hirschman Model", *Social Sciences Information* 13:1, 1974

Seton-Watson, Hugh: *Nations and States: An Enquiry into the Origins of Nations and the Politics of Nationalism,* London 1977

Sievers, Kai Detlev (ed.): *Beiträge zur Frage der ethnischen Identifikation des Bundes deutscher Nordschleswiger*, Sankelmark 1975

Sievers, Kai Detlev: "Einige prinzipielle Bemerkungen zu Troels Finks Kritik...", *Sønderjysk Månedsskrift*, 1976

Smith, Anthony D.: "Nationalism, Ethnic Separatism and the Intelligentia", in Williams, Colin (ed.): *National Separatism*, Cardiff 1982

Smith, Anthony D.: *The Ethnic Origins of Nations*, Oxford 1986

Smith, Anthony D.: *Theories of Nationalism*, London 1971

Stokes, Gale: "Cognition and the Function of Nationalism", *Journal of Interdisciplinary History* 1, 1974

Strayer, Joseph R.: *On the Medieval Origins of the Modern State*, Princeton, N.J. 1970

Svanberg, Ingvar–Runblom, Harald (eds.): *Det mångkulturella Sverige. En handbok om etniska grupper och minoriteter*, Stockholm 1989

Taylor, Peter J.: *Political Geography, World Economy, Nation-State and Loyalty*, Singapore 1985

Tägil, Sven (ed.): *Regions in Upheaval: Ethnic Conflict and Political Mobilization*, Lund Studies in International History 22, Lund 1984

Tägil, Sven, et al.: *Studying Boundary Conflicts*, Lund Studies in International History 9, Lund 1970

Wallerstein, Immanuel: *The Modern World System*, New York and London 1974

Williams, Colin: "The Question of National Congruence", in Johnston, R.J.–Taylor, P.J. (eds.): *A World in Crisis*, Oxford 1986

PART TWO

THE EMERGENCE OF
NATIONALISM IN ICELAND

Gunnar Karlsson

Introduction

In 1814, when Denmark ceded Norway to Sweden, three Norwegian dependencies in and beyond the Atlantic Ocean were left behind under Denmark. If this was not due to a pure lack of historical knowledge on the part of the Swedish negotiators, it is at any rate evidence of little interest in these remote parts of the old Norwegian realm.[1] As a consequence, Iceland, the Faroes and Greenland acquired an inaccurately defined and somewhat different status under the Danish monarchy. The inhabitants of these islands formed three ethnic minorities in the kingdom, and all of them were to use their individual ethnic distinctions to demand a separate constitutional status, Home Rule, and in Iceland's case, complete secession and establishment of an independent state. Their demands were rooted in very different social and economic soils, and therefore one can find here three different variants of a trend which has characterized world history over the last few centuries: the birth of nation states. In this

[1] I say this in spite of Finn Gad's argumentation in his article, "La Grönlande, les Isles de Ferröe et l'Islande non comprises", 1979. Although he may be right that Britain wished the dependencies to be kept under the Danish monarchy, it is nevertheless true, as Gad actually points out (p. 189), that the Swedish representative at the peace conference in 1814 wrote to his Foreign Minister that "Iceland, Greenland and the Faroes have never belonged to Norway ...".

article I shall describe and try to explain the origin and success of national consciousness and political nationalism in Iceland, the most populous of the three dependencies.

As Sven Tägil has mentioned in his contribution to this book, nationalism is the wish for ethnic and political boundaries to coincide. (See p. 19). In a multi-ethnic kingdom, like the Danish one in the age of absolutism, this wish can be met in two ways. Either two or more ethnic groups can adopt a common ethnicity, the same language, one identity etc., or each ethnic group can build a political unit, in or outside the realm.

In the United Kingdom, integration has been the dominating solution to the problem of nationalism. An overwhelming majority of non-English-speaking inhabitants of the British Isles, Celts and speakers of Nordic dialects alike, have adopted English and united with the English people in a polity which for most purposes plays the role of a state. The people of Shetland, the northernmost outpost of the Kingdom, did not change their language from the Nordic dialect (Norn) to English until the 17th and 18th centuries.[2] In the Danish kingdom, and in Scandinavia generally, the separatist solution has prevailed, at any rate if the development is seen from the viewpoint of ethnic and linguistic groups. If, on the other hand, we look at it from the position of the individual, the process of integration has no doubt been active too. Although practically all inhabitants of Denmark in the age of absolutism may have looked upon themselves as Danes, and all Norwegians probably knew that they were Norwegians if they were asked, they were not attached to their state, nation or fatherland in the same way as their descendants around the turn of the 20th century. A Norwegian representative of the old type can be found in Henrik Ibsen's play, *Peer Gynt*, written in the 1860s. In this play a man appears who cuts off his finger to avoid conscription into his fatherland's army. But he rebuilds his farm twice when it is devastated by a flood and an avalanche, and he

---

[2] Schei: *The Shetland Story*, pp. 85–86.

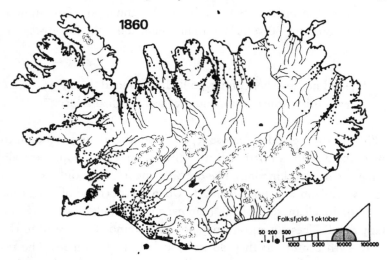

Iceland: Settlements in 1860.
Source: Helga Þórarinsdóttir et al. (eds.): *Eldur er í norðri*, Reykjavík 1982, p. 427.

demonstrates bravery and devotion in bringing up his children. At his funeral the priest says:

His horizon was narrow. Apart from the few
Who were nearest to him, nothing else existed.
The ringing words that rouse other men's hearts
Meant nothing to him, more than a tinkle of bells.
Mankind, the fatherland, the highest ambitions
Of men, were only misty figures to him.
––––
He was a poor patriot. To State
And Church, an unproductive tree. But there
On the brow of the hill, within the narrow
Circle of family, where his work was done,
There he was great, because he was himself.[3]

[3] Ibsen: *Peer Gynt,* pp. 136–37.

A similar observation was made by the Icelandic poet Guðmundur
Friðjónsson some 30 years later in his poem about the Widow by the
Stream:

> She did not love her country, only her plot and shack,
> A few yards of the stream, and the lava, rough and black.[4]

Why did the Icelanders choose separatism rather than integration to
meet the demand of nationalism? Why did they not adopt the main
language of their kingdom, like the Shetlanders? Why did they learn
to love Iceland and not Denmark, when the doctrine of 19th century nationalism told them that everyone should love only the
fatherland? These questions may not have sounded as absurd in the
early 19th century as they do now, at least to Icelanders. The re-
nowned Danish linguist Rasmus Christian Rask stayed in Iceland in
the years 1813–15 to study Icelandic. He came to the conclusion
that the language was retreating rapidly before Danish, especially in
Reykjavík, and forecast that it would die out in the town within a
century and in the whole of Iceland within three centuries.[5] But this
development took a sharp turn, and within half a century after
Rask's forecast it must have been completely clear to any observer
that Iceland had chosen the other way to meet the principle of nationalism.

Obviously it was crucial for the Icelanders that they lived in a
country hundreds of miles away from all other countries, and that
practically all of them lived there, and there alone. The Icelandic
population was exceptionally distinct from others and ethnically almost as homogeneous as possible. Even though Rask felt that the
Danish influence on the Icelandic language was so strong that he
feared its extinction, there was no Danish-speaking population in
Iceland, only a handful of Danish merchant families. Admittedly, it

[4] Guðmundur Friðjónsson: *Úr heimahögum*, p. 121.—My translation.
[5] Rask: "Brjef frá Rask", p. 56.

Table 1. The Population of Iceland and Reykjavík, 1703–1920 [6]

Year	Iceland	Reykjavík
1703	50,358	69 [7]
1801	47,240	307
1840	57,094	890
1850	59,157	1,149
1870	69,763	2,024
1901	78,470	6,682
1920	94,690	17,679

was said about the people in Eyrarbakki, a small village where a Danish merchant was more influential than was elsewhere the case, that they put on their best clothes on Sundays and spoke Danish. But, even if that was true, they had six days a week for Icelandic. And although the language of the people in Reykjavík may have been strongly influenced by Danish, the town had only a few hundred inhabitants when Rask was there, about 1% of the population of the whole country.

Furthermore, Iceland had a good historical tradition for nurturing 19th-century nationalism. The country had been free and independent for more than three centuries in the Middle Ages, a kind of republic it was said. In that period the Icelanders had written the sagas, a genre of literature which was highly respected throughout Northern and Western Europe in the Romantic era.

So there were several things that spoke for a national movement

6 *Tölfrædihandbók 1974*, pp. 7, 14–15.

7 In 1703 Reykjavík was only a farmstead with six crofts. I include the total population of the farm and all the crofts, although some of them were to fall outside the town's boundaries when it was officially established in 1787.—*Manntal á Íslandi árið 1703*, pp. 24–25.

in Iceland. But there were also things that spoke against it. The very distance from other countries, which afterwards makes it look so natural for Iceland to be a separate political unit, deprived it of any tradition of heroic defence against foreigners. Its subjection to the King of Norway in the years 1262–64 had been brought about by a treaty between the King and representatives of the Icelanders, without any bloodshed. Also, by all normal 19th-century standards the population of Iceland was far too small to deserve any kind of autonomy. While the Icelanders were demanding a status of practical independence, for a population of 60,000, the Belgians and Portuguese, with around four million inhabitants each, were ridiculed in Europe for thinking that they could last as independent nations because they were thought to be too small.[8] So, if the Icelanders had become good Danish citizens in the 19th century, that development could also be explained. Therefore, the alternative they elected needs further explanation.

The Birth of a Nationalist Movement, 1830–1850

Everything that we know indicates that the Icelanders were for the most part at ease with their status within the Danish–Norwegian monarchy during the age of absolutism, well into the 19th century. Positive evidence for this is an episode that took place in Iceland in 1809. At that time all foreign trade in the country was by law restricted to the subjects of the Danish King, but because of England's attack on Denmark during the Napoleonic wars, all communication between Iceland and Denmark was extremely difficult and in effect broken off. An English merchant tried to utilize the situation to trade with Iceland. As an interpreter he hired a Danish prisoner of war, by the name of Jørgen Jørgensen. When they arrived in Iceland, the Danish Governor in Reykjavík hesitated to allow the Icelanders

[8] Hobsbawm: *Nations and nationalism since 1780*, pp. 30–32.—Cf. Mitchell: *European Historical Statistics*, pp. 19, 22.

to trade with them. The crew responded by arresting the Governor, and Jørgensen assumed the task of ruling the country. Immediately he declared all Danish authority in Iceland abolished and promised to introduce a democratic form of government, independent but protected by the British state. It seems that most Icelanders were content with this, and most of the Icelandic officials continued in their offices under Jørgensen's rule. But two months later, when Jørgensen was arrested by an English admiral and Danish rule was restored in Iceland, no one lifted a finger or uttered a word to defend the young Icelandic independence. People did not seem to care at all.[9]

There is no sign of a political movement in Iceland for more than twenty years after Jørgensen's coup. The secession of Norway from Denmark in 1814 does not seem to have attracted great attention in Iceland and, as far as we know, no Icelander expressed a wish to follow suit.[10] It was not until the 1830s, when the Danish King began to plan the establishment of consultative assemblies in his kingdom, that a group of Icelandic intellectuals in Copenhagen raised the first political demands on their country's behalf. In Iceland a medieval assembly, the *Alþing*, had survived in its original place, Þingvellir, mainly as an appellate court, until 1800. The Icelanders in Copenhagen now wanted this assembly to be reestablished as a separate consultative body for Iceland. They won a victory in 1845, when the Icelandic *Alþing* was reestablished, but, to the great disappointment of many of them, this occurred in Reykjavík and not at Þingvellir. About that time Jón Sigurðsson, a philologist living in Copenhagen, became the generally acknowledged leader of the national movement, a status he enjoyed for thirty years.

In 1848, when the King abolished absolute monarchy, Jón Sigurðsson proposed a theory that was to form the basis for Iceland's struggle for independence for seven decades. He argued that Iceland had been subjected to the Norwegian King in 1262–64, not to the

---

[9] Helgi P. Briem: *Byltingin 1809*.
[10] *Saga Íslendinga* VII, p. 331 (Þorkell Jóhannesson).

Norwegian people. Thereby Iceland entered a personal union with Norway which was transferred into a union with Denmark when the Norwegian Crown was subjected to that of Denmark in the late 14th century. Later, in 1662, the Icelanders had accepted the absolute rule of the Danish King, not the Danish people. Therefore, the King could not give his power over Iceland to his Danish subjects, but only to the Icelanders. Under Jón Sigurðsson's influence Iceland's struggle for independence was to be mostly based on juridical and historical arguments. It was stressed that Iceland had the right to rule itself. The feasibility of doing so was more tacitly taken for granted, although some grievances, especially concerning the monopoly trade in Iceland, were also pointed out.[11]

Already in the revolutionary year of 1848 Jón Sigurðsson's theory was at least partly accepted by the King, when he promised that Iceland's constitutional status within the kingdom would not be "finally decided on until after the Icelanders have been heard in their own assembly in the country."[12] In accordance with this pledge, Iceland was not mentioned in the Danish Constitution of 1849, and the country was never represented in the Danish parliament.

As a fulfilment of the royal pledge of 1848 a National Assembly, elected by most male farmers and a few others, met in Reykjavík in 1851. By then the radical wave of 1848 had ebbed and the Danish government could not offer Iceland anything more than a communal status, like that wich the Faroes received in the following year, and representation in the Danish parliament. From the Icelandic standpoint this meant an incorporation into the new, democratic Danish state. The majority of the National Assembly, under Jón Sigurðsson's leadership, made a different proposal, which in practice meant that Iceland would be a separate state in a personal union with Denmark, although the term "state" was never used, probably

[11] Gunnar Karlsson: "Icelandic Nationalism and the Inspiration of History", pp. 81–88.

[12] *Lovsamling for Island* XIV, p. 185.—My translation.

for tactical reasons. Only those affairs that both parties agreed on would be administered jointly, and in practice by Danish authorities. It was obvious that no agreement could be reached, and the Assembly was dissolved before it had passed any bill on the constitutional status of the country.

The party division over the two alternative proposals at the National Assembly in 1851 is the first solid evidence that nationalism had penetrated the population of Icelandic farmers. It is a *terminus ante quem* for the emergence of nationalism in Iceland. In all, 43 representatives met at the Assembly, 37 elected and six appointed by the King. There was never any vote on the main issue of the Assembly, as it was dissolved prematurely, but the reaction of the representatives to the dissolution shows unequivocally their attitude. Altogether 36 representatives, 35 elected and one with a royal appointment, protested actively against the dissolution, while the two remaining elected representatives must be considered neutral. Evidence for this is that only five royally appointed representatives, and none of the elected ones, came to a banquet which the Governor held after the dissolution. The 36-man strong opposition consisted of 13 clergymen, 11 farmers, four university students and young academics without a permanent post, three district magistrates *(sýslumenn* and *bæjarfógetar)*, two teachers, one physician, one merchant and one shop manager.[13]

It would no doubt be an exaggeration to say that the whole population supported the majority of the National Assembly in their protest. An Icelandic farmer's son, born in 1836, has written in his autobiography that his father subscribed to the Parliamentary Gazette and a political periodical and started to read from them aloud for the people at his home, instead of reading sagas or chanting epic poems (*rímur*). "Old people and farm hands" did not like this change, he says, and they spoke contemptuously about this political

---

[13] Páll Eggert Ólason: *Jón Sigurðsson* II, pp. 464–66, 475–76; III, pp. 10–12.—Cf. *Alþingismannatal 1845–1930.*

stuff as the "new porridge".[14] But the people had no alternative politics. The independence movement was the only political movement in the country.

This situation lasted for more than half a century. During the 67 years following the National Assembly, Icelandic politics revolved around the struggle for independence, a struggle which led to legislative power for the Icelandic *Alþing* in 1874, Home Rule with an Icelandic minister in Reykjavík in 1904, and the establishment of an Icelandic state in a personal union with Denmark in 1918. In this period, for many people, the word "politics" became synonymous with "struggle for independence"; nothing else was considered real politics. Those who were interested in practical progress, like the improvement of education or communications, sometimes complained that the whole attention of the people was directed towards the demand for independence.[15]

To be sure, there was often a bitter disagreement among the Icelanders in this struggle, but that was nearly always a disagreement about ways, and not principles. Most often they disagreed on how radical demands should be raised at a definite point in time and how imperfect offers of improvement should be accepted. No one doubted the general course, that Iceland should head for greater autonomy. Iceland never had a Union Party like the Faroe Islands.

The Danish Attitude

Of course the provisional failure and final success of Iceland in its struggle for independence must partly be ascribed to the attitude of Denmark. Why, in the first place, did the Danes oppose Iceland's secession? And having done so, why did they finally give in?

Since the trade monopoly was lifted in Iceland in the 1780s,

---

[14] Jakob Hálfdanarson: *Sjálfsævisaga*, p. 19.
[15] Gunnar Karlsson: *Frá endurskoðun til valtýsku*, pp. 36–37, 106–08, 131–37.

Denmark had no major economic interests connected with Iceland. When Iceland raised the claim for separate finances, it even faced the awkward dilemma that the income which the state collected there did not cover its expenditures in the country. If the standard of public services was not to be lowered or the taxes raised, one had to secure an annual contribution from the state treasury of Denmark to the treasury of Iceland. Jón Sigurðsson saved the pride of his fellow countrymen by arguing that the contribution was a refund for goods and valuables that had been taken from Iceland to Denmark during the time of their union. The Danish never accepted this view, but nevertheless they annually paid a considerable sum of money to Iceland in the years between 1874 and 1918.[16]

It must mainly have been a question of pride for Denmark to keep its hold on Iceland. Since the 17th century, Danish and Swedish intellectuals had known that the Icelanders had written down and preserved on parchment sagas of their own kings and heroes from a very distant past (later called *fornaldarsögur Norðurlanda*). These sagas could even be used as evidence in the long-lasting dispute between Denmark and Sweden on the issue of which of the kingdoms was the oldest.[17] Furthermore, the Icelanders proved to be able to read these manuscripts without any special training, whereby one concluded—with some exaggeration of course—that modern Icelandic was in fact an old common language of the Scandinavian countries. Even a competent scholar like Rasmus Christian Rask presented Icelandic as the mother tongue of the other Nordic languages and used the term "Icelandic" for any Scandinavian language spoken in Scandinavia in the Viking Age. Thus, according to Rask's terminology, Icelandic was spoken in all of Scandinavia in those

---

[16] Einar Arnórsson: *Alþingi og frelsisbaráttan 1845–1874*, pp. 71–80, 104–08, 178–81, 184–85.—Björn Þórðarson: *Alþingi og frelsisbaráttan 1874–1944*, p. 342.

[17] Andersson: *The Problem of Icelandic Saga Origins*, pp. 1–2.

times.[18] This extraordinary status given to the Icelandic language naturally fostered a high esteem for Iceland in Scandinavia.

Iceland's esteem must have grown in strength during the age of Romanticism in the first half of the 19th century.[19] When King Frederik VI announced his intention of founding consultative assemblies in his kingdom and having Iceland represented at the assembly for the Danish Islands, no less than three Danish authors reacted by proposing that the Icelandic *Alþing* should be restored as a consultative assembly for Iceland. The first to mention the matter was F. A. Holstein, Count of Ledreborg. The others were Jens Møller, Professor of Theology, and Orla Lehmann, later one of the leaders of the National-Liberal Party in Danish politics, then only 22 years old.[20] On this occasion Orla Lehmann wrote that he

> honestly knows no better way of expressing what it is that draws our imagination so forcefully to the naked mountains [of Iceland] than [to say] that in them we see our own past, a gigantic monument raised over a distant time, which in severe loneliness projects into a World, where everything is new and altered. Thus, in the old days a number of Scandinavians emigrated to the country and introduced there the life and customs of the old North. A life so rich in alteration and transition has, since that time, almost transformed for us the surface of the Earth and its inhabitants; the mighty hand of Civilization has plowed up almost every trace of the life of these ancient times and everything that moved within it. But, as if frozen between the distant icy mountains, where the storms of time never reached, it persists in almost complete purity in Iceland, so that there we can see a living past, an eloquent picture of past life.— Therefore, every Scandinavian is bound to feel affection for the Icelandic people, and we should definitely be able to find, in the character, mode of life and customs of present day Icelanders, traces of

[18] Lindroth: "Þegar íslenzkan var álitin móðurmál Norðurlandamálanna", pp. 117–18.—Jón Pétur Ragnarsson: *Entstehung und Entwicklung des Nationalbewusstseins in Island*, pp. 85, 87.

[19] Cf. Sverrir Kristjánsson: "Endurreisn alþingis", pp. 108–09.

[20] Páll Eggert Ólason: *Jón Sigurðsson* II, pp. 37–39.

our own old physiognomy, which we would look for in vain in our crumbled ruins or lifeless annals.[21]

For people with this attitude it would have been devastating to do anything to introduce a modern Danish culture in Iceland; it was much more suitable for them to help the Icelanders reestablish a medieval assembly. On the other hand, when the Icelanders began to demand real autonomy and seek political segregation from Denmark, it was a serious blow for many a Danish friend of Iceland. Orla Lehmann came to be considered one of Iceland's most dangerous opponents among Danish politicians.[22]

Nevertheless, since Iceland was a small jewel in the Danish Crown, and not a source of income or a military stronghold, Danish nationalists could not find great pleasure in keeping it within its boundaries against the will of the Icelanders. In fact they had no other choice than to give in step by step.

Back to the Question of Nationalism in Iceland

As Sven Tägil mentions (pp. 34–36), many authors have connected the emergence of nationalism with the advent of the bourgeoisie and industrialization. Of course this opinion must allow for a number of cases of earlier proto-nationalism or ethnic roots of the modern nationalism proper.[23] Nonetheless, I shall here use as a theoretical background the theories of one of the most implacable proponents of the modernist view of nationalism, the English sociologist Ernest Gellner.

According to Gellner, agrarian people do not normally desire a coincidence of cultural and political boundaries. Some societies even prefer foreigners as rulers in order to minimize corruption, as their links of kinship are assumed to be unlikely to influence their official

---

21 *Maanedsskrift for Litteratur* VII, pp. 523–24.—My translation.

22 Páll Eggert Ólason: *Jón Sigurðsson* V, pp. 5–14, 19–22.

23 Cf. Smith: *The Ethnic Origins of Nations*, pp. 13–16.—Hobsbawm: *Nations and nationalism since 1780*, pp. 46–79.

duties. Another important feature of agrarian societies is that only a few people can read; literacy is a monopoly of an administrative/religious elite, the *clerisy*. The literate high culture often extends over large areas, much larger than one political unit. The illiterate low culture, on the other hand, is locally based and divided by dialectical and other differences. Normally the high culture tends to exaggerate rather than underplay the difference between the two cultures. Contrary to this, an industrial society needs constant mobility; people must be able to move between classes and other social groups, which demands general literacy and a homogeneous culture. This, in turn, calls for a standardized educational system which only the state can provide. For this reason the culture must have the same boundaries as the state, and this is the very essence of nationalism.[24]

I do not choose Gellner's theory as a point of departure because it applies very well to Iceland. On the contrary, I choose it because it seems convincing generally, and Iceland appears to offer an interesting exception to the theory, an exception which definitely does not "prove the rule", but may nonetheless give it some support and throw a new light on its validity.

There was practically no technical or industrial modernization in Iceland in 1850. Although the first half of the 19th century was a period of considerable economic growth in the country, this growth took place entirely within the boundaries of the old society, and in the long run it led to overpopulation within rural areas, a protracted economic and demographic crisis and emigration to America in the second half of the century.[25] In 1860, 80% of the population were still engaged in agriculture and 10% in fishing (the boundaries between the two occupations being rather diffuse), but only 3% in industry and trade.[26] No semblance of an industrial revolution

[24] Gellner: *Nations and Nationalism*, pp. 8–38.

[25] Aðalgeir Kristjánsson and Gísli Ágúst Gunnlaugsson: "Félags- og hagþróun á Íslandi á fyrri hluta 19. aldar".—Guðmundur Hálfdanarson: "Aðdragandi iðnbyltingar á 19. öld".

[26] *Tölfræðihandbók 1974*, p. 32.

emerged in Iceland until after the turn of the century, with the introduction of the mechanization of fishing.[27]

It cannot be said either that the proponents of nationalism in Iceland stressed the most important role of the nation state, which is, according to Gellner, to standardize and expand literate high culture through an educational system. Compulsary school attendance was not introduced until 1907, almost a century later than in Denmark. To be sure, parents had been required to teach their children to read since the 18th century, and in 1880 writing and arithmetic were added to the list. But that was all. On the other hand, a Theological Seminary was established in Reykjavík in 1847, a Medical School in 1876, a Law School in 1908 and a University, where a Faculty of Arts was added to the other institutions, in 1911.[28] It was obviously thought to be more important in Iceland to reproduce the cultural élite than to spread its high culture to the lower classes through a general school system.

There is still one way left to connect the origin of Icelandic nationalism with the process of modernization. It can be assumed that Iceland's demand for autonomy was a reaction against progressive development in Denmark. Seen in this way, the case of Iceland would fall into a well-known and much discussed group of periphery-nationalisms (cf. Tägil's contribution, p. 27). And of course Iceland was a periphery. There was a striking difference between the standards of living and visible culture in Denmark and Iceland in the first half of the 19th century, a difference which must have had a strong effect on Icelandic students in Copenhagen, who became the pioneers of Icelandic nationalism. The second half of the 18th century had been a prosperous time in Denmark while Iceland was blighted by a cold climate and a catastro-

[27] Gísli Gunnarsson: "Kenningar um útbreiðslu þróaðs hagkerfis", pp. 20–22.—Jón Þ. Þór: "Vélvæðing í íslenskum atvinnuvegum í upphafi 20. aldar", pp. 35–43.

[28] Guðmundur Finnbogason: *Alþingi og menntamálin*, pp. 8–22, 97–108.

phic volcanic eruption.[29] Table 1 (p. 37) demonstrates this, as it
shows that the population of Iceland fell by some 3,000 during the
18th century. Nevertheless, Icelandic nationalism starts too early to
be explained as a reaction to an industrial breakthrough in Denmark, which first occurs in the second half of the 19th century.[30]
There is no doubt that Denmark's superiority was a provocative
example for Iceland, but that alone is not a sufficient explanation for
the early occurence of nationalism, especially as it comes exceptionally
early by general European standards. According to Eric Hobsbawm,
the nationalism of minority groups was rarely a serious problem for
the rulers of European states until the 1880s.[31] Anthony D. Smith
sets the beginning of the disruptive phase of nationalism in Europe
at 1871 (cf. Tägil's contribution, p. 24–25). We must therefore seek
other explanations for the origin of nationalism in Iceland.

The Cultural Heritage

In the first place, the Icelanders were a highly historical people, both
politically and culturally.[32] The existence of an independent society
in Iceland in the Middle Ages was well documented: in an extensive
law code, in a treaty whereby Iceland was subjected to the King of
Norway, and not least in the sagas. It may be asked whether the historic tradition of Iceland is anything but a romantic invention. Anthony D. Smith has argued, convincingly, that the myth of a golden
age is universal; all peoples discover it in their past when they need
it.[33] It has also been said about the golden age of Iceland that it was a
myth; the Danish anthropologist Kirsten Hastrup has argued that it

[29] Gunnar Karlsson: "Icelandic Nationalism and the Inspiration of History", pp. 84–85.

[30] Olsen: *Danmarks økonomiske historie siden 1750*, pp. 120–21.

[31] Hobsbawm: *Nations and nationalism since 1780*, pp. 43–45.

[32] Cf. Gunnar Karlsson: "Icelandic Nationalism and the Inspiration of
History", pp. 77–89.

[33] Smith: *The Ethnic Origins of Nations*, pp. 191–200.

had already been created in the Middle Ages: "By means of an optical illusion the authors of twelfth- and thirteenth-century Icelandic literature created an image of an original 'free state' as the essence of Icelandic social identity. The separate law was interpreted as political sovereignty, the noble heathen as a statesman."[34] But perhaps just because Iceland had preserved in the sagas a medieval tradition of a golden age, it was unusually well-equipped for a nationalist struggle in the age of Romanticism, especially as the sagas also had material which could easily interest the country's larger neighbours.

Actually, the interest in old Icelandic history and literature originated in Iceland. In the 16th century the country was repeatedly described in European geographical literature as the home of a most exotic and primitive people. In 1593 an Icelandic clergyman, Arngrímur Jónsson, published a book in Latin, *Brevis commentarius de Islandia*, in which he tried to reject what he saw as slander about his fatherland. Sixteen years later Arngrímur followed up his work with a history of Iceland, *Crymogæa* (literally "Iceland" in Greek, although the book was written in Latin). The book is permeated with European humanism in an Icelandic variant, where the country's past and the Icelandic language are glorified. It was mostly through these writings of Arngrímur that Scandinavians got to know about Icelandic saga literature and Iceland's history.[35] Their interest not only led to a high esteem for Iceland in Scandinavia, as mentioned above, but must also have given the Icelanders a higher degree of self-esteem, even though it did not have any political consequences for the time being. There could be no doubt that the Icelanders were a people of their own, a *þjóð* as it is called in Icelandic.

Admittedly, one can find quite anti-national opinions among Icelanders in the age of Danish absolutism. "I do not only see it as

[34] Hastrup: "Defining a Society", pp. 250–51.

[35] Jakob Benediktsson: "Inngangur", pp. 13–50.—Jakob Benediktsson: "Den vågnende interesse for sagalitteraturen på Island i 1600-tallet", pp. 157–70.—Andersson: *The Problem of Icelandic Saga Origins*, pp. 3–4.

useless but as directly harmful to keep using the Icelandic language," the principal of one of the two Latin schools wrote in 1771, and wanted his fellow countrymen to adopt Danish.[36] But one also constantly finds people who want to keep Icelandic culture alive, people who love their land and their language, without displaying a trace of political nationalism. On the contrary, sometimes the most enthusiastic patriots, like the poet Eggert Ólafsson (1726–68), are those who praise their monarch in the highest terms.[37]

Although Iceland is not included in Miroslav Hroch's study of nationalism among ethnic minorities in Europe, it ought to be possible to place Iceland's development within his three phases of nationalism.[38] Phase A, when only a group of intellectuals are interested in popular culture, language and history, can be said to have lasted for more than two centuries in Iceland, from about 1600, when Arngrímur Jónsson started his work, until about 1830, when Icelandic intellectuals in Copenhagen began to argue publicly for the cultural and political restoration of Iceland. This deep cultural root is no doubt an important prerequisite for political nationalism in Iceland. But it is not a sufficient explanation of its origin. A not altogether unlikely outcome would have been a fairly common nostalgic national sentiment, restricted to glorification of old Icelandic language and literature, while political and industrial modernization would have paved the way for foreign culture in the country. This was the case in Wales, where a few people kept writing beautiful poems in Welsh, while the majority of the population forgot the language, adopted English and never raised the demand for a Welsh nation state.[39]

[36] Jón Jónsson Aðils: *Dagrenning,* pp. 23n–24n.—My translation.

[37] Halldór Hermannsson: *Eggert Ólafsson,* pp. 14–16, 29–33, 40–44.—Jón Pétur Ragnarsson: *Entstehung und Entwicklung des Nationalbewusstseins in Island,* pp. 7–11.

[38] Hroch: *Die Vorkämpfer der nationalen Bewegung,* pp. 24–26.—Cf. Tägil pp. 36–37 .

[39] Williams: "Wales—the Cultural Bases of Nineteenth and Twentieth Century Nationalism", pp. 119–29.

Political Power in Iceland

Iceland was under the absolute monarchy of the Danish King in the period 1662–1874. Although absolutism in its strict Danish form did not allow for any formal autonomy for any part of the realm, Icelandic society may have been fairly independent in real terms. In this respect the most important factor is not that Iceland was a separate legislative district, nor that the Icelandic *Alþing* met annually until 1800. Legislation became more and more Danish or Danish/Norwegian during the age of absolutism, and the former legislative assembly was little more than a court of law. The important thing for Iceland's selfrule was that it had, for the most part, its own native class of officials. There were in all 78 district magistrates in office in the country during the period 1721–90. Only three of them were born in Denmark, the remaining 75 in Iceland. More than half of the higher Crown officials, governors (*stiftamtmenn*), sub-governors (*amtmenn*), bailiffs (*landfógetar*) and chief justices (*lögmenn*), were of Icelandic origin.[40] All bishops in Iceland after the Reformation, and practically all clergymen, were Icelanders. To be sure, the officials had the role and duty to carry out the King's will, as it was mediated through Danish royal officials in Copenhagen. Only one Icelander in the 18th century, Jón Eiríksson, reached a top post in the administration of Iceland in Copenhagen. But, according to Harald Gustafsson, a Swedish historian who has written his dissertation on the subject, it was in most cases the will of the Icelandic officials in Iceland which was carried out. If they were unanimous in saying "This can not be done in Iceland," no Danish person had the knowledge to challenge their opinion.[41] Iceland and Denmark were very dissimilar countries with entirely different economies and juridical systems, in spite of a certain amount of Danish influence in Iceland during the absolutist period.

[40] Gustafsson: *Mellan kung och allmoge,* pp. 78–79, 290–93.
[41] Ibid. pp. 161, 168–69, 237–40, 274–82.

The class of Icelandic officials was to a large extent identical with the landowners. Up into the 18th century the post of district magistrate was sometimes a kind of sideline for the richest landowners of the country, who had most of their income in the form of land-rent from their tenants. As education became a more important prerequisite for royal offices, in the 18th century, this class kept well in step with this development. They made good use of the two Latin schools in Iceland and the privileges which Icelandic students enjoyed in Copenhagen, where they got free food and lodging at the students' hostel for three years. In the 18th century the district magistrates in Iceland were considerably better educated than governors and sub-governors in Denmark and Norway.[42]

From this point of view the struggle for the independence of Iceland can be seen as defensive. In 1848 the old regime in Denmark, a regime that had secured considerable internal selfrule for Iceland, went to pieces. The Danes built up a new form of government based on representative democracy. The crucial question for the Icelandic nationalists, in the first phase, was to prevent Iceland from being incorporated into the new Danish form of government much more thoroughly than it had ever been incorporated in the old one. In this struggle there was a general agreement between quite conservative and radical forces in Iceland, in sociopolitical terms. It has even been argued that Icelandic farmers supported the nationalist cause mainly in order to preserve the traditional Icelandic society against liberal ideas coming in from Denmark.[43] Although there is no doubt some truth in this opinion, Icelandic farmers were surely also under some influence from liberal ideas,[44] and the form of government that the Icelanders wanted to

[42] Ibid. pp. 84–85, 101.
[43] Guðmundur Hálfdanarson: "Takmörkun giftinga eða einstaklingsfrelsi", pp. 464–67.
[44] Guðmundur Jónsson and Gunnar Karlsson: "Skiptar skoðanir: Frelsisþrá í sjálfstæðisbaráttu Íslendinga", pp. 60–66.

establish was from the very beginning a democratic one, no less so than that of their neighbouring countries.

Cultural Homogeneity

Nevertheless, Icelandic nationalism was much more than a tactical play for power. One must look deeper into the structure of society to explain how easily the pioneers of nationalism gained support among the common people of the country. Let us start our third explanation with a quotation from Ernest Gellner:

> Industrial societies are quite inegalitarian in providing their citizens with a wide variety of social positions, some very much more advantageous than others; but they are also egalitarian in that this system of posts forms a kind of continuum (there are no radical discontinuities along it), and that there is a widespread belief, possibly exaggerated but not wholly devoid of truth, that it is possible to move up and down, and that rigid barriers in the system are illegitimate. [45]

As incredible as it may sound, this description is strongly reminiscent of the old Icelandic agricultural society. There were enormous differences in wealth and possibilities between the richest and the poorest, but nowhere on the long continuum between them was there an absolute barrier; the society was not divided into segregated groups of any kind.

Starting at the bottom, the working class, over 40% of the adult population, consisted for the most part of domestic servants who lived unmarried in the homes of their employers. Some of these servants had children, but largely the class was "socially infertile"; for social reasons it was excluded from having children and had therefore to be reproduced by the farming class. Most domestic servants were thus children of farmers and their wives. According to figures

[45] Gellner: *Nations and Nationalism*, p. 67.

collected from two districts in the census of 1801, over 80% of the boys under five years of age were sons of farmers. In the age group 15–24, around 90% of the men were servants, in their parents' homes or elsewhere. After that the number of servants fell rapidly, and in the group of 40–59-year-old men, 80% were farmers and 10% servants.[46] These numbers show that for most men the status of a servant was a step on the way towards that of a farmer, and not a lifelong occupation. For women the situation must have been somewhat different. More of them remained in the servant class, because they were more numerous than the men and had therefore less chance of marrying (839 men to 1,000 women in 1801).[47] Nevertheless, this proves that the working class was for the most part recruited from the farming class, and a large part of it was young people who would, in the future, establish their own homes. For each individual of both sexes there was always a possibility, at least theoretically and in many cases in reality, of moving up into the farming class. One needed nothing but the good luck of getting married to someone who owned or could rent a farm. (One of the present author's grandfathers, born in 1864, was a poor servant when he married the widow of a rather well-to-do farmer, some seven years older than he was, and in due time he became one of the wealthiest farmers of the neighbourhood.)

Within the farming class, too, there was a great difference between the richest and the poorest. About half of the land was owned by private individuals, while the other half was the property of the Church and the Crown. Around the year 1700, the privately owned property was divided among some 1,300 owners, almost all of them Icelandic. This meant that one out of every six families owned some land, but half of it (a quarter of the whole landed property in the

[46] Guðmundur Hálfdanarson: "Aðdragandi iðnbyltingar á 19. öld", pp. 28–29.
[47] *Tölfræðihandbók 1974*, p. 7.

country) was owned by some 80 persons (6%), while the remaining 1,220 (94%) shared the other half.[48]

However, this does not mean that the farming class was divided into two groups, the rich landowners and the poor farmers who had no or very little land of their own. The whole farming class can be ordered along an uninterrupted continuum from those who owned no land to those who possessed up to 60 farms. There was practically no difference in status between tenants who owned no land and those 400 persons who owned from one twentieth to one third of an average farm. There was no barrier either between those who owned one third of an average farm and those who owned half a farm or a small and poor farm, nor between the latter and the farmers who possessed one average farm. In this way one could go on up along the whole continuum without finding, anywhere, a dividing line which would have been considered a class difference by contemporary people. In practice the difference between the top and the bottom was of course great, but in theory all farmers belonged to the same class, and there constantly existed a theoretical and a real chance to move up the scale a bit.

This social mobility was mirrored by a great geographical mobility. A study has been made of this in a parish of 37 farms in Western Iceland in the period 1754–81. Only three farms were farmed by the same person throughout the period. Twelve were farmed by two or three persons, eleven by four farmers and another eleven farms by five to eight farmers. In almost 40% of the cases, the time a farmer stayed at a farm was only one to four years. Only three times in the period did a son succeed his father at a farm. In 1816 about 25% of the farmers and farmers' wives were born within the parish, 15% in neighbouring parishes, but 60% in distant districts. A study of a district in Northern Iceland in the 19th century shows a similar trend. If we count only people who were farmers more than ten years in their lifetime, more than half of them lived on three or more farms.

---

[48] Bragi Guðmundsson: *Efnamenn og eignir þeirra um 1700*, pp. 31–35.

Everything thus indicates that the mobility of Icelandic farmers was considerably greater than that among their peers in Scandinavia.[49] A substantial part of the rich landowners were simultaneously officials, almost all of them Icelandic. Among the 80 magnates who owned half of the privately-owned property around the year 1700, there were 21 Crown officials and 22 clergymen (bishops and provosts included).[50] This was the real upper class of the country, and to a great extent it reproduced itself. But, again, there was a real possibility to get ahead from the farming class into this upper class. In the 18th century, around 40% of Crown officials in Iceland were sons of Icelandic farmers.[51] Of course, most of them were sons of wealthy farmers who possessed considerable property, and who were again, some of them, sons of officials. It was this wealthy section of farmers who connected the farming class and the officials and ensured that no barrier between the two groups could be perceived.

The lack of absolute barriers in the old Icelandic society has been observed by earlier scholars as insignificant class consciousness among the Icelanders.[52] Furthermore, it has produced the myth that Iceland was a society without class divisions. The myth was nurtured by the nationalist historians in the first half of this century, and it has proved to be tenacious. As recently as 1984 a member of Parliament, and an educated teacher, discussed the teaching of history at the *Alþing* and pointed out

...that through the centuries the equality between the rich and the poor was often a very outstanding feature. A skipper did not survive if his boat went down. He perished together with the ship. Leaders in political confrontations in this land did not sit at home and send

[49] Loftur Guttormsson: "Staðfesti í flokkusamfélagi?", pp. 18–23, 29–33, 40.

[50] Bragi Guðmundsson: *Efnamenn og eignir þeirra um 1700*, pp. 50–51.

[51] Gustafsson: *Mellan kung och allmoge*, p. 78.

[52] Jón Pétur Ragnarsson: *Entstehung und Entwicklung des Nationalbewusstseins in Island*, p. 4.

their troops to the battlefield. They fell with weapons in their hands, together with their followers. When famines raged, not only the peasants in the South suffered, but also the episcopal seat. ... Thus I believe that those who want to demonstrate a classridden society forget that the Icelanders were in many situations all in the same boat.[53]

Needless to say, this is a very superficial interpretation. But it has not emerged from nothing, and what it has emerged from, apart from wishful thinking, is that the contrasts in Icelandic society were hidden, informal and mobile, and not completely different from those of an industrial, capitalist society, as Gellner describes it. One could disregard them, were one politically interested in doing so.

It could be assumed that this lack of obvious class divisions in Iceland has fostered a relatively homogeneous culture. On the one hand, literacy was rather common, probably around 50% among adults, even before any real attempts were made to increase literacy, under the influence of pietism, in the mid-18th century.[54] On the other hand, cultural activity did not extend very far, after the demise of saga-writing in the late Middle Ages. The well-educated district magistrates and clergymen, like poor farmers, were for the most part content with composing *rímur*, extremely long epic poems, with material from old sagas and other histories. *Rímur* were made according to the same tradition, generation after generation and century after century, without any original creative contribution, and sung or chanted to traditional, monotonous melodies.

It is probably also a sign of a greater cultural homogeneity in Iceland than elsewhere in the Nordic countries that Iceland adopted hardly a trace of home mission or other religious awakenings in the 19th century. Apart from a few people who became Mormons and

53 *Alþingistíðindi 1983–84* B, p. 2746 .—My translation.

54 Hallgrímur Hallgrímsson: *Íslensk alþýðumentun á 18. öld*, p. 70.— Loftur Guttormsson: "Island. Læsefærdighed og folkeuddannelse 1540– 1800", pp. 141–148, 158, 169.

emigrated to America, no religious initiative was taken outside the National Church until the end of the century, when new groups like the Salvation Army and YMCA/YWCA began to gain support among Reykjavík's growing population.[55] The awakenings, within and outside the Church, were among the very first popular movements in Scandinavia, and they are usually seen as a sign of a cultural cleavage between the official Church and the common people. In Iceland the clergymen seem to have been sufficiently close to the people to respond to their religious and social needs. To this point can be added the lack of local differences in popular culture in Iceland. One example of this is that dialect differences in the Icelandic language are insignificant and far less than in Danish and Faroese, even though these languages were spoken in much smaller countries and, at least in Denmark, with far better means of communication. Linguists have even discussed whether it was right to talk about dialects in Icelandic at all.[56]

Iceland and the Theories of Nationalism

The opinion which has been proposed here, that the Icelanders were exceptionally receptive to nationalism earlier than can be explained by their place in the process of modernization, because of their unusual social mobility, can be supported by the findings of Miroslav Hroch. He concludes, that "the national movement found ... reception and followers quicker among the more socially mobile and communicating social groups, also among the more communicating and mobile parts of those groups."[57] Nevertheless, Ernest Gellner's stringent theory of the connection between nationalism and industrialism would seem to provide a deeper understanding of the special case of Iceland.

[55] Pétur Pétursson: "Trúarlegar hreyfingar í Reykjavík" I, pp. 201–06.

[56] Dahlstedt: "Íslenzk mállýzkulandafræði", pp. 29–31.—Stefán Karlsson: "Tungan", pp. 52–53.

[57] Hroch: *Die Vorkämpfer der nationalen Bewegung*, p. 168.

Of course Gellner has not said that cultural homogeneity leads to nationalism. He says that industrialization needs homogeneity, which "appears on the surface in the form of nationalism", or "is reflected in nationalism."[58] What is borrowed from Gellner here is the idea that there is a strong relationship between cultural homogeneity and social mobility on the one hand and national identification on the other, in other words, that it was easier, and more natural for an Icelander to identify with his or her people than it was for most Europeans in the first half of the 19th century, because the Icelander had so little else to identify with—no estate or class, no district or region. Paradoxical as it may seem, Iceland may have been more of a nation state during the age of absolutism than most European societies at the time.

LITERATURE

The names of Icelandic authors are placed in the alphabetic order of the first names, according to Icelandic practice.

Aðalgeir Kristjánsson and Gísli Ágúst Gunnlaugsson: "Félags- og hagþróun á Íslandi á fyrri hluta 19. aldar." *Saga* XXVIII, 1990

Alþingismannatal, konungsfulltrúa, landshöfðingja, ráðherra o.fl., 1845–1930. Reykjavík 1930

Alþingistíðindi 1983–84. B. *Umræður með aðalefnisyfirliti.* Reykjavík 1987

Andersson, Theodore M.: *The Problem of Icelandic Saga Origins. A Historical Survey.* New Haven 1964

Björn Þórðarson: *Alþingi og frelsisbaráttan 1874–1944.* Reykjavík 1951 (*Saga Alþingis* III)

Bragi Guðmundsson: *Efnamenn og eignir þeirra um 1700. Athugun á íslenskum gósseigendum í jarðabók Árna og Páls og fleiri heimildum.* Reykjavík 1985 (*Ritsafn Sagnfræðistofnunar* XIV)

Dahlstedt, Karl-Hampus: "Íslenzk mállýzkulandafræði. Nokkrar athuganir." *Skírnir* CXXXII, 1958

---

[58] Gellner: *Nations and Nationalism*, pp. 39, 46.

60	Gunnar Karlsson

Einar Arnórsson: *Alþingi og frelsisbaráttan 1845–1874*. Reykjavík 1949 (*Saga Alþingis* II)

Gad, Finn: "'La Grönlande, les Isles de Ferröe et l'Islande non comprises.' A new look at the origins of the addition to Article IV of the Treaty of Kiel of 1814." *Scandinavian Journal of History* IV, 1979

Gellner, Ernest: *Nations and Nationalism*. Oxford 1983

Gísli Gunnarsson: "Kenningar um útbreiðslu þróaðs hagkerfis." *Iðnbylting á Íslandi. Umsköpun atvinnulífs um 1880 til 1940*. Reykjavík 1987

Guðmundur Finnbogason: *Alþingi og menntamálin*. Reykjavík 1947 (*Saga Alþingis* V)

Guðmundur Friðjónsson: *Úr heimahögum. Kvæði*. Reykjavík 1902

Guðmundur Hálfdanarson: "Aðdragandi iðnbyltingar á 19. öld." *Iðnbylting á Íslandi. Umsköpun atvinnulífs um 1880 til 1940*. Reykjavík 1987

Guðmundur Hálfdanarson: "Takmörkun giftinga eða einstaklingsfrelsi. Íhaldssemi og frjálslyndi á fyrstu árum hins endurreista alþingis." *Tímarit Máls og menningar* XLVII, 1986

Guðmundur Jónsson and Gunnar Karlsson: "Skiptar skoðanir: Frelsisþrá í sjálfstæðisbaráttu Íslendinga. Hófst sjálfstæðisbaráttan sem andsvar við frjálslyndum hugmyndum úr Evrópu?" *Ný saga* I, 1987

Gunnar Karlsson: *Frá endurskoðun til valtýsku*. Reykjavík 1972 (*Sagnfræðirannsóknir* I)

Gunnar Karlsson: "Icelandic Nationalism and the Inspiration of History", in Mitchison, Rosalind (ed.): *The Roots of Nationalism. Studies in Northern Europe*. Edinburgh 1980

Gustafsson, Harald: *Mellan kung och allmoge—ämbetsmän, beslutsprocess och inflytande på 1700-talets Island*. Stockholm 1985 (*Acta Universitatis Stockholmiensis* XXXIII)

Halldór Hermannsson: *Eggert Ólafsson. A Biographical Sketch*. Ithaca 1925 (*Islandica* XVI)

Hallgrímur Hallgrímsson: *Íslensk alþýðumentun á 18. öld*. Sérprentun úr Tímanum. Reykjavík 1925

Hastrup, Kirsten: "Defining a Society: the Icelandic Free State between two Worlds." *Scandinavian Studies* LVI, 1984

Helgi P. Briem: *Byltingin 1809*. Reykjavík 1936

Hobsbawm, E.J.: *Nations and nationalism since 1780. Programme, myth, reality*. Cambridge 1990

Hroch, Miroslav: *Die Vorkämpfer der nationalen Bewegung bei den kleinen Völkern Europas. Eine vergleichende Analyse zur gesellschaftlichen Schichtung der patriotischen Gruppen.* Praha 1968

Ibsen, Henrik: *Peer Gynt. Play in Five Acts.* Ed. by James Walter McFarlane. English version by Christopher Fry, based on a literal translation by Johan Fillinger. London 1970

Jakob Benediktsson: "Den vågnende interesse for sagalitteraturen på Island i 1600-tallet." *Maal og minne* 1981

Jakob Benediktsson: "Inngangur", in Arngrímur Jónsson: *Crymogæa. Þættir úr sögu Íslands.* Reykjavík 1985

Jakob Hálfdanarson: *Sjálfsævisaga. Bernskuár Kaupfélags Þingeyinga.* Reykjavík 1982

Jón Jónsson Aðils: *Dagrenning. Fimm alþýðuerindi.* Reykjavík 1910

Jón Pétur Ragnarsson: *Entstehung und Entwicklung des Nationalbewusstseins in Island.* Inaugural-Dissertation zur Erlangung des Doktorgrades einer Hohen Philosophischen Fakultät der Eberhard-Karls-Universität zu Tübingen. Tübingen 1959

Jón Þ. Þór: "Vélvæðing í íslenskum atvinnuvegum í upphafi 20. aldar." *Iðnbylting á Íslandi. Umsköpun atvinnulífs um 1880 til 1940.* Reykjavík 1987

Lindroth, Hjalmar: "Þegar íslenzkan var álitin móðurmál Norðurlandamálanna." *Skírnir* CXI, 1937

Loftur Guttormsson: "Island. Læsefærdighed og folkeuddannelse 1540–1800." *Ur nordisk kulturhistoria. Läskunnighet och folkbildning före folkskoleväsendet. XVIII Nordiska historikermötet, Jyväskylä 1981. Mötesrapport* III. Jyväskylä 1981

Loftur Guttormsson: "Staðfesti í flökkusamfélagi? Ábúðarhættir í Reykholtsprestakalli á 18. öld." *Skírnir* CLXIII, 1989

Lovsamling for Island. Samlet og udgivet af Oddgeir Stephensen og Jón Sigurðsson. XIV. Kjøbenhavn 1868

Maanedsskrift for Litteratur. Udgivet af et Selskab. VII, 1832

Manntal á Íslandi árið 1703. Tekið að tilhlutun Árna Magnússonar og Páls Vídalín. Ásamt manntali 1729 í þrem sýslum. Reykjavík 1924–47

Mitchell, B.R.: *European Historical Statistics 1750–1970.* London 1975

Olsen, Erling: *Danmarks økonomiske historie siden 1750.* København 1967 (*Studier fra Københavns Universitets økonomiske institut* III)

62	*Gunnar Karlsson*

Páll Eggert Ólason: *Jón Sigurðsson* II–V. Reykjavík 1930–33
Pétur Pétursson: "Trúarlegar hreyfingar í Reykjavík tvo fyrstu áratugi 20. aldar. Fyrsti hluti." *Saga* XVIII, 1980
Rask, Rasmus Christian: "Brjef frá Rask." *Tímarit hins íslenzka bókmentafélags* IX, 1888
Saga Íslendinga VII. *Tímabilið 1770–1830. Upplýsingaröld.* Samið hefir Þorkell Jóhannesson. Reykjavík 1950
Schei, Liv Kjørsvik: *The Shetland Story.* London 1988
Smith, Anthony D.: *The Ethnic Origins of Nations.* Oxford 1986
Stefán Karlsson: "Tungan." *Íslensk þjóðmenning* VI. Reykjavík 1989
Sverrir Kristjánsson: "Endurreisn alþingis." *Saga* IX, 1971.—Reprinted in Sverrir Kristjánsson: *Ritsafn* I. Reykjavík 1981
Tölfræðihandbók 1974. Statistical Abstracts of Iceland 1974. Reykjavík 1976 (*Hagskýrslur Íslands* II:63)
Williams, Glanmor: "Wales—the Cultural Bases of Nineteenth and Twentieth Century Nationalism", in Mitchison, Rosalind (ed.): *The Roots of Nationalism: Studies in Northern Europe.* Edinburgh 1980

THE FORMATION OF A NATION: THE FAROE ISLANDS

Hans Jacob Debes

Introduction[1]

The Faroe Islands are an archipelago in the North Atlantic, consisting of 17 inhabited islands, covering an area of 1,400 square km. with a population of about 50,000. A people of Nordic origin has inhabited these islands since the time of the Vikings. During a period of a thousand years they have had the possibility of developing their own history and language and, as a whole, a culture of their own, dependent on the possibilities and limitations of the land and the sea. In this country all the objective historical factors for the creation and the formation of a nation should be present .

The Faroe Islands were the last of the Nordic countries in which nationalist sentiments arose in the 19th century, and within the Kingdom of Denmark this rise of a national consciousness took place after it had done so in Iceland, and before Greenland. In 1946 a majority of the Faroese voted for independence and secession from Denmark in a national plebiscite—about 80 years after the first awakening and organizing of Faroese nationalism. But no Faroese state was established; instead a majority of the Faroese accepted a home-rule status as "a self-governing community within the Danish state".

This outcome of very dramatic political events (especially during the Second World War when the Faroese had to govern them-

[1] Notes are limited to an absolute minimum, especially references to sources and literature written in the Faroese language.

selves after the German occupation of Denmark) raises the question whether in a historical-theoretical context the Faroese example is unique or universal, and how it can be related to diverse theories on nationalism. And because a considerable part of the Faroese people constantly feel themselves to be confronted with unsettled national problems, nationalism in the Faroe Islands is a more active political reality than in ethnic groups which—through nationalism—have achieved political independence, almost as a logical consequence.[2]

Here we attempt to find and explain the preconditions of Faroese nationalism, from the preparatory or formative period in the first decades of the 19th century, its breakthrough in the 1870s and 1880s, and, from the turn of the century, its development as a political movement for a higher degree of selfrule, and ultimately secession from the Danish state. An effort will also be made to place this development in the Faroe Islands in a larger historical and theoretical context.

Preconditions

The preconditions for the Faroese to develop and recognize a separate nationality can be placed in rather traditional definitions of the subject.[3] The geographical factor itself, combined with the small physical extent of the country, must in the course of time create a high degree of cultural homogeneity. Being of common origin, history, language, religion and culture in the broadest sense, it would have been historically illogical if the Faroese were to have developed into any group but a nation.[4] Denmark was far away, and the element of Danish popula-

[2] Debes: *Nú er tann stundin* , passim.—Kedourie: *Nationalism*, pp. 118–140.—Gellner: *Nations and Nationalism*, pp. 3–7.—Barclay: *Revolutions of Our Time*, pp. 79–120.

[3] Kohn: *The Idea of Nationalism*, pp. 13–18.—Kemiläinen: "The Idea of Nationalism", pp. 48–49.—Same author: *Nation, Nationality (Volkstum) and the Factors of National Consciousness in Modern Europe*, p. 5.

[4] Kemiläinen: *Nation, Nationality* , p. 5.

tion in the islands, amounting to only about 10 individuals, was too small to produce any major cultural influence.

Even if about half of the land after the Reformation belonged to the Crown, it was hired out to Faroese tenants. No Danes in their private capacity ever bought land in the islands. The "scotization" of Orkney and Shetland emphasizes the importance of distance between central authorities and subordinate peripheries. Even if one can accept the view that nationalism is "a doctrine",[5] it is hardly right to describe it generally as "invented" [6] or "imagined".[7] A moralizing attitude, as to whether nationalism be good or evil, has no scholarly significance. Empirical knowledge has proved clearly enough that such an attitude has been used for both purposes, which again makes it evident that not only one of the consequences is unavoidable. In the nature of nationalism there is probably "room for both the Sleeping Beauty and the Frankenstein's monster view of nationalism".[8] Nationalism is first and foremost "a state of mind" and "an idea",[9] the consciousness of being a nation from objective and subjective criteria, and a cultural and political force that can also justify itself as a "principle" of the right of self-determination and the forming of an independent state as its ultimate aim.[10] Nevertheless, the Faroese example demonstrates that this end of the process cannot always be presupposed.[11]

---

[5] Kedourie: *Nationalism*, p. 9.

[6] Ibid.—Hobsbawm & Ranger: *The Invention of Tradition*, pp. 1–14.—Hobsbawm: *The Age of Capital*, pp. 103–121.—Same author: *The Age of Revolution*, pp. 306–335.

[7] Anderson: *Imagined Communities*, pp. 14–16.

[8] Minogue: *Nationalism*, pp. 154–155.

[9] Kohn: *The Idea of Nationalism*, pp. 1–10.

[10] Ibid., pp. 13–18.—Kemiläinen: *Nationalism: Problems Concerning the Word, the Concept and Classification*, pp. 13–59.—Same author: *The Idea of Nationalism*, pp. 31–63.

[11] Ibid., p. 48: "The nation was not necessarily political; it also existed without forming a state."

The Faroe Islands were never considered a Norwegian or a Danish province. From the 13th century until the Peace of Kiel in 1814 they were constitutionally a "land" (country) under the Norwegian Crown and preserved their old social and political institutions, the legal basis being the same, i.e. Norwegian laws, supplemented with special judical precepts for the islands.

To the outer world the Faroese were represented by the *Lawthing* ("Løgting"), which was also a superior court (with 6 inferior local courts), with the *Lawman* ("løgmaður") as chairman and chief judge. He was always a native, and so were his 36, later 48, co-judges. This was also the case with the 6 local sheriffs, many of the court secretaries and always some of the priests, deans and headmasters of the Latin school (grammar school), who were educated in divinity at the University of Copenhagen after preparatory education at the Latin school. In the service of the royal monopoly trade, Faroese men often occupied leading positions. Occasionally there were Faroese commandants of the royal fort in the capital. The royal bailiff was the representative of the Crown or the feudal lord, the public prosecutor and the man responsible for the official revenues. He was generally a Dane, but he only resided in the islands from late spring to early autumn; in his absence a Faroese was temporarily appointed. As in Iceland, it was a class of Faroese officials (recruited among well-to-do farmers)—"between the king and the common people"[12]—who virtually ruled the country.

It is striking that the Faroese in documents to Danish authorities never identified themselves as other than Faroese—never e.g. as Norwegians or Danes. Common terms in royal documents to the Faroese are "subjects" or "farmers" in "Our land the Faroe Islands". No Norwegian or Danish writer ever took the Faroese for anything but one of the Nordic peoples.

It is evident from the sources that of the identity-creating preconditions, the common language was the most important for the

---

[12] Gustafsson: *Mellan kung och allmoge*, pp. 278–288.

later national identification.[13] During the Middle Ages, Faroese developed into a separate Nordic language.[14] The Norwegians became more distant kinsmen than before. As a whole the old ties between the Faroe Islands and Norway loosened after the Reformation, especially in the 17th and 18th centuries.

Even if Faroese had disappeared as a written language around 1500, it continued to be the spoken language of the people. No sections of the Faroese people became Danish-speaking, while Danish became the language of the authorities, in church, court, trade and the administration at large. The records of the Lawthing (preserved from 1615) are all written in Danish. But the Faroese language was not only an instrument of communication in the daily toil of the people; it was also the preserver of an old culture, manifest in an extensive oral tradition of ballads ("kvæði") and legends which still constitute classic Faroese literature.

Among preconditions for the awakening of a nationalist movement in an ethnic group, the degree of literacy and the industrialization of a given territory, deliberately promoted by central authorities but producing an "unequal" development in the center and periphery respectively, has generally been assumed.[15] But this "explanation" can hardly be accepted as universally valid. In the Faroese model, however, there can be no doubt that the factor of literacy was important in the process of national identification. Yet it was in no way consciously promoted by central authorities to meet the needs of industrial society for literacy and homogeneity, in con-

[13] Cf. Kedourie: *Nationalism*, pp. 62–73.—Nash: *The Cauldron of Ethnicity in the Modern World*, p. 12.—Smith: *The Ethnic Origins of Nations*, pp. 26–28.

[14] Matras: "Færøsk sprog", pp. 80–84.

[15] Gellner: *Nations and Nationalism*, pp. 8–18, 29–35.—Kedourie: *Nationalism*, p. 148.—Minogue: *Nationalism*, pp. 81–113, 149–152.—Barclay: *Revolutions of Our Time*, pp. 79–120.—Coleman (ed.): *The Study of Africa*, pp. 156–188.—Legum: *Panafrikanismen*, pp. 40–41.

trast to the illiterate society where such needs are not likely to be felt.[16]

The Faroese society was to a very high degree literate. A long tradition of interest in learning and intellectual competence can be documented.[17] Instrumental in bringing to the islands the changing temporal and spiritual currents of the time was the Latin school in Tórshavn (mentioned for the first time in 1547) and the University of Copenhagen. Those pupils of the Latin school who did not or could not go to the university went back to their home villages, where they could teach others the arts of reading and writing to the extent that the headmaster, priest, and dean (and in that capacity responsible for the educational level in his deanery), Lucas Jacobsen Debes, in his classic description of the Faroe Islands (1673), writes that "most of the men in the country can read in books".[18] Several visiting foreigners express in written sources their surprise at the unexpectedly high level of general knowledge.[19]

The National Awakening

The enlightened environment which arose at the capital at the beginning of the 19th century and gained momentum throughout the century had its roots in the Enlightenment and its interest in the past as a condition for understanding the present in order to make reasonable plans for the future. The outstanding Faroese exponent of that Age was the polymath Jens Christian Svabo (1746–1824), educated in economics and natural sciences at the University of Copenhagen. His main work is the "Report" he drew up for the Royal Danish Exchequer in 1782 on the general conditions in the islands, with proposals for improvements in keeping with the

[16] Gellner: *Nations and Nationalism*, pp. 33–38.

[17] West: *The History of the Faroe Islands, 1709–1816*, 1, pp. 76–79.

[18] Debes: *Færoa & Færoa reserata*, p. 313.

[19] For references, see Debes: *Omkring formationen af en nation*, notes 25–29, 31.

spirit of the age. For two centuries, this great topological work has been an inexhaustible source of information on all aspects of Faroese life, including its distant past.[20] His great collection of Faroese words and his manuscript of a Faroese-Danish-Latin dictionary laid the foundation for all subsequent scientific work on the Faroese language.[21]

Because Faroese did not exist as a written language, Svabo constructed a relatively stringent, phonetically based orthography. But over the future of his native language he was not an optimist. In his own words his work was a last desperate effort to save what could be saved for the future, as "samples" of his native language wich seemed doomed to extinction. He visualized the necessity of introducing Danish to the Faroe Islands also as the spoken language. But Svabo was not only a pragmatic scientist and an antiquarian. His love of and his longing for his "native land" is repeatedly expressed in his works. Without knowing it Svabo had, in all his pessimism, laid the foundation for a later optimistic tradition which prevented his dismal prophecies from coming true.

In the years after 1800 several books were printed (in Denmark) in the Faroese language, e.g. a collection of ballads, the first biblical texts in Faroese, and the "Saga of the Faroese". The tradition of writing ballads in the classical style was revived, manifest both as political satire and as a nostalgic retrospect to an old Faroese "grandeur" which had come to a tragic end with the loss of self-government to the rule of foreigners. One interesting example is the demand of a Faroese student, in 1840, to all his countrymen to teach themselves to read and write Faroese.[22] It was no accident that this young man was the son of one of the leading men in the enlightened environment. New sentiments and new ideas were awakening.

But the realization of this categorical imperative was quite illu-

---

[20] Svabo: *Indberetninger fra en Reise i Færø 1781 og 1782*, passim.
[21] Svabo: *Dictionarium Færoense*, passim.
[22] Jacobsen: *Úr bókmentasøgu okkara*, p. 24.

sory as long as a formal Faroese grammar and a normalized ortho-graphy did not exist. Out of the "high culture" which grew up around Svabo's person and influence came the man who removed those hindrances, the learned priest V. U. Hammershaimb (1819–1909), the fourth generation of an immigrant family of high offi-cials, who had married into the most influential families in the is-lands. The importance of his "Faroese Grammar", printed in 1854,[23] cannot be overestimated. Besides being a new literary instrument for both creation and preservation, it also made Faroese visible as a Nor-dic language.

When the first generation of Danish politicians tried in 1845 to introduce Danish schools in the Faroe Islands, the language of in-struction was to be Danish, a language unknown to children in the islands. This experiment was stopped after eight years, the worst of its effects having been that the traditional private instruction in the pupils' homes had come to nothing. But Tórshavn preserved its long school tradition, and in addition a secondary school was established in 1861 at which boys could be prepared for grammar schools in Denmark, and there, in turn, for admission to the University of Copenhagen. In 1870, two years before the introduction of compul-sory school attendance (for all children between 7 and 14 years of age), a teachers' training school was started in Tórshavn. These two institutions produced a Faroese intelligentsia who eventually became the catalysts of the awakening national movement. The sources show that this new sentiment of identification arose both as protest and inspiration in these Danish schools where no subject related to Faroese society and culture existed.[24] Inspiration also came from the Danish Folk High Schools where national pride and respect for the common people were fundamental elements. The establishing, on a private basis, of the Faroese Folk High School in 1899 meant a con-

[23] Hammershaimb: *Færøisk Sproglære.*—Cf. Matras: "Det færøske skrift-sprog af 1846", passim.

[24] Cf. R. Effersøe in the newspaper *Dimmalætting,* 10 November 1888.

siderable strengthening of the nationalist movement and its transition into a political movement. It was the first school in the islands
where Faroese was taught. The influence of Icelandic and Norwegian nationalism can also be detected.

A New Political Framework

The events of 1814 when the Danish king had to cede Norway to
the Swedish king while the Faroe Islands (like Iceland and Greenland) remained with Denmark, seem not to have provoked any emotional reaction among the Faroese. After the abolition of the old Faroese Lawthing in 1816 and the consequent elimination of every Faroese element in the administration of the country, the Faroe Islands
were ruled by a handful of Danish officials, from 1821 as a Danish
county ("amt"), always before having been a country ("land"). This
also meant that the distinction between what was Faroese and what
was Danish was more visible than before. Another effect was the social degradation of old Faroese families from which many of the civil
servants of the country, through intermarriage, had been recruited.
The abolition of the Latin school in 1794 made it almost impossible
for Faroese to get any higher education. Nevertheless, the traditions
of that institution lived on.

The establishment of political institutions in Denmark in the
transition from Absolutism to Constitutional Monarchy (1834–
1849) confronted the Danish authorities with the problem of the
constitutional status of the ethnic minorities within the realm, i.e.
Iceland, the Faroe Islands and Slesvig, when considering their
forms of representation in the new political system constructed and
dominated by ethnic Danes, who, although politically the "core" of
the state, were only tiny minorities in the Faroe Islands and Iceland.

The Faroese were denied their own advisory assembly in 1846 for
the official reason that they only "constitute 7,000 individuals, consisting of simple people devoid of any higher culture" and, therefore,

could not sustain such an institution.[25] They were not represented in the bodies that prepared the new Danish Constitution of 1849, which was extended to apply also to the Faroe Islands the following year. From 1851 they were represented in the Danish parliament ("Rigsdag") by 2 members. In 1852 the Danish parliament passed a special act for an advisory county council in the Faroe Islands, bearing the old name of Løgting, although its functions were quite different. The two highest Danish officials, the chief of administration ("amtmand") and the dean, became ex officio members of the council, the former as chairman (until 1923).

The creation of new political institutions and elections for them was bound to produce new forms of communal life and of communication. The Faroese elected their own politicians, the radical faction being led by the lawyer N. C. Winther (1822–1892), rather than Danish candidates (officials). Winther was first and foremost a radical democrat. Nationalist claims, e.g. greater rights for the Faroese language, are hardly to be found in his struggle. He fought for a new political order, but he writes in the introduction to his book "The Ancient History of the Faroe Islands" that the purpose of his work had been to give the Faroese people some "knowledge of the events of the past" to awaken in them "a national consciousness" because only that would make them strong enough "to throw off the yoke under which they have been sighing far too long".[26]

The Breakthrough of Nationalism

The breakthrough of Faroese nationalism in a "diaspora-group" in Copenhagen shows many parallels to related movements in similar environments, e.g. among foreign students at universities in their

[25] *Stændertidende for Østifterne* (Copenhagen, 1844, 1), pp. 467–469; (1846, 2), pp. 2730–2731.

[26] Winther: *Færøernes Oldtidshistorie,* passim.

"mother countries".²⁷ The alienation²⁸ of Faroese students in Copenhagen can be traced back to the 17th and 18th centuries, clearly showing the sense of a Faroese identity. In both centuries words like "fatherland" and "patriot" can be found in written sources, and in 1766 the Faroese are for the first time described as a "nation".²⁹ This last manifestation coincides clearly with the general development of the chronology of nationalism.

In the last quarter of the 19th century, quite new preconditions had developed: a new intellectual background, the influence of Icelandic, Norwegian and Danish nationalism, Scandinavianism, the Folk High School movement, and European late Romanticism in general.

The Faroese society must be susceptible to new ideas and currents. During the period 1801–1901 the population almost trebled (from 5,262 to 15,530), the greatest growth taking place in the last quarter of the century, a development quite different from that of Iceland and Shetland.³⁰ The Faroese did not take part in the large-scale emigration from the Nordic countries and Shetland which characterized this period. From 1840 to 1910, when the population grew from about 7,000 to about 18,000, only about 600 Faroese emigrated, almost exclusively to Denmark, and very few to America.³¹ These developments can only be explained in terms of a general rise in the standard of living. The growth of inshore fishing

²⁷ Mykland: *Cappelens Norges Historie 9*, pp. 41–46.—Þorleifsson: *Íslandssaga eftir 1830*, pp. 12–33.—Guðmundsson & Karlsson: *Uppruni nútímans*, pp. 107–203, 261–282.—Coleman (ed.): *The Study of Africa*, pp. 156–188.—Sørensen: *Danmark-Grønland i det 20. århundrede*, pp. 199–245.—Dahl: *Arktisk selvstyre*, pp. 13–77.—Minogue: *Nationalism*, pp. 294–295.

²⁸ Kohn: *The Idea of Nationalism*, pp. 294–295.

²⁹ In a book by the lawyer and Lawman Hans Jacobsen Debes.

³⁰ On Shetland, see Nicolson: *Shetland*, pp. 89–92, 128–142, 209–211.—Goodlad: *Shetland Fishing Saga*, passim.—Smith: *Shetland Life and Trade 1550–1914*, pp. 155–206.

³¹ Patursson: *Fólkaflytingin úr Føroyum*, pp. 3–4, 26.

throughout the century, the cultivation of virgin land, new possibilities for private enterprise after the abolition of the royal monopoly trade (1856), the rapid growth of villages where the new economic activities were located, the revolution in the deep-sea fisheries in distant waters (1872: 1 vessel, 1906: 128), the relative decline of agriculture in the economy, the transition from a subsistence to money economy[32]—all these factors had disintegrating effects on the old social structure. Nor could the traditional culture survive unaffected by these economic and social transformations in such a short span of time, in which, furthermore, the connection with the rest of the world was tremendously intensified in comparision to earlier times, both as a consequence of the deep-sea fisheries and the establishment of Danish and Norwegian steamship routes in the North Atlantic.

This also meant a cultural challenge. But in the middle of disintegration there was also an integrating factor: The new economic base and its demand for manpower created a much higher degree of geographical and social mobility. These circumstances necessarily facilitated the transition from concrete local patriotism to abstract nationalism.[33]

The breakthrough of Faroese nationalism can be precisely dated, starting with a meeting of Faroese students in Copenhagen in February 1876. Many of the students who participated had personal connections to the enlightened environment described above and to V. U. Hammershaimb personally. It was no coincidence that the leader of that group of students, at Hammershaimb's suggestion, had attended the Latin school in Reykjavík in order to learn Icelandic, and thereby develop an interest in the Faroese language. These were years of intense nationalist agitation in Iceland, and from let-

[32] In the Faroese Savings Bank (established in 1832) 32,400 kroner were deposited in 1873 on 291 accounts, in 1906 478,500 kr. on 1,527 accounts.

[33] Kohn: *The Idea of Nationalism*, pp. 1–10.

ters which this young man sent home it is clear that he had considered his national identity, especially the question of what it was "to be a Faroese" and "a nation".[34]

This meeting of Faroese students in Copenhagen became a regular annual event, for wich the first Faroese patriotic songs were written, all expressing anguished and painful love of the fatherland and the mother tongue. In 1881 the nationalist movement was organized in the Association of the Faroese ("Føringafelag"). It is characteristic that at its first meeting, the elderly Hammershaimb was invited to speak on "the love of one's fatherland."[35]

In the Faroe Islands, the nationalist breakthrough came both as intellectual inspiration from outside and as reaction against the changes in the old way of life, resulting from economic and social changes that were experienced as the decay of old values. This reaction also had religious overtones.

The culmination of an intense debate on the position of the Faroese language in the Faroese society in the only existing newspaper (since 1878, written in Danish) in the autumn of 1888 was the meeting in the house of the Lawthing in Tórshavn on 26 December the same year—since then always referred to as "The Christmas Meeting". It can rightly be described as an epoch-making event in Faroese history. The emotional and poignant debate, lead by several of the most respected and enlightened men in the country, all with connections to the nationalist movement in Copenhagen, concluded with a resolution which demanded greater rights for the Faroese language in the schools, in the churches and in the courts. The speakers were unanimous that the nationality of the Faroese manifested itself first and foremost in their language. If that was lost—which many of the speakers considered a distinct possibility in such a time of change —the Faroese people would disappear as a nation, at best living on as miserable wretches.[36]

---

[34] Letters in the Library of the University of the Faroe Islands.
[35] Minutes in the National Faroese Library.

The Christmas Meeting marked a new starting point in Faroese history. In January 1889 the movement was organized in the "Føringafelag", as a parallel to the organization in Denmark, with the following programme: 1. "To bring the Faroese language to honour", and 2. "To make the Faroese stick together in order to be independent" (in the sense of being able to provide for themselves).[37] The great support accorded this nationalist union and its messenger, The News of the Faroese ("Føringatíðindi"), the first periodical written in the Faroese language, proves that new needs for identification had emerged.

Nationalism and Politics

After Rasmus Effersøe, the real leader of the nationalist movement soon became Jóannes Patursson (1866–1946). With him the movement added a Norwegian impulse—together with a new Faroese dimension—to its Icelandic and Danish influences. As heir to the largest farm in the islands, the old episcopal residence of Kirkjubøur, he had received an agricultural education in Norway at a time of militant nationalism in the 1880s. His father had brought him up to feel a special national responsibility which made him the leading personality in Faroese independence politics until his death.[38] His wife was Icelandic, which facilitated contacts with leading Icelandic cultural and political leaders.

It was against him personally that the opponents of the national movement—especially the Danish officials in the islands—directed their most severe attacks. They were the guardians of one of the outskirts of the realm, and were naturally vigilant after the catastrophe of 1864. At the turn of the century a fusion can be seen be-

---

[36] *Dimmalætting* (Detailed reports 5 and 12 January 1889).

[37] *Dimmalætting* (2 February 1889).

[38] Cf. J. Patursson's memoirs *Tættir úr Kirkjubøar søgu*, pp. 23–24, 106–107, 110–125, 147.

tween the opposition of the Danish officials and the conservative wing of the nationalist movement, directed against Jóannes Patursson's radical line.

As a cultural movement, organized nationalism was now past its peek. The period of national salvation belonged to the past. Faroese had become a literary language, both written and spoken. In 1900 old Hammershaimb could look back on his work with satisfaction when writing that "the Faroese tongue has been loosened".[39]

The conservatives were fully aware of their national identity; they did not regard themselves as Danes, but they were afraid of the political and economic consequences of the new political movement. They also saw a danger of cultural isolation if the use of Danish was to be reduced in favour of Faroese.

On the other hand, the radical wing felt it natural and necessary to move the nationalist struggle into the field of politics. In 1901 Jóannes Patursson was elected Faroese member of the Danish parliament and a member of the Faroese Lawthing.

In the period 1901–1906, Jóannes Patursson formulated the Faroese self-rule policy on a pragmatic and historical basis.[40] No doubt the Icelandic home-rule status within the Danish Kingdom in 1904 was one of his sources of inspiration. In 1906 he returned from Copenhagen with a "Proposal" (so always referred to in Faroese history and politics) from the Danish government for a higher degree of self-rule for the islands. The substance of it was the transfer to the Lawthing of more financial responsibility, a definition of what was to be administered as "Danish" and "Faroese" matters, and an annual Danish financial contribution from the state.[41] The Lawthing was to decide on the "proposal", which consequently became the

[39] *Ársbók Førja Bókafelags* (1900).
[40] Patursson: *Færøsk Politik*, passim.
[41] *Tillæg til Lagtingssamlingen for 1906. Beretning om den overordentlige Samling i Maj 1906*, pp. 12–13.

main question in the electoral campaigns of 1906, for the Lawthing and both chambers of the Danish "Rigsdag".

The "Proposal" seems to have come as a shock to the Faroese electorate, and in the political debate it was distorted almost out of recognition.[42] Opponents of the "Proposal" won all three elections in the summer of 1906.

From "National Idea" to "National Principle"

The events of 1906 resulted in the formation of two political parties, the Unionist Party ("Sambandsflokkurin"), advocating the closest possible relations with Denmark, and the Self-Rule Party ("Sjálvstýrisflokkurin"), wich regarded additional political responsibility as a logical consequence of the nationalist movement. This laid the foundations of Faroese politics in the 20th century. For a long time, the question of language rights was the most pressing issue in Faroese politics, social issues being of much less importance. These old, frozen battle lines were to some extent dissolved by the growth in the 1930s of the Social Democratic Party ("Javnaðarflokkurin"), with a unionist confession but at the same time much more sympathetic towards nationalist claims (such as language and flag) than the old Unionist Party. Only in 1938 did the Danish authorities recognize Faroese as the language of instruction, and from the following year it could also be used in the services of the church.[43]

Because of the German occupation of Denmark in April 1940 and the consequent interruption of all connections between Denmark and the Faroe Islands, it became necessary for the Faroese, under "friendly" British occupation, to govern themselves on the basis of a "provisional constitution" passed by the Lawthing in May 1940. This reality, together with the economic boom which the is-

---

[42] Debes: *Nú er tann stundin*, pp. 292–314.

[43] On Faroese as a religious language see Rasmussen: *Den færøske sprogrejsning*, passim.

lands experienced during the war as deliverers of fish to the British market (with heavy human and material losses) must be seen as the background of a remarkable intensification of nationalist agitation and the growing support for the self-rule movement, reorganized in 1940 (now more than earlier an independence movement) in the People's Party ("Fólkaflokkurin"), which lacked only one seat of having an absolute majority in the Lawthing.

After the war it was not politically possible to return to the pre-war "amt" status. Negotiations between representatives of the Faroese political parties and the Danish government achieved no result apart from a restrictive Danish ultimatum for the Lawthing to accept or reject. When it became evident that a majority would vote against it, the Lawthing decided that a plebiscite should be held in which the voters were to choose between acceptance of the government proposal and secession from the Danish kingdom.

Nobody seems to have expected the result of the plebiscite on 14 September 1946: a majority in favour of independence. Apparently, the Faroese had moved from "the national idea" to "the national principle". The instant reaction of the Danish Prime Minister was that the consequence must be secession,[44] and Danish jurists reflected on the practical aspects of that process.[45] But Faroese, and Danish, politicians now began to discuss whether it had been a facultative or a consultative referendum. Objectively, there can be no doubt that everybody regarded the result as binding. The political agitation before the referendum and the Prime Minister's first reaction are proof of that. This problem only arose because the result was unexpected. When the majority in the Lawthing began to make preparations for the establishment of governmental institutions, this was declared illegal by the Danish government, which made the

---

[44] Interview in the Danish newspaper *Politiken* (16 September 1946).

[45] Professor Alf Ross, interview in the Danish newspaper *Social–Demokraten* (20 September 1946).

King dissolve the Lawthing. A later election gave the opponents of independence a solid majority.

The result of subsequent negotiations was the Home Rule Act of 1948, passed by the Danish parliament and sanctioned by a majority in the Lawthing.[46] This is done on the grounds of the "special status that the Faroe Islands enjoy within the realm, nationally, historically and geographically"; they constitute "a self-governing community within the Danish state", and a Faroese is defined as "a Danish subject living in the Faroese Islands". According to the Home Rule Act Faroese is "the principal language", but Danish can be used as well as Faroese in all official matters. A special Faroese flag, which was for several decades the core of discord in Faroese–Danish relations, is recognized. By delegation the Lawthing is competent to legislate in all matters transferred to home-rule authorities. Executive functions are administered by the Home Government ("Landsstýri"), led by the Lawman ("Løgmaður"), who is elected by the Lawthing. The Faroese elect 2 representatives to the Danish parliament in Copenhagen. Most matters, with the exception of defence, foreign policy and the judiciary, can be taken over by the home-rule authorities. When in 1985 Faroese was also recognized as "the principal language in the Court of the Faroe Islands", the third of the main demands of the "Christmas Meeting" had been complied with, after a lapse of a hundred years. The Danish government is represented by a "rigsombudsmand" responsible for the Danish part of the administration.[47] The Faroese political system has been characterized by a Danish jurist as "a municipal self-rule of an unusually extensive kind".[48] For Denmark is not a federal but a unitary state.

Interpreted in the light of the programmes of the different politi-

[46] *Løgtingstíðindi 1945. Skjøl frá sendinevnd Føroya Løgtings til samráðingar í Keypmannahavn januar–mars 1946.—Løgtingstíðindi 1946– 1947*, pp. 256–285.—Debes: "Fólkaatkvøðan 14. September 1946".— Harder: *De dansk-færøske forhold 1945–48*, passim.

[47] "Lov om Færøernes Hjemmestyre", pp. 822–825.

[48] Ross: *Dansk Statsforfatningsret*, p. 493.

cal parties and their general support in elections it may, with some simplification, be concluded that while about half of the Faroese want a higher degree of self-determination, in a spectrum reaching from somewhat more than the present Home Rule status to full independence, another half do not regard a recognized Faroese nationality as incompatible with the status of a national minority within a larger political unit, i. e., the Kingdom of Denmark. The tendency, however, is towards extended self-responsibility.

Conclusion

Nationalism is traditionally described as a bourgeois phenomenon.[49] If that is accepted as a general rule, the existence of a bourgeoisie, and hence a certain kind of economic and social development, must be presupposed. It seems to be difficult to place the Faroese example in such a model. Very few families in the country could be reckoned in that social category at the time of the nationalist breakthrough. It was not a capitalist middle class which, from the turn of the century, supported the fledgling self-rule movement. Rather the opposite was the case. These families were mainly of Danish origin. Numerically this group was of little importance as voters. The political struggle was about the votes of the fishermen's families, a group who ought not to be supporters of nationalism if a bourgeoisie and nationalism should be symbiotic. It was not special socio-economic structures, but rather tradition established in the different constituencies early in the century, which became decisive for the geographical location of Faroese nationalism and its political manifestations.

Furthermore, it may be difficult to fit the Faroese development into narrow chronological phases. Miroslav Hroch's 3 phases might, at least at first glance, seem plausible: one intellectual (A: 1780–

---

[49] Kedourie, *Nationalism*, p. 147: "Nationalism is an expression of bourgeois interest."—Hroch: *Die Vorkämpfer der nationalen Bewegung*, pp. 163–171.

1901/06), one characterized by political agitation (B: 1901/06–
1940), and the final struggle for independence (C: 1940–1946/48).
But no Faroese state was established, and, therefore, a term for the
"relapse" phase in the Faroese example seems to be missing in
various theories of nationalism.

It may be of historical importance that the climax of Faroese nationalism, the plebiscite of 1946, happened before the age of decolonization, which might have given the plebiscite another perspective. This time factor, also in the light of the radicalism of the 1960s,
may partly explain the fact that the Greenlanders in the course of
only about 15 years of political struggle won as much political influence (with their Home Rule Act of 1979) as the Faroese had
gained over about half a century. Part of the explanation must be
that within the Kingdom an applicable model existed.

In conclusion, it must be admitted that the Faroese, from objective historical preconditions, have lived through the national idea
and have carried through the national principle without the creation
of a state as the ultimate political consequence of that principle. The
question of whether this consequence could be considered inevitable
in a comparative context has to remain open.

LITERATURE

Anderson, Benedict: *Imagined Communities*, London 1987
Årsbók Førja Bókafelags, Tórshavn 1900
Barclay, Glen St. J.: *Revolutions of Our Time. 20th Century Nationalism*,
    New York 1962
Coleman, James (ed.): *The Study of Africa*, London 1967
Dahl, J.: *Arktisk selvstyre*, Copenhagen 1986
Debes, H.J.: "Fólkaatkvøðan 14. September 1946". Newspaper *14. Septem-
    ber* (13 September 1986).
Debes, Hans J.: *Nú er tann stundin*, Tórshavn 1986. (Doctoral thesis, writ-
    ten in Faroese, on the rise of Faroese nationalism and its development
    into a self-rule movement)

Debes, Hans J.: *Omkring formationen af en nation. Færøerne som unikt og komparabelt eksempel. Et forsøg*, Tórshavn 1991

Debes, Lucas Jacobsen: *Færoa & Færoæ reserata*, Copenhagen 1673

Dimmalætting (newspaper), 10 November 1888, 5 and 12 January 1889, 2 February 1889

Gellner, Ernest: *Nations and Nationalism*, Oxford 1984

Goodlad, C.A.: *Shetland Fishing Saga*, London 1971

Guðmundsson, B. & Karlsson, G.: *Uppruni nútímans*, Reykjavík 1988

Gustafsson, Harald: *Mellan kung och allmoge—ämbetsmän, beslutsprocess och inflytande på 1700-talets Island*, Stockholm 1985

Hammershaimb, V.U.: *Færøisk Sproglære*, Copenhagen 1854

Harder, Kirsten: *De dansk-færøske forhold 1945–48*, Odense 1979

Hobsbawm, E.: *The Age of Capital*, Reading 1988

Hobsbawm, E.: *The Age of Revolution. Europe 1789–1848*, Reading 1988

Hobsbawm, E. & Ranger, T.: *The Invention of Tradition*, Cambridge 1987

Hroch, Miroslav: *Die Vorkämpfer der nationalen Bewegung bei den kleinen Völkern Europas*, Praha 1968

Jacobsen, M.A.: *Úr bókmentasøgu okkara*, Tórshavn 1921, 1974

Kedourie, Elie: *Nationalism*, London 1985

Kemiläinen, Aira: *Nation, Nationality (Volkstum) and the Factors of National Consciousness in Modern Europe*, Stockholm 1985

Kemiläinen, Aira: *Nationalism: Problems Concerning the Word, the Concept and Classification*, Jyväskylä 1964

Kemiläinen, Aira: "The Idea of Nationalism", *Scandinavian Journal of History* 9:1, 1984

Kohn, Hans: *The Idea of Nationalism*, New York 1961

Legum, Colin: *Panafrikanismen*, Oslo 1966

"Lov om Færøernes Hjemmestyre", *Føroyskt lógsavn*, Tórshavn 1953

Løgtingstíðindi 1945. Skjøl frá sendinevnd Føroya Løgtings til samráðingar í Keypmannahavn januar–mars 1946.

Løgtingstíðindi 1946–1947

Matras, Chr.: "Det færøske skriftsprog af 1846", *Scripta Islandica* 1951

Matras, Chr.: "Færøsk sprog", *Kulturhistorisk leksikon for nordisk middelalder, 5*, Copenhagen 1981

Minogue, K.R.: *Nationalism*, London 1967

Mykland, K.: *Cappelens Norges Historie 9*, Oslo 1978

Nash, Manning: *The Cauldron of Ethnicity in the Modern World*, Chicago 1989

Nicolson, J.R.: *Shetland*, New Abbot 1984

Patursson, E.: *Fólkaflytingin úr Føroyum*, Copenhagen 1942

Patursson, J.: *Førøsk Politik*, Copenhagen 1903

Patursson, J.: *Tættir úr Kirkjubøar søgu*, Tórshavn 1966

Politiken (Danish newspaper) 16 September 1946

Rasmussen, P.M.: *Den føroyske sprogrejsning*, Tórshavn 1987

Ross, Alf: *Dansk Statsforfatningsret*, Copenhagen 1966

Smith, A.D.: *The Ethnic Origin of Nations*, Oxford 1989

Smith, Hance D.: *Shetland Life and Trade 1550–1914*, Edinburgh 1984

Social-Demokraten (Danish newspaper) 20 September 1946

Sørensen, A.K.: *Danmark-Grønland i det 20. århundrede*, Copenhagen 1983

Stændertidende for Østifterne, Copenhagen 1844, 1; 1846, 2

Svabo, J.C.: *Dictionarium Færoense. 1 Ordbogen. 2 Indledning og registre* (Matras, Chr. ed.), Copenhagen 1970

Svabo, J.C.: *Indberetninger fra en Reise i Færø 1781 og 1782*, (Djurhuus, N. ed.), Copenhagen 1958, 1976

Tillæg til Lagtingssamlingen for 1906. Beretning om den overordentlige Samling i Maj 1906

Þorleifsson, H.: *Íslandssaga eftir 1830*, Reykjavík 1973

West, John F.: *The History of the Faroe Islands, 1709–1816*, 1, Copenhagen 1985

Winther, N.C.: *Færøernes Oldtidshistorie*, Copenhagen 1875; Tórshavn 1985. (Preface by H.J. Debes)

GREENLAND: FROM COLONY TO HOME RULE

Axel Kjær Sørensen

The Viking Age Contact

Greenland is huge, cold, and far, far away. More exactly stated, it covers two million square kilometers, although only 342,000 of it is free from a permanent ice-cap. It is situated 4,000 kilometers northwest of Denmark and has a population today of 50,000.

Greenland has been populated from two directions. The immigration from the northwest came across the narrow strait between Greenland and Arctic Canada. The oldest known settlements of the early immigrants can be dated to around 2500 B.C. The latest of several groups came about 1000 A.D. They were the Eskimos related to their kinsmen in Canada, Alaska and Siberia. These people supported themselves by hunting and gathering and 80 per cent of the present population in Greenland have some of their ancestors among these tribes.

The immigration from the second direction, the southeast, came in two waves. The first, during the Viking Age, was very similar to the immigration into the Faroe Islands and Iceland. However, this time the Vikings came from Iceland and took land in the southern part of Greenland, which at that time was uninhabited. Some archaeological evidence as well as some medieval written evidence suggests that later on some contact with the Eskimos developed, friendly as well as hostile. As the medieval society in Greenland in 1261 came under the Norwegian king, it came under the Danish-Norwegian crown in 1380. Greenland, however, remained with Denmark when Norway was ceded to Sweden in 1814. In this respect it has had the same course as Iceland and the Faroe Islands. But it was different in another, because the communication with the European world dwindled from about A.D. 1400. About 1500 the Norse settlements vanished, which has not yet been fully explained. Scholars do agree, however, that a period of colder climate, which is a fact, was detrimental to the Norse peasant society and favoured the Eskimo way of life. Fighting over hunting grounds has also been suggested.

Adjusting to the Colonizer 1721 to About 1900

During the next two centuries the Danish king made several attempts to reach the coast of Greenland, but he did not succeed on a permanent basis until 1721. That was the second wave. By that time all the old Norse population had disappeared; only the Eskimos remained. To call the second contact with Greenland a wave is of an exaggeration; only a handful of men came to trade and to preach Christianity. Up to the Second World War, they numbered only a few hundred among a population that grew from 5,000 to 20,000 during the same period.

To everyone else this looked like any commercial colonization at that time, but for the Danish king it was different. It was resuming contact with one of his possessions which for so long had been missing, but never forgotten. The driving force behind the second colonization was the desire by the Norwegian clergyman Hans Egede to find "the old Norwegians," as the Norsemen were called at that time, and convert them to the proper Lutheran faith. He found none, and preached instead to the heathens. This was part of his purpose as well. The trade with the Greenlanders was meant to finance the Christian mission. It could not, and in 1731 the king was ready to give it all up, but by then some fifty Greenlanders had been baptized. To abandon them to paganism was more than the Christian conscience of Hans Egede and the king could permit. Since then, no Danish government has tried to back out of Greenland.

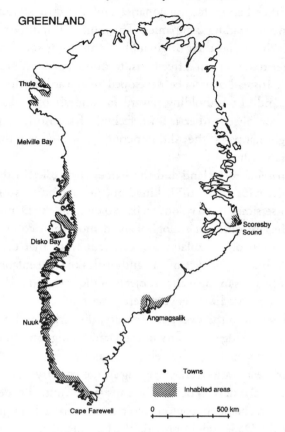

Greenland has been the meeting place between a population with origins in American-Asian Arctic culture and people from Northern Europe, more precisely from the Danish realm. This duality has marked the history of Greenland. Its political conditions have reflected the mixture of being in a colonial situation and being an ordinary part of the Danish realm. Thus, one must look for parallels to the Greenlandic development in other European colonial empires as well as in Iceland and the Faroe Islands. The colonial situation was in the relationship between, on the one hand, the Greenlanders and, on the other hand, the missionaries and the civil servants of the crown and its trading companies. The Christian faith was imposed on the Eskimos and their original Shamanism was soon rooted out. The barter trade was on a free basis, to mutual benefit. No coercion was used. Instead a practice developed of rewarding the approved behavior and of withholding reward for undesirable behavior. The Eskimos complied, either from a feeling of inferiority and fear of what might happen if they did not comply, or to obtain the benefits of the relationship.

The parallel to Iceland and the Faroe Islands lies in the age-old connection with the Danish kingdom. Greenland was one of the king's possessions, not a colony to be exploited by the Danish people. Due to the very different ecological and demographic conditions, the administration of Greenland was different from that of mainland Denmark, but in the eyes of the authorities the Greenlanders were, like other peoples in the realm, subjects of the king and had to be protected and provided with government services.

Until well into the twentieth century, the Greenlanders felt little anxiety about being a minority in the Danish kingdom. In their own country they were an overwhelming majority. The few Danes (or other European nationalities) staying in the country were no threat to the Greenlanders. The two groups were mutually dependent. Only the Greenlanders could exploit the country's living resources, and only the Danes could provide the Greenlanders with the European goods on which they had gradually become dependent, especially firearms and ammunition, and iron for tools. Furthermore, the Danes did not settle in the country. They stayed there for shorter or longer periods. When pension age arrived, they usually retired to Denmark. This was the rule even in families which for generations had their employment in Greenland. When the building of trading and mission stations along the west coast was completed before 1800, the coast was consequently sealed for other nations and for companies other than the Royal Greenland Trade Department, established in 1776.

The distribution of roles between Europeans and Greenlanders was fairly clear during the first period of the colonization. The Europeans were missionaries and traders, craftsmen and sailors needed for collecting the Greenlandic products and distributing the European ones. The Greenlanders, so named by the Danes—*inuit* (people) or *kalaallit* (a word of uncertain origin) by themselves— were left alone to hunt the sea mammals. But soon the Greenlanders, too, were included in the colonization process. First came the assistants to the mission, the catechists. A teachers' college was founded in Nuuk in 1845 to train them. Well into the 19th century Greenland was as Christian a society as any. Not much later a new development called for more helpers.

The period after 1825 was a prosperous time, in which good prices were obtained for the Greenlandic products. Greenlanders, too, were employed as craftsmen and workers in the growth of trade which followed. This group were mostly the offspring of mixed marriages (Greenlandic mother and European father), which meant that their fathers could not teach them the Greenlandic way of making a living. Furthermore, they were cheaper labour than the people called in from Europe. From this "Europeanized" élite came most of the Greenlandic spokesmen. There were no racial prejudices in marriages, so many of which were mixed that at the end of the 19th century the authorities gave up distinguishing between Europeans, Greenlanders, and people of mixed origin in the censuses. From then on, they only counted Europeans and Greenlanders, the people of mixed origin falling into the latter category. Only in the remotest parts of the vast country was it possible to find people with no European blood.

The progress in Greenland was turned into higher living standards. Wooden boards were imported to cover the turf walls, and so were coal-fired stoves to heat them. Hence the valuable blubber, the traditional source of heating, was saved for sale. The teaching of children had its origin in preparation for Christianizing. In good Lutheran fashion the task was to reach the souls in their own tongue. From the very beginning of the colonization the missionaries had written the

Greenlandic language as it was spoken, and not until 1871 did the Moravian Brother Samuel Kleinschmidt create a grammar as well as an orthography for the language. It is still in use, after slight modernization in the early 1970s. The ability to read, which all children were being taught, might be used for more than clerical purposes. By 1861 the first periodical in Greenlandic, *Atuagagdliutit*, was published in Nuuk; it still exists and since 1951, has been bilingual.

The bourgeois democracy, which emerged victorious in Europe in the middle of the 19th century (in Denmark it did so in 1849) , was felt in Greenland as well. In the 1860s local councils with Greenlanders participating were created in each of the 13 colony districts. Their task was to administer poor relief and the unwritten rules which regulated civil affairs between the Greenlanders. Thus, the political development in Greenland was a (later) copy of the development in Denmark, as it was in Iceland and the Faroe Islands. In that way these areas were far ahead of the other European colonial empires, but neither of the Danish North Atlantic dependencies were colonies in that sense.

In Iceland and the Faroe Islands, the material development in the late 19th century brought an extra dimension to nationalism. It was there already on a cultural basis and, for Iceland, on a constitutional basis as well. What took place was that the greater part of a peasant society had to make its living from a new occupation: fishing and its concomitant employment. Such changes will easily give rise to second thoughts about one's origin in adjusting to the new times. In Greenland too, the material development gave reason to contemplate oneself and one's origin. The background was a rising population and perhaps a falling, or at last not a rising number of animals to hunt. Of greater importance, maybe, was that on the world market, mineral oils were replacing animal fat, a main product of Greenland. At the turn of the century the Royal Greenland Trade Department, which administered the country as well, made major efforts to find alternative occupations for the population. They tried sheep-breeding and fishing from motorized vessels. The rearing of sheep

was successful but never became a large industry due to the sparseness of suitable pastures. The future lay in fishing, but the climatic
conditions for that did not arise until a quarter of a century later.

Seeking Equality with the Colonizer 1900–1970

The Greenlandic élite, consisting of the most outstanding hunters
and the clergy, were aware of this trend and discussed it. The discussion has hitherto been little noticed outside Greenland, because it
took place mainly in Greenlandic in the two Greenlandic periodicals, *Atuagagdliutit* and *Avangnâmiok*, and in literature. In the debate the progressives supported the new ways of earning a living, arguing that their agents ought to be considered as genuine Greenlanders as the hunters. The traditionalists praised the hunting from the
kayak as second to none, precisely in Greenland and just for Greenlanders. The poems had a religious and naturalistic content, as well
as clearly praising the new times and reminding the people of their
own cultural values. A good representative of this line of thinking
was the poet clergyman in Narssaq, Henrik Lund.[1] His national anthem (in my translation) will illustrate this point:

> Kalâtdlit,[2] forward! Arise!
> A human life is worth your while.
> Begin believing in your own ability!

Some of this debate was clearly patriotic as it had visions of a future
modern Greenland without Danes. But it was hardly nationalistic,
as it had no argument with other nations. The Danish civil servants
in Greenland—no other Danes were there—were perceived as good
allies and not as representatives for suppressors.

---

[1] The description of the Greenlandic debate is based on Langgaard:
Henrik Lunds Verdslige Digtning and Thuesen: *Fremad, opad.*
[2] *Kalâtdlit* = *kalaallit* = Greenlanders.

To a high degree, this group of benevolent civil servants took the initiative for reforms in Greenland, presumably in accord with the progressive sector of the Greenlandic élite. This has always been so, right from the beginning of establishing of inspectorates in the early 1780s, the commissions in the middle of the 19th century, and the local councils in the 1860s.

The period from the turn of the century to 1912 was just such a period of reform. At the political level it resulted in establishing municipal councils and two Provincial Councils (1911), one for Northern Greenland from Disko Bay to Melville Bay, and one for the South from Disko Bay to the southern tip at Cape Farewell. Colonization on the east coast was established at Angmassalik in 1894 and at Scoresby Sound in 1925. At Thule (north of Melville Bay) a private mission and trading station was set up in 1910, to be taken over by the state in 1937. These districts were governed directly from Copenhagen and were not the responsibility of the authorities on the west coast until 1950.

Unlike similar political councils in the French and British colonies, only native Greenlanders were eligible for the Provincial Councils, and no civil servants were represented except as chairmen. Through these advisory councils the Greenlanders got a platform to formulate their political wishes and demands so they could be heard in Denmark. National self-consciousness existed but in no rebellious spirit. The Danish civil servants and their principals in Denmark were meant to be used to forward the Greenlandic cause, politically and economically.

To that end a political philosophy took shape which stressed the need for making the society as Danish (European) as possible and as Greenlandic as necessary. The philosophy made itself felt in the policy for primary schools for which prominent Greenlanders inside and outside the Provincial Councils were spokesmen: The children had to learn Danish to acquire the abilities which were needed in the modern occupations, foremost fishing and the fishing industry. The Danes could hardly believe this was meant seriously and did not give in to the wish before 1925. At that time no Greenlandic fear existed of the cultural impact which this policy would lead to. Later on, in the 1960s, this fear became outspoken.

Seen from a nationalist point of view, the Provincial Councils would seem rather tame and not much aware of using the meetings for political manifestations. Most of the agendas were filled with issues brought forward by the Greenland Administration. Some of the issues were raised by the members themselves, however, and that section grew through the period between the two World Wars. These issues mostly dealt with minor improvements in daily life, but at times occasions arose which made the Provincial Councils protest bluntly against the government in Copenhagen.

In 1924 Denmark had agreed to let Norwegians hunt in the uninhabited areas of East Greenland, at that time not included in the authority of the two councils, which consequently were not consulted. They, however, put the question on the agenda themselves. They were indignant at the assumed injuries to the Greenlandic hunting, but especially at not being consulted. In the South the tone was serious. The Council found the agreement "quite incomprehensible" and pronounced that the Greenlanders' "trust in the Danes" might weaken. In the North the tone was severe. "Denmark had deserted the Greenlanders," and "shattered all the expectations which the Greenlanders had placed in Denmark for the future." A proper understanding of the position of the nationality question in international politics is found in hunter Ludvig Siegestad's speech (in my translation from Danish):

"...Even if the Greenlanders are insignificant people, they are very well aware that the custom in other parts of the world is not to make decisions of fundamental significance for a whole people without consulting the people concerned. And they had expected that Denmark would ask the Greenlanders before decisions were made concerning the country which the Greenlanders consider their own."

The biting words, mildly stated, endow the speech—even through the Danish interpreter—with an unmistakably Greenlandic tone. Disappointment, not hostility, is expressed. A friend had let you down; no enemy had dealt a blow. As outspoken was the joy in Greenland in 1933 when the International Court of Justice at The Hague awarded the whole of Greenland to Denmark. Certain people in Norway held the view that Greenland was rightfully a Norwegian possession and had acted accordingly in East Greenland.

Between the Wars the climate grew milder, which strengthened the need to change from hunting sea mammals to fishing. Between 1915 and 1920 the surface temperature in the Greenlandic waters rose by 1° Celsius. This change displaced the seals northward, and shoals of cod moved in. In just ten years the value from cod fishing rose from insignificance to exceed the value of blubber in 1926, and to be three times higher in 1930. This change shifted the political and the economical weight from Disko Bay in the north to the open-water zones of the central and southern part of the west coast.

At the political level this development made the civil servants and the Greenlanders increase their efforts to supply the country with facilities for the new business. Also, the development whetted the appetite of outside competitors whom they had to fight off.

The Greenland Administration was able to avert one threat. Combining a nationalist urge with a desire to stimulate sheep breeding in Greenland, some Danish politicians wanted to let Danish sheep farmers settle in Greenland. The Greenlanders were not interested in the settlement of such people; nevertheless, the admission of Danish sheep farmers was legalized in 1929. According to the minutes the Provincial Council had no comments, but wrote to the Greenland Committee of the Parliament directly, strongly opposing "the idea that the land was given to Danes as long as the Greenlanders had not occupied what they wanted and were able to farm...." The settling of Danish sheep farmers came to nothing. In 1939 the director of the Greenland Administration could (rejoicingly?) announce that the settlement authority had not been used, "as no mood existed in favour."

Another attack was more difficult to avert than the Norwegian desire for possession of East Greenland and the settlement of Danish sheep farmers in South Greenland. The issue was Faroese fishing in Greenlandic waters. The Faroe Islanders were being ousted from their usual fishing grounds by British and German fishermen, whose trawls spoiled the opportunities for the Faroese hand-line and long-line fishery. The Faroese used comparatively small boats and were highly dependent on landing stations near to the fishing grounds. As Danish subjects, therefore, they put their demand for access to landing stations in Greenland to the Danish government. This request was highly inconvenient for the Greenland policy. To admit the Faroese would mean abandoning the centuries-old policy of no admission, as the prohibition could hardly be upheld towards other nations once exemption was given. The monopoly trade would be endangered as well, since an unavoidable, unauthorized trade would follow in the wake of the intensified traffic. The core of the protective element in closing the country was at stake, as international fishery in Greenlandic waters would hamper the Greenlandic fishery and the intensified traffic might scare the remaining game (seals etc) away.

In spite of the warnings from the Greenlanders as well as from the Greenland Administration, the Faroe Islanders got increased access to landing stations in Greenland. Permission was given in 1925 for a single harbour, and by 1939 this had grown to four harbours, Færingerhavn (Faroese Harbour) being the largest. Furthermore, Færingerhavn was also opened to ships of all nationalities in 1939.

The Provincial Councils had fought a rear-guard action against this development. Under strong pressure from the Danish authorities they had given in to each extension in the hope that this concession would be the last. When in 1939 they accepted an invitation to discuss the Greenlandic situation in a joint committee in Copenhagen, it was their clear intention to get something in return for the concessions to the Faroese, i.e. to obtain resources for developing the Greenlandic society, so a free interaction with the rest of the world could be established.

From the Danish side the interest in the committee work was somewhat mixed. Clear economic and nationalist concerns were expressed from the political opposition (right-wing parties), while the governing parties (liberal and social-democratic) supported the Greenland Administration's efforts to avoid too radical changes.

Not much resulted from the committee work. From the Danish point of view it was self-evident that the development of Greenland must respect the doctrine of financial self-support, the common doctrine of all colonial powers at that time. No extra funds were available to the Greenland Administration, which could barely manage even by practising strict economy. The negotiations were quickly adjourned when the war between Germany and Poland broke out on September 1, 1939. As it developed into a full scale world war, the situation for Greenland became decisively changed.

The Second World War had a tremendous impact on Greenlandic development by creating new circumstances to be dealt with after the war. The actual wartime period was mostly a continuation of the prewar policy and conditions, although some changes dictated by wartime conditions were introduced. The period can briefly be characterized in the following way:

- ❖ The existing regime in Greenland continued unchallenged with the change that the authorities in Greenland, the two *landsfogeds* (chief administrative officers), exercized the authority formerly exercized from Copenhagen.
- ❖ All existing laws and regulations were upheld including the monopoly of trade. Purchase and sale now took place in the USA and Canada and some other places. However, the Royal Greenland Trade Department still managed all distribution in Greenland.
- ❖ It furthermore meant continuing to deny foreigners ad-

mission to the country. The American military bases, which in agreement with the Greenland authorities were established after 1941, lay mostly far from inhabited places. Intercourse with the local population was forbidden and, as far as is known, took place to no greater extent than would be expected when the nights were as light as the days and curiosity was equally great on both sides.

❖ Greenland did not receive any material aid from either the USA or Canada. It paid for its imports out of its own exports (cryolite and fish) and even ran a surplus.

In the new international atmosphere after the war, the Danish civil servants in Greenland and the Greenlandic élite became firmly convinced that the seclusion of the country could not be maintained. The preparation to enable Greenland to communicate freely with the outside world, a political aim since the 1920s, had to be accelerated. The fact that Greenland had managed on its own resources during the war, even when it was cut off from Denmark, gave a strengthened belief in its feasibility.

The Danish politicians agreed that the five years' separation as well as the development in Greenland during those five years called for new plans for the country. The Provincial Councils in Greenland came to terms on their wishes at a joint meeting in 1945. A tone of seeking equality with Denmark and the Danes as a society and as individuals was expressed.

❖ They wanted to keep the unit administration in Nuuk, established during the war. There should be only one governor *(landsfoged)* and one Provincial Council with greater authority than before.

❖ They wanted to maintain the system of a few transit harbours and distribution along the coast by minor ships. Their argument was concern for "the affinity of the Greenlandic people."

- ❖ They wanted to be represented in the Greenland Committee of the Danish parliament.
- ❖ They wanted teaching in Danish expanded, including establishment of boarding schools using only the Danish language.
- ❖ They wanted some of the fringe benefits of the Danish civil servants for the Greenlanders as well, at least where equal education and occupation were concerned.

Moderate claims, one would think, but going further than anything before, but also not as far as some suggestions during the debate. Those included abolition of the trade monopoly and the seclusion of the country, permission for immigration from Denmark, and a master scheme to make all Greenlanders bilingual.

The Danish politicians surely realized that an extra effort had to be made in Greenland. They advocated a much stronger effort in material development than the Provincial Councils had proposed, but they were reluctant to unite the political and administrative systems under one head in Greenland. Only by a close examination of the internal documents does the real reason for this resistance emerge: the fear of setting off a Greenlandic separatism. Maybe the reluctance of the Greenland Administration for too radical changes went hand in hand with the politicians' regard for the Danish nationalist feelings intensified by the preceding war.

Even if the Greenlandic wishes were not fulfilled in every respect, the five year plan of 1946 was so promising on the material level that the Provincial Councils complied with it. Some critical remarks on its defects were made by individuals, especially Danes who had spent the wartime in Greenland, and also by a few Greenlanders. Other than that, the plan facilitated the work in the beginning.

Yet, this state of affairs did not last for the entire five year period. The reasons were that Greenland had become an issue in international as well as national politics to a degree that the Greenland Administration was not able to run affairs without interference from outside, as before the war. As a member of the United Nations,

Denmark had to make up its mind if it had some "non-selfgovern-ing territories," which according to the UN Charter should be re-ported. Such a description was appropriate for Greenland, and after an internal weighing of the advantage of serving as an example to other nations against the risk of international interference in Danish affairs, Greenland was reported "non-selfgoverning" in the autumn of 1946. This resulted in an experience not especially desired. Not that conditions in Greenland were criticized in the UN assemblies, but as the pressure and criticism against the colonial system grew, it was unpleasant to be seen in company with the colonial powers. An amendment to the Danish Constitution in 1953 placed Greenland on equal footing with the continental part of the kingdom, and Denmark could leave the unpleasant company. The Greenlandic politicians were aware of the UN relation, but never took advantage of it to try their own hand.

The US military bases in Greenland also raised the Greenland issue to the highest political level. Denmark wanted to get rid of the bases, but the USA was unwilling and dragged out the negotiations until the bases could serve as NATO bases after the formation of this organization in 1949. The Weather Service was to be taken over by the Danes, and that brought a row of ministries into the administra-tion of Greenland affairs.

Danish private business had never taken much interest in Green-land, partly because there was little to attract investment, partly be-cause admission was restricted. After the war, however, as fishermen from Esbjerg felt the pressure in the North Sea from vessels of other countries, they looked further north and had their organizations urge the government for admission to Greenland waters.

In November 1947 a new Social-Democratic government in Denmark took over. Faced with the complex situation, it decided to set relations with Greenland on a new footing. The keyword was equality. The trade monopoly and the seclusion of Greenland should be abolished. The state should provide for a proper infra-structure in housing, medical service, schooling, and communications. Private business in Denmark should be allowed to operate in Greenland, under close state supervision, to teach the Greenlanders how to operate a private business, especially in industrial fisheries. As the period of construction was assumed to be short, it was planned to use Danish workers, so that the Greenlanders could concentrate on primary production. An enthusiastic prime minister convinced everyone, from the Danish politicians to the Provincial Councils in Greenland, that the time had come to reverse the course of the Greenland policy in this direction. At the political level the wish to have one and only one Provincial Council was met, although its authority was not expanded. The Greenlanders were to be represented in the Greenland Committee of the Danish Parliament, as they had wished, and because they turned down—for reasons unknown—a proposition to elect their own representatives to Parliament. Not until 1953 was this part of the "New Order of 1950," as the reform was called, realized, as mentioned above.

Seen in an international perspective, this effort was tremendous, costing about DKR 100 million over 10–15 years. Similar development programmes were carried out in the British and French colonies. Counted per receiver, the French contribution in Africa was 20 times less, but counted per taxpayer, the Danes had only a quarter of the burden of the French taxpayers. Certainly, it was easier for four million Danes to provide for 20,000 Greenlanders than it was for 40 million French to provide for 20 million in the African colonies and 40 million elsewhere in the world.[3]

It is safe to say that this effort overwhelmed the Greenlanders. Surely, the material buildup was highly desired, but the consequences of being spectators of the construction of a new society left its marks in decreasing self-respect followed by all kinds of social problems. For the ordinary Greenlander it was hard to adjust to town life, based on formal education and governed by the clock. Nevertheless, 15 years later, in 1964, no other course was seen feas-

[3] Albertini: *Dekolonisation*, p. 491.

ible than to continue the chosen path. A change to public ownership of the fishing industry was the only amendment, as the opportunities and conditions for doing business in Greenland had not attracted sufficient private Danish capital anyway.

Most frustrating for the leading Greenlanders, however, was the shortage in equal opportunities with the Danes in Greenland. Although the political and civil rights became equal, salaries were not. The reason for this was the main idea behind the "New Order". It was a tremendous buildup, financed by the Danish government, to make Greenlandic society able to provide for itself on an acceptable level. Therefore, wages and salaries had to be adjusted to the capability of the Greenlandic economy. This wage level was insufficient to attract the Danish labour force, which consequently was paid according to standards in European Denmark plus a Greenland increment. Such conditions had existed for centuries and had caused no political problems while the Europeans were few and their tasks different from those of the Greenlanders. But now that there were many of them (soon up to a fifth of the population), the problem became noticeable, especially to the Greenlandic élite, who essentially had the same kind of work as the Danes. But since no increment was given to Greenlanders for working in Greenland, they had to tolerate a lower salary than that enjoyed by their Danish colleagues. This became the most delicate political issue. It could not be solved on the given premises, and only in 1989, after ten years of Home Rule, were the first steps taken to nullify the differences.

Doing Without the Colonizer

It took a new generation of Greenlandic politicians to get the Danish-Greenlandic relations moving. They agreed with the old generation in criticism of the inequalities in salaries. However they devised a new social strategy: they wanted a more Greenlandic Greenland, i.e. a society as Greenlandic as possible and as Danish as necessary.

The new politicians, two of whom were elected in 1971 to the Provincial Council and one to the Danish Parliament, wanted first to free Greenland from the Danish dominance, so that the Greenlanders by their own lights could make policy and administer society accordingly. Part of this political philosophy was to appeal to the non-Danish and non-European by underlining the Greenlandic, the Eskimo, in their cultural heritage. The language was the most important—and best preserved—part of it. It was a budding nationalism, where the nation asserts its equal worth with other nations but makes no claims to be superior to them.[4] One may say that the new politicians began to fulfil what the old ones at the turn of the century had hoped for: self-reliance and equality with other nations.

The new generation of Greenlandic politicians prudently used the currents of the time. Decolonization had mainly taken place in the world at large in the 1950s and 1960s. Denmark avoided having its relations with Greenland mingled with this issue as the constitutional amendment in 1953 took it off the hook, as mentioned above. But it got caught in its aftermath as decolonization went further to embrace the Fourth World conception. The idea was claiming nation rights for the aboriginal peoples who had become minorities in their own territories, such as the Aborigines in Australia and the Indians in America. The Greenlandic politicians attached their cause to this issue which was much alive in the beginning of the 1970s. Their kinsmen in the west were also active in this respect, and their organizations, Alaska Native Federation and Inuit Tapirisat of Canada, gave inspiration to the Greenlanders, as did the struggle of the Sami in Scandinavia to get their rights respected by the majority society. Although the Greenlanders were no minority in Greenland, they were so in the Danish realm, and now they wanted to have a greater say in their own country. The new politicians later (in 1977) formed the Siumut party (meaning forward)

---

[4] See Sørensen: *Grønlandsk nationalisme.*

and the Inuit Ataqatigit party in 1979 (meaning the Inuit Union), while the "old" politicians gathered around the Atassut (meaning connection) party also formed in 1977. Since then, the two parties in Greenlandic politics have been roughly of equal size.

The Danish entry into the Common Market in 1972 was the clearest single impetus which got the political development in Greenland moving. A referendum was taken all over the realm. Denmark (continental) was in favour, while Greenland voted against. Due to its Home Rule (of 1948), the Faroe Islands could decide for themselves, and the Løgting turned affiliation down. Greenland, however, had to follow Denmark in joining the EC. The new politicians had argued against joining, and after the referendum they took the initiative to change the constitutional relations to Denmark to get out again. Although Greenland got favourable arrangements for fishing products and developmental aid, the Greenlandic politicians stuck to the wish to leave the EC as soon as possible. They succeeded in 1985 after nearly six years of Home Rule. The reason was, no doubt, that they did not want to exchange jurisdiction from Copenhagen for jurisdiction from Brussels. They were most anxious to minimize any outside authority.

It took five years of Greenlandic-Danish negotiations to agree on Home Rule status for Greenland. It was implemented in May 1979. Like the Home Rule Act for the Faroe Islands, the Act for Greenland declares that Greenland is a self-governing community within the Danish realm. Governmental matters are divided into three parts:

1. Matters of especial concern to Greenland which the Greenlanders (meaning the electorate in Greenland) shall determine exclusively. Such matters may be transferred to local decision by unilateral decision of the Greenlanders or by the Danish government. The expenses for them must be paid by the Greenlandic community. Such matters are: issues concerning Home Rule organization, taxes and dues, mu-

nicipal affairs, fishing in inshore waters, hunting and farming.

2. Matters of especial concern to Greenland which will be
   funded from Denmark. The Danish minister keeps the
   overall surveillance of the particular law by which the matter
   is transferred. Such matters are: church and religion, social
   security, labour market legislation, primary schools, culture
   and business, health services, housing legislation, the supply
   of goods, transport and environmental protection

3. Matters which remain with the state authorities: the Constitution and the ensuing Human Rights, defence and
   foreign policy, the courts, civil and criminal jurisdiction,
   currency etc. The state pays for these matters.

The first group in paragraph 2 was transferred almost immediately,
and some of the second group have followed. The listing of matters
in this paragraph was not meant to be exhaustive. More may follow
by mutual agreement. A particular area, much debated during the
five years of negotiation, got its own law, namely mineral extraction,
which was made a joint venture. The commission thus bypassed the
crucial question of who owned the minerals in the ground. The
Greenlanders think they do, and for the time being hold a veto right
concerning mining activity.

The first decade since establishing of Home Rule in Greenland
was a success. Nobody in either place thinks of reversing it, and
everybody is ready to expand it on its own terms. It derives its character from history and from the situation of Greenland as part of the
Danish realm. It appears to be stable as long as the prevailing conditions exist. It must be kept in mind that Greenland in its present
state can in no way be financially self-sufficient. If that situation
should change—and the opportunity lies in the subsoil minerals—a
new situation will arise, not seen since the colonization started almost three centuries ago. Shrewdly, the politicians do not discuss a
non-existent situation. However, Greenlandic society in that event

would want to be even more independent, perhaps only having the head of state and foreign affairs in common with Denmark. On that, it is likely to come to terms with the Danish government.

LITERATURE

Albertini, Rudolf von: *Dekolonisation*, Köln 1966
Gad, Finn: *The History of Greenland I–III*, London (and Copenhagen) 1970–1975. (Covering the period to 1808.)
Handbook of North American Indians, Volume 5, Washington 1984. (The book has 200 pages on Greenland, written by several authors.)
Kalaallit Oqaluttuarisaanerat 1925-p tungaanut, Nuuk 1987. (History of the Greenlanders to 1925)
Langgaard, Karen: *Henrik Lunds Verdslige Digtning*, Copenhagen 1984. (Henrik Lund's Secular Poetry. Non-published student thesis, Institute for Eskimology, University of Copenhagen)
Sørensen, Axel Kjær: *Danmark–Grønland i det 20. århundrede*, København 1983. (Denmark–Greenland in the 20th century)
Sørensen, Axel Kjær: *Grønlandsk nationalisme*, Historie XIII, 1–2, Århus 1979. (Greenlandic Nationalism)
Thuesen, Søren: *Fremad, opad*, Copenhagen 1988. (Forward, Upwards. The book traces the beginning of the modern Greenlandic national self-consciousness, especially in the lay revival movement, Peqatigîngniat.)

PART THREE

SAMI ÆDNAN:
FOUR STATES—ONE NATION?
NORDIC MINORITY POLICY AND
THE HISTORY OF THE SAMI

Helge Salvesen

The Area of Enquiry

An examination of the Sami as an ethnic or national minority, in the context of the history of the Nordic minorities, must start with six propositions:

❖ The Sami, seen historically, are a unique linguistic, cultural, and ethnic people, with their roots in Nordkalotten (the Northern Cap*) stretching so far back that no-one today can say with certainty where they came from or at what time after the last Ice Age they arrived in the area.

❖ The Sami have always been accorded the status of a minority, in one form or another, within the various states which have sprung up in Nordkalotten since the Middle Ages, even though, in some areas, they have formed a majority of the population.

❖ The Sami have never, throughout their history, ever identified with the majority population in the states they have lived in.

* "The Northern Cap" is the Scandinavian name for (roughly) the area north of the Arctic Circle.

❖ The Sami feel that, in their dealings with the majority culture, they have never been able to dictate terms, but have always been on the receiving end, seen as the losing party, territorially, economically, demographically and as regards their cultural identity.

❖ The Sami lived in areas that soon attracted the interest of their powerful neighbours, who, little by little, shared them out among themselves.

❖ The Sami way of life has evolved in different ways in the four states—Norway, Sweden, Finland and the Soviet Union/Russia—which, in drawing up their borders, have divided the *Sami ædnan* —the Sami country—among them.

In order to understand the conduct of Nordic nation states towards the Sami, as well as the situation of the Sami today—both as they see it and as regards the strategies they employ in confronting the majority culture—it is necessary to follow the interplay of political action and reaction, between the minority and majority cultures, in Nordkalotten, over several hundred years. Politics, in this context, must be interpreted widely, both as regards the arena it occupies and its borders with the non-political activities.

Ideally, in this context, it would be desirable to analyse all those areas, where significant choices are made, that are of consequence for the conduct of the majority society towards the Sami, as well as the Sami view of themselves and of "those others", with whom they do not identify. In practice, however, we must restrict ourselves to the following:

❖ An historical account of the natural conditions and economic geography of the area in which the majority and minority cultures have confronted each other.

❖ A clarification of some of the key concepts used in the problems under discussion.

❖ An analytical sketch of the legal and macropolitical stages through which the minority policies of the individual states have passed, and the pattern of organizational reaction to this, by the Sami themselves.

❖ A locating of the history of minority policy within the ideological currents affecting society, including an analysis of research and intellectual activities, as an important source of premises for political actions.

As regards conditions in the various countries, those in Norway will be examined most, those in Sweden more closely than those in Finland, whilst least light will be thrown on Russia.

An Historical Geography and a Definition of Terms

There are good grounds for asserting that the *Sami ædnan*—the Sami settlement area—covered most of Fennoskandia. This stretched from the White Sea to the Atlantic, from the Gulf of Bothnia to the Arctic Ocean. Just as it is difficult today to draw definite frontiers around the area of Sami settlement, so it was in the past.

The northern part of the Sami settlement area lies, for natural geographical reasons, on the northernmost border of human settlement. Most of the area is covered by woods, bogs and lakes. Compared to other areas so far north, heterogeneity is the most striking feature of the natural environment. The animal and plant life of this small territory is remarkably varied, seen in an arctic context. The icefree coast has been the most reliable source of food.

The closer one comes to the border of human settlement, the more restrictive are the conditions set by physical geography for economic and cultural life. Traditionally the Sami supported themselves by drawing on the organization and techniques of a hunting society in order to exploit the natural environment. Unlike other Arctic peoples, the Sami have had access to an open sea throughout the year. Seals and seabirds were an important resource in earlier times. Fish from the seas, rivers and lakes have always been of great consequence for the Sami. Among land animals, the reindeer has always occupied pride of place; in earlier times the wild reindeer, in recent centuries the semi-tame variety. Climate and vegetation have influenced the migratory habits of the reindeer, which in turn have set limits to Sami cultural expression, first for the hunters of the reindeer and later for those who herded them.

The Sami culture of the chase was founded upon fishing, hunting and, to a lesser extent, reindeer herding. The pattern of the year was divided up into a series of seasonally determined migrations, so as to exploit a variety of resources and to avoid their over-exploitation. Family and kin were custodians of the old way of life. *Sii'da* was the name given to the local groupings of families who together exploited a particular hunting and pastoral area. The size of the *Sii'da* varied from a handful up to 20–30 families, comprising several hundred individuals.

Reindeer herding became the main support, at least of the mountain Sami, no later than the 1500s to 1600s. This represented a more intensive use of resources as compared to pure hunting. The first step towards this new, technically more advanced management of resources came with the use of tame reindeer as decoys, in order to ensure enough food. A further intensification occurred when the herds were followed, protected from predators and tended. Gradually the herds grew bigger and bigger, though not until this century were herds containing thousands of animals the norm.

In the course of the Middle Ages, Nordkalotten and the Sami settlement area attracted the interest of three states; namely Denmark-Norway, Russia and Sweden-Finland. The right to tax and trade with the Sami was, however, placed under royal authority via the King's personal representatives. All these states sought to extend or protect their positions through the granting of trading privileges, taxes, military expeditions and later by state directed missionary and colonization initiatives.

The taxation of the Sami was of significance not only as a source of income but as the basis of a claim for sovereignty over the area.

For long periods the Sami in the "common areas" paid tax to all three states at the same time. One must ask why the Sami went along with this. It is unlikely that any of the states had the power to enforce payment. The nature of the physical environment occupied by the Sami gave the states few opportunities for the use of force. We must remember that Fennoskandia was very thinly populated and the scattered groups of hunter-gatherers scarcely comprised more than a few thousand people, spread over an area twice the size of Norway today (323,878 km^2). The only sanction was to deny the Sami the right of admittance to various markets—these being their most important sources of trade—if they did not pay the taxes placed upon them. The taxes should then be seen more as trading dues rather than state taxes which might eventually be cited as evidence of territorial rights.

From as early as the thirteenth century, the constitutional position of the Sami areas of settlement was the object of lengthy negotiations between the neighbouring states. Map 1 gives a summary view of the final disposition of the frontiers in Fennoskandia. The border between Denmark-Norway and Sweden-Finland was fixed by a treaty of 1751, the origin of which was the peace of 1720 that brought to an end the Great Northern War. A codicil to the border treaty, the so-called *Lappecodicillen*, guaranteed the Sami the rights of passage and economic exploitation of their traditional areas, without regard for the newly agreed frontiers. This meant they could continue to use their old migratory routes, irrespective of frontiers or citizenship. Furthermore the codicil guaranteed a legal right to land and water on the basis of customary practice. In addition the Sami were to be liable to taxes in only one country, but were to retain their rights in both.[1]

The border between Norway and Russia east of Varanger was not fixed until 1826.[2] Sweden had been forced to give up Finland in

[1] *Norges offentlige utredninger* (NOU) 1984:18, pp. 166–200.

[2] The standard work on the border question is O.A. Johnsen: *Finnmarkens politiske historie aktmæssig fremstillet*, Oslo 1923.

Fennoskandia: International Borders on the Northern Cap

1751 The border between Sweden and Norway finally determined. Norway took over Karasjok, Kautokeino and Utsjoki on the north side of the River Tana (Polmak). The rest of the common area went to Sweden.
1809 Sweden gave up Finland which became a Grand Duchy under Russia.
1826 The border between Russia and Norway finally determined. The common areas south and east of Varanger were shared.
1944 Finland's border with the Soviet Union revised. Petsamo and Suenjel, which had belonged to Finland since 1918, were lost to the Soviet Union.

Source: *Ottar*, No. 84, 1975, p. 41.

1809 and this became a Grand Duchy under the Russian crown. The *Lappecodicillen* was not binding on Russia. The area on the southern side of Varanger Fjord continued to be held in common, without fixed frontiers; both the Norwegian and Russian authorities

collected taxes from the so-called "Østerhavsbyene", Neiden, Pasvik
and Peisen.

Negotiations on the frontier were begun in 1816 and concluded
in 1826, the result being the frontiers we know today. Who got
most out of the negotiations has often been discussed. The question
of who lost the most is, however, not in doubt. It was the *Skoltesami*
whose migratory routes lay in the frontier zone. Though the treaty
secured their rights to hunt and fish on both sides of the border, this
was only for a limited period and only for so long as the two kingdoms wished. The *Skoltesami* did not then get the same rights—
guaranteed by treaty for all time—as the reindeer-herding Sami had
obtained in regard to the Norwegian-Swedish border. Under pressure from the two states, the *Skoltesami* were forced to choose to be
citizens of one or the other. In the long run this meant that the area
they could exploit became more and more limited—definitely from
the 1920s—to that held by the state in which they held citizenship.
As early as 1826 religious affiliation was taken to be the only criterion for Norwegian or Russian citizenship. The 67 individuals in the
common territory who were of the Evangelical-Lutheran persuasion
were considered to be Norwegian citizens, whilst the 82 who were
Greek Orthodox were considered to be Russian.

After the First World War, that part of the common territory occupied by the *Skoltesami* which had previously belonged to Russia
was transferred to the new state of Finland. Thus some of the *Skoltesami* became Finnish citizens since most of the area they exploited
lay within Finland. However, some who lived further east, but yet
had close kin and cultural ties with their Finnish compatriots, became Russian. Thus this tiny group of *Skoltesami* was divided
amongst three states. They had a hard time too during the Second
World War. They were evacuated from the war zone, but since the
war the new settlements allocated to them by the Finnish government have shown signs of breaking up.

The *Skoltesami* are a classic example of how the border policies of
neighbouring states can turn a weak minority into a shuttlecock, sac-

rificed to the interests of powerful forces, with virtual extinction the result, even though this was not at all what the parties involved wished. Quite the opposite: they tried to accommodate the wishes of the minorities. But for many the ethnic ties were cut. In the eyes of the states, the frontier agreements of 1752 and 1826, which produced fixed borders, were to be preferred to the messy common area. The Sami, on the other hand, were fundamentally uninterested in national frontiers. First and foremost they wished to pursue their livelihood and meet their trading needs without interference from the state.

The trade goods of the Sami—principally furs and fish—were of considerable economic importance. Fundamentally, however, the economic foundation of the states formed in the Middle Ages was the surplus produced by the settled farmers. The state could identify with such people far more easily than with the nomadic hunter-gatherers. For the structure of the agrarian culture—its stationary population and stable institutions—was guaranteed to meet, year in and year out, the tax objectives of the state. As a consequence, it is easy to understand that the legal thinking of the state authorities would be attuned to the need of the agrarian society for order and regulation. This is because there lies at the heart of the agrarian culture the need to accumulate investment goods from generation to generation; hence the need for rules governing inheritance and the protection of property. Naturally this has been of great significance when two such different cultures as those of the settled farmers and the nomadic hunters have come into conflict with one another. It goes, almost without saying, given the basic ideology of the law, which group will turn out to be the winner.

An awareness of one's own identity first occurs when relations with "others" are established. With the Sami, it is impossible to determine when such relationships came into being. What we do know is that the Sami represent the only minority population among the Nordic countries whose roots stretch so far back that their arrival is as clouded in the mists of time as is that of the Germanic peoples. Naturally that does not mean that the point of entry is not of political interest. And, of course, it is central to an understanding of just who the Sami are. One saw that in the last century when efforts were made to strengthen the Norwegian national identity. The first generation of Norwegian historians carried on a long and heated debate as to whether or not the Germanic tribes had entered Scandinavia from the North, thus reaching Norway first, only then to spread southwards into Sweden and Denmark.[3] The arrival of the Sami in Scandinavia had similar ideological overtones. Who came first? Are the Sami really an indigenous people? How far back can the Sami document their presence?

In more recent historical time, that is to say after 1500, the Sami have occupied all those areas of the Nordic Countries in which they have permanent settlements today (see Map 2). These are to be found between 62° and 71° North and between 10° and 40° East. In Norway these are bordered on the south by Engerdal in Hedmark (Femundsmarka) and in Sweden by Idre in Dalarne. From there the settlement area stretches north across the Scandinavian peninsula and over Northern Finland. In the latter, however, settlement is limited to just the northern part of Lapplands Län, principally the administrative districts of Utsjoki, Enontekiö, Inari and the northern part of Sodankylä. The entire northern part of the Kola peninsula is reckoned to have been an ancient Sami settlement area. Today the Sami population is confined, for the most part, to Lowozero in the middle of the Kola Peninsula. Thus the Sami are settled in four states.

It is difficult to say just how many Sami there are, partly because of the problem of identification and partly because of migration. One comes to a different result according to the criteria used, e.g. first language; the language of the home today; social class; genetic origin; personal preference. The essence of being a Sami, in the eyes of the Sami themselves, lies not least in such intangibles as the sense

[3] Dahl: *Norsk historieforskning*, pp. 40 ff.

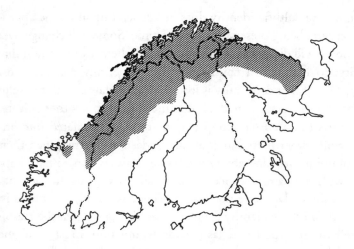

The Spread of Sami Settlement

The shaded area shows the approximate area of Sami settlement in the twentieth century. The greater part of the population within this area nevertheless consists of the majority population of the respective country: Norwegians, Swedes, Finns and Russians.

Source: *Ottar*, No. 84, 1975, p. 33.

of belonging to a district, to a way of life, a group, a family. Individual cultural characteristics and ways of articulating one's personality such as language, terminology, body language, traditional dress, music (the *joik* being the traditional musical form of the Sami), and religious expression—here Laestadianism (a Lutheran revivalist movement) is both the dominant faith and a significant identification factor—are further ways of pinning down the essence of being a Sami.[4] Just how many Sami there are is thus a matter that no census can determine.

---

[4] *NOU* 1984:18, p. 69.

An overall cultural identity does not depend upon all the appropriate criteria being present at the same time. Some will change over time. Some will disappear to be replaced by others. But to retain that identity, to maintain a consistency over time, any changes must overlap. For if that continuity is lost, then assimilation is not long in coming; that is to say a gradual identification with another culture. Some parts of an ethnic group may be totally assimilated into another, while other parts can continue, indeed even strengthen their cultural uniqueness and ability to survive. This appears to have happened with the Sami over recent centuries. In view of the fact that the Sami themselves have not always been consistently interested in making their ethnic identity explicit, it would appear that the reason for their mixed experiences, as regards assimilation, must lie in the pressure brought to bear upon them by the other inhabitants of Scandinavia, Finland and Russia, together with the deliberate policies pursued by the authorities in those countries towards their minorities.

At a rough estimate the Sami population has, with certain reservations, been put at around 50,000. Of these about 30,000, or 60%, live in Norway, some 15,000 in Sweden, 5,000 in Finland and 2,000 in Russia.[5] It would also appear that about two thirds of all Sami master at least one of the nine main dialect groups into which the Sami language can be divided (see Map 3). However, the dialects vary so much that communication between those speaking only one of them (e.g. North Sami on the one hand, South Sami on the other) is all but impossible. Some three quarters of all who use the Sami language speak or can understand North Sami, which is the dialect most used by the press and on radio and television. Besides, the majority of Sami who have a mastery of the language are—willingly or not—bilingual; that is to say they also have a mastery of the majority language of the state in which they live.

The Sami, then, are a people with shared ethnic and cultural

[5] Aarseth: "Samene", p. 388.

Sami Dialect Districts

Sami dialect groups:

1. South Sami
2. Ume Sami
3. Pite Sami
4. Lule Sami
5. North Sami

6. Enare Sami
7. Skolte Sami
8. Kildin Sami
9. Ter Sami

Source: B. Aarseth: "Samene", 1977, p. 388, according to K. Nickul: *Saamelaiset*, 1970—English edition available.

characteristics who are now citizens of four sovereign states. Today, more and more of the Sami themselves talk of a nation spread across four states. The Sami expression "Sapmi" is to be found in all the Sami dialects. It refers both to the geographical area which has traditionally been settled by the Sami people themselves, or, put another way, to the Sami country, the Sami people and the Sami nation. The

term "Sami"—which is how the Sami people describe themselves—
has replaced the previously used "Finn" or "Lapp", in all the Nordic
languages. Gradually the term Sami has entered into international
use, especially in academic circles, e.g. among the English.

In the earliest literature we find expressions that are linguistically linked with the term "Finn". It is possible, however, that the
term includes Finns *qua* Finns as well as Sami. The expression first
appears in the year 98 B.C. in Tacitus' *Germania,* in the form
fenni. Here it would appear Tacitus is referring to the Sami. On
the other hand the astronomer Ptolemy of Alexandria (ca. 100
B.C.) speaks—in so far as our interpretation of his geographical
study is correct—of two *phinnoi* people; the one lived in an area of
Weichsel, the other in the northern part of Scandinavia. This
would suggest that there was already a division between Finns and
Sami. If this is the case, then it lends some support to the theory
that the Sami, who around Christ's birth were spread across the
whole of Finland, were subsequently forced northwards. Seen from
that perspective a plausible hypothesis might be that the Sami gradually pushed south across the Scandinavian peninsula at the same
time as they were being forced northwards in Finland. The first oc-
currence in Norwegian sources of the term "Finn" (plural
"Finnas"), in the sense of Sami, appears in the account written by
Ottar, the north Norwegian chieftain, around AD 900. This was
included in King Alfred's translation of the history of the world
written by Orosius.[6] The term "Finn" is not an "in-group" one.
Rather it is part of the tradition that has characterized most of what
has been written about the Sami: namely a description of the Sami
for non-Sami by non-Sami.

If one takes as one's starting point Tägil's definition of a nation
(see above pp. 23–25), the Sami might be expected to strive for their
own state, that is to say a politically and territorially circumscribed
entity. Such an aspiration would be based on their feelings of cultu-

---

[6] Itkonen: "Finnar", pp. 276–278.

ral community, for which we have argued in the preceeding pages. There are no doubt grounds for suggesting that the Sami sense of nationhood does not go as far as that. Rather it might be thought to involve—at the aspirational level at least—a common desire to create a society whose members are united one with another and are only separated in certain ways from the other members of the states in which they live.

Why have the Sami developed this nationalism, this exclusive sense of ethnic loyalty which separates them from the nation states in which they reside? Is it that the nation states are seen as a threat to the cultural and ethnic sense of belonging which the Sami feel gives them their identity? Nationalism is always the result of an historical process, and like ethnicity it has always had to do with relationships to "others". Ethnic identity is thus a result of contact with other groups with which one does not identify. For the Sami there has always been contact with a majority culture which, to a great extent, has determined the conditions of such contact and brought about an "ethnic anaemia" in the Sami culture. The way this contact has turned out will, to a great extent, determine the content of Sami nationalism and Sami identity. A diachronic analysis of relations between the minority policies and of the minority response to them will therefore contribute, among other things, to an understanding of what constitutes ethnic minorities.

The pattern of Sami settlement today, and in recent centuries, has comprised a more or less clearly defined concentration within a general area of settlement. In certain areas such as the interior of Finnmark or in Utsjoki-Inari, the Sami are the dominant population. Elsewhere they have formed more or less clearly defined neighbourhoods along the coasts and in the fjords of Finnmark and North-Troms as well as in scattered rural enclaves further south, where they have always been in a minority. Around the spring and winter encampments of the Swedish reindeer-herding Sami have sprung up *"lappebyer"* (Lapp towns) which are now occupied throughout the year. In addition to this, most large towns in Fen-

noskandia contain greater or smaller groups of Sami migrants. For
example Oslo is thought to contain around 2,000 Sami.

Thus the Sami population locally, both today and in the past, has
had mixed fortunes regarding its minority/majority status. Both
from this and other experiences, the Sami view the question of assimilation in a variety of ways. These extend from a desire to be assimilated fully into the majority culture, through a wish for what
one might call "unity but not uniformity", and ending up with a call
for the greatest possible isolation from the majority culture, including a desire for positive discrimination in favour of the Samis' exclusive rights to, for example, certain natural resources. This last position has been held more strongly by Sami who form a majority
within their local community than it has by those in a minority, and
still less by those who are scattered amongst the majority population,
such as the "sea Sami" in Norway. The explanation would seem to
be that the mechanisms employed by the majority culture to isolate
and/or assimilate the Sami living as a minority within a local society
have been so strong that the solution to the problems of ethnic
identity has been to become "more Catholic than the Pope". How
has this pressure come about?

National Interests—Integration without Assimilation

Neither legally nor politically has there been a common Nordic approach to the Sami minority. Both Norway and Sweden have, however, each viewed their Sami and Kven populations in the same light
without necessarily pursuing the same policies towards them. There
are, therefore, good grounds for periodizing the history of the
policies directed at the Sami minority in the same way that Niemi
has done with the Kven (see pp. 163–198).

Ever since the end of the seventeenth century, Sami language and
culture have been viewed in two different ways. The one would suggest that the Sami ought to disappear, to give up their language and
their culture, that is to say their traditional way of life, practices,

dress etc, and assimilate with the majority population in whatever country they happen to reside. The alternative was that the Sami should be preserved as a separate people and that their language and culture should be protected, that is to say their ethnic identity should be reinforced. Churchmen, given their missionary interests, were the first to take an unambiguous position on the Sami culture. They justified assimilation because they wanted to drive out the old Sami religion. The spirit of a pietistic and nationalistic protestantism demanded that the old paganism be eradicated from the minds and hearts of the Sami, to be replaced by the one true message; this being presented in a "simple, clear and intelligible language". Paradoxically these same aims could produce a contrary strategy; not eradication and assimilation, but support and understanding. For the first step was to win the Sami's confidence. This was to be brought about by giving the Sami textbooks in their own language, as well as education and religious instruction through the same medium. It was also important to understand the Sami religion. That way it could be undermined from within. A missionary college was founded in Copenhagen in 1714 with the aim of providing clergy for the Danish colony in India and for the Sami in Finnmark. Under the leadership of Thomas von Westen the strategy of support and understanding was the one adopted, though it was not pursued habitually. The choice of strategy was to have far-reaching consequences for the preservation or abandonment of the Sami language and culture.

Both approaches—that of assimilation and that of protection—have had their supporters and opponents, within and outside the church, throughout the entire 300 years that have passed since a clear position was first enunciated. There are, however, grounds for believing that neither the Danish-Norwegian nor the Swedish authorities saw any matters of principle separating the interests of the state and those who championed the Sami cause. This applied throughout the eighteenth century and even in the first half of the nineteenth.

There was, in any case, seldom any conflict of interest between

Church and State in the Nordic countries. For since the Reformation the Church had strongly identified itself with the State. It was not remarkable, therefore, that the missionary activities of a Protestant State Church should be seen as an instrument for building up state power.

The *Lappecodicil* of 1751 well illustrates that, even in the eighteenth century, there was nothing controversial about a measure which sought to secure both the economic interests of the Sami and the foreign policy interests of the State. The development of permanent, centralised states in Fennoscandinavia by the Norwegians, Swedes and Russians, in the period from ca. 1100–1350, posed no threat to the Sami organization of the *Sii'da*. The territorial "campaign over Sameland" did not become a campaign *against* the Sami, but rather one *about* the Sami. What happened with the Codicil of 1751 was that, for the first time, an unambiguous border was drawn through the Sami area of settlement and economic interests, and it was confirmed by the highest law of the land. In reality the Codicil can be seen as the keystone in a long process, where the surrounding states demanded the right first to tax the Sami, then to create an administration, and then to exercise ecclesiastical and secular jurisdiction—not least through the building of churches and monasteries and, the development of missionary activities by an ever-expanding church.

The *Lappecodicil* contains rules concerning neutrality in the case of war; internal Sami administration, including a limited administration of justice, together with the legal confirmation of ancient Sami customs. But the most pressing matter was to determine the constitutional and economic rights of the Sami, now that a dividing line had been drawn through Sameland. First the nomadic Sami must be given citizenship in one of the countries. Here one had to avoid either making the Sami stateless or giving them dual nationality. Secondly, one needed to regulate the future herding of reindeer across the frontier. The newly drawn national borders ran right across some areas that were of vital importance for the Sami. Neither state wished to destroy the use to which these were put. Seventeenth-century opinion on natural rights, such as we find in the writings of Grotius and Pufendorf, took the view that groups and communities could occupy uncultivated or uncultivable areas such as rivers, lakes, bogs, woods and rugged mountains. Thus the parties to the Treaty believed that the ancient customary rights of the Sami should be given legal recognition and protection. Schnitler writes in his examination of border records that the Lapp nation were a free people in ancient times until their Norwegian, Swedish and Novgorod Russian neighbours forcibly made them liable to taxes.[7]

How the Sami had made use of the country was crucial for the drawing of the border itself. Where nature allowed, the old view that the watershed should be the frontier was adhered to. In the far north, Sami land use was of particular importance for the line of the border. At the same time a key aim of the Codicil was to secure for the Swedish Sami their old rights to herd reindeer on what was now Norwegian territory, and likewise for the Norwegian Sami on Swedish territory. This can be seen as a willingness to reduce the drawbacks of the new borders for the Sami.

A corresponding goodwill was also shown, at the outset, in the drawing of the border between Russia and Norway in 1826. The Sami were given the right to use the land on both sides of the border, but this was now for a limited period and only so long as both kingdoms wished it. The actual consequences of this can be seen in the fate of the *Skoltesami*. However, while the *Lappecodicil* gave the Sami an immutable right to cross the border between Denmark-Norway and Sweden, according to their ancient customs, even if both countries should be at war with one another, the subsequent agreement between Russia and Norway led to a gradual cutting off of that right so far as the border between Norway and Russia was concerned, until finally it was closed completely.

[7] *Major Peter Schnitlers grenseeksaminasjonsprotokoller, 1742–1745*, p. 10.

If, even in the middle of the eighteenth century, one looked positively on the need to secure the Sami land use rights, this attitude did not pervade the view of Sami culture as a whole. Nevertheless there was in seventeenth-century Sweden a willingness to preserve Sami language and culture. When churches were built in the "Lappmarken", one tried to provide clergy who could speak Sami. Around 1600, Karl IX entered into an agreement to *force* Sami boys to go to Uppsala, there to study for ministry. Naturally the venture failed, but it can be seen as one of a number of attempts to realize the Protestant belief that the gospel be preached in the mother tongue. In that way at least, the Sami culture was given the same status as the Nordic cultures.

The Swedish state was also interested in acquiring reliable information about Sami culture. Schefferus' work *Lapponia*, which came out in 1673, must be seen in this context. The book is for the most part based on information gathered from clergy in the north. Interest was also shown in the publication of writings in Sami, especially biblical titles. Johan Ohrling produced a Sami-Latin-Swedish dictionary. This came out in 1780. It is still of value today for linguistic research and linguistic development. Sami schools were set up in towns which had churches, after the pattern of the *Skytteanska* school which was founded in 1632 in Lycksele and which was to play an important role in raising the educational level of the Sami in general, and for the spread of Swedish and Christian culture in particular. All these schools were under the control of the *Lappmark Ecclesiastical Authority*. The pupils who graduated from these schools were given prizes for spreading reading skills and Christianity among their nearest neighbours and kin. Underpinning most of this work was a generally positive approach to Sami culture and the active use of the Sami language.

It would appear that both Russia and Sweden started systematic missionary activity among the Sami earlier than Denmark-Norway. As far back as the sixteenth century, Russian monks had founded monasteries and chapels right up to the coasts of the Kola Peninsula and westwards to Neiden in South Varanger. The Swedish Church, for its part, had established chapels as far north as the Tana River (Talvadas), and to within a day's journey south of Kautokeino (Raunola). Danish-Norwegian churches in the northern territories were, at this time, only established along the coast where Norwegian fishing settlements were to be found, although a certain amount of missionary activity no doubt took place up the fjords and in the interior.[8]

In the eighteenth century there was a greatly increased interest in the Sami on the part of both Sweden and Denmark-Norway. This stemmed from pietistic ideology and the economic and political interests of the states. But the eighteenth century also witnessed an ideological and economic upheaval. The ambivalence inherent in the cultural policy was soon to be expressed in friction, at the national level, between a Sami and a Dano-Norwegian approach. The status of the Sami language was strengthened until well into the second half of the eighteenth century. The growth of rationalism, however, in the second half of that century undoubtedly resulted in a harder line being taken with regard to the Sami. Several concrete expressions of this appeared in Denmark-Norway from the 1700s onwards, including the closing of the *Seminarium Lapponicum* in Trondheim and on order to reduce the use of Sami as a teaching and preaching language with a view to its complete abandonment.

There appear to be two reasons for the weakening of the policies that had been so supportive of the Sami. The first seems to have been the development of some form of antagonism between the clergy who were recruited from the Sami areas and those who came from outside. This was particularly so in the Finnish areas. The second reason arose out of an aggressive agricultural colonization. From the end of the seventeenth century, colonists in Sami settlement areas had been accorded liberties and rights aimed at stimulating the

[8] Widén: "Religionsskiftet från hedendom i Nord-Skandinavien", passim; Steen: *Samenes kristning,* passim.

permanent settlement of a farming population. An important assumption behind this was the belief that the colonists and the Sami exploited different natural resources and therefore would not be in competition with each other. In fact it turned out that an active, state-supported colonization was not easily to be combined with a pluralistic policy, one aspect of which was that particular attention be paid to the special interests of the Sami.

1850–1950: the Effect of a Century of Assimilation Policies

By the beginning of the nineteenth century interest in the Sami language, and through that also in the Sami culture, was in decline among the clergy, the schools and the authorities generally. The most important reason for the weakening of the Sami language both in churches and schools was the agricultural colonization that occurred in both Norway and Sweden. The Sami in Finland had been pushed northwards for several centuries by the expansion of Finnish culture. Nordkalotten became a "frontier" area in the course of the nineteenth century, performing a function similar to that of the "frontier" in America; namely as an outlet for an expanding population.

The colonization in Sweden took the form of a movement northwards from the established farming communities of Jämtland, as well as inland from the coast. During the first three decades of the nineteenth century the position of the Sami in Sweden was markedly weakened. Obstacles were systematically placed in the way of the Sami reindeer herders so as to protect the colonists' farms. In Norway the Sami and Norwegian populations had occupied the same areas, though often contact between them had been limited. This was due to the fact that migration there had been mostly to the coastal regions of Finnmark, whilst the Sami had concentrated on the interior (Finnmarksvidda).

Increased contact between the Norwegian and Swedish farmer-fishermen colonists on the one hand and the Sami on the other, in the course of the nineteenth century, resulted in the need for further legal regulation of the interests of the two groups. Sweden was the first to do this. If Swedish cultural policies had tended towards the assimilation of the Sami, legal changes at this time began to favour their interests. A turning point in the policy of the Swedish state regarding the areas of Sami settlement occurred around 1840. From a one-sided policy of furthering the power of the state, there now developed a greater interest in drawing up regulations that aimed at protecting the Sami. This new approach resulted in agreements in 1867 on limiting the cultivated area, and a common Norwegian-Swedish initiative in 1883, and again in 1897, to regulate the grazing of reindeer. These aimed at regularizing the relations between the reindeer herders on the one hand and the agricultural settlers on the other.

What lay behind these laws was the clash of interests not only between farmers and Sami but also between the two minorities themselves in Norway and Sweden respectively. That the Norwegians and Swedes got together to promulgate the laws came about, first and foremost, because of a persistent demand from the Norwegians to draw up detailed and restrictive regulations aimed at favouring the settled agricultural population. In Troms, in particular, the reindeer herding Sami and the farmers had come into conflict.

The joint regulations also introduced, among other things, detailed rules for dividing up the various areas, controlling the migratory routes along which the reindeer passed, and compensation for damage caused by the reindeer. The aim of this comprehensive and detailed set of regulations was to establish a system that would meet the agricultural population's demand for an effective arrangement for compensating them for damage caused by the reindeer. The intention was not to get involved in the internal arrangements of the Sami herders. Seen, however, from the Sami side, the demarcation of grazing areas which was carried out gradually on the Norwegian side of the border (Troms, 1883; Trøndelag-Hedmark, 1894 and 1909; Nordland, 1898), was a threat to their right to exist.

When the union between Norway and Sweden came to be dissolved in 1905, the question of the rights of the nomadic Sami turned out to be one of the biggest and most difficult problems during the final critical phase of the discussions. The old demands, on the Norwegian side, of the settled farming population for a restriction of Sami rights and complaints over damage caused by reindeer, together with inadequate compensation for such damage, had not ceased after the law of 1883. Within Norway itself these demands and complaints were met in 1897 when new regulations (outside Finnmark) dramatically reduced the rights of the reindeer-herding Sami. But so long as the joint Swedish/Norwegian agreements of 1883 remained in force, the law of 1897 could not curtail the rights of the Swedish Sami in Norway. It was hoped that what the Norwegian parliament *(Storting)* had not been able to achieve in 1897, because of a concern for the union and for human rights, would now be achieved with the dissolution of the Union in 1905.

Up to this point the assimilation policies of Norway had been based, among other things, on security interests in the northern border areas around 1900, and the dominant view that the reindeer nomads and the Sami culture in general were inferior. In addition, the nationalist feeling generated on the Norwegian side by the conflict surrounding the dissolution of the union increasingly caused the "reindeer grazing question" to be seen as just one element of relations with Sweden, and one which could involve Norway in a position of "servitude" *vis-à-vis* that country in the years to come. The Norwegians were unanimous in wanting to leave the Union without any future obligations to Sweden.

The cross-border rights of the Sami nomads were only reluctantly accepted by the Norwegian authorities. The result in the end was based upon a sober assessment of the human rights position of the Sami nomads. There is no doubt that the official Norwegian view (and, it would seem, that of Sweden) in 1905 was that the state, in line with the current human rights position, was obliged to respect the continuance of cross-border reindeer herding by the Sami.

As the Norwegian prime minister Michelsen put it, this was based on the "centuries-old rights of the country's indigenous population". The two states negotiated several new agreements in later years. On each occasion Norway wanted to restrict the grazing rights of the Swedish Sami on its side of the border. The Swedes went along with this in 1919 regarding the extent and use of the grazing area in Troms county. As a result of the Norwegian demands for restrictions in order to protect farming and forestry interests, the Swedish reindeer herding Sami were forced to move their animals from the north to south Sami areas.

How did the Sami react to the new legal regulations that have appeared since the second half of the nineteenth century? Around 1900 the Sami in the northern and southern areas mobilized. For a brief period the Swedish Sami in Västerbotten managed to establish a national organization. The Sami areas in the south, in both Norway and Sweden, had long been under pressure, especially since the second half of the nineteenth century, from the neighbouring agricultural settlements. Swedish agricultural society reached its maximum geographical extent towards the end of the nineteenth century. This brought conflicts of interest between the reindeer herders and the agriculturalists. The state attempted to regulate these through the law. The Sami reacted by forming their own pressure groups. Such organizations were intended to present a united front in an economic conflict where the law appeared to impose unfair restrictions on reindeer herders.

The Norwegian Sami attempted to secure their interests in the face of the threat from the authorities in two ways. In the early 1900s the northern Sami aroused the Sami nationally, much as the Norwegians had been aroused during the closing decades of the nineteenth century, as a result of the conflict over the Union with Sweden. The southern Sami had followed in the tracks of their Swedish counterparts and taken up the campaign to protect their reindeer herding interests. From 1910–1913 the southern Sami had their own newspaper, *Waren Sardne*. This helped keep together the various Sami organizations that had been founded. In Finnmark a national organization was set up amongst the Sami with its roots in *Sagai Muittalaegje,* a paper that appeared in 1904–1911. The most important result of this movement was the election of a member of the *Storting* for the period 1906–1912. This was made possible through an alliance with the Norwegian socialists. It is worth noting that the Sami political movement came into being at about the same time that the labour movement first entered *Storting.*

Attempts to rouse the Sami politically had occurred as early as the 1870s, but they had failed. This time an effort was made to raise the level of awareness among the Sami. This, it was thought, would contribute to a more active Sami involvement in official bodies through which they could themselves further their own interests.

The Sami movement in North Norway, with its strong national undertones, was a reaction to the harsh assimilation policy being pursued by the authorities. This policy aimed at getting both the Sami and the Kven to give up their language and their culture. Paradoxically the Sami activists were inspired by the very same Norwegian nationalistic movement which was itself the source of the increased pressure for assimilation. The first phase of Sami political activism ended around 1912–13 and some years elapsed before the movement managed to get back on its feet. A second characteristic of this phase was that most of the activity took place in those areas where contact with the Norwegian population was greatest, namely in the southern Sami area and in the fjord areas of Finnmark. Whether this was because there the need to mobilize against the majority culture was greatest, or because more was known of the organizational methods of the Norwegians, is difficult to say. Probably both were of importance.

The next period of organized Sami resistance was in 1912–1921. The characteristic feature of this phase was the holding of a series of large assemblies. In 1917 the Sami held their first national congress—in Trondheim. This meeting proved to be an inspiration for the Sami, both in Sweden and in Norway. It also led to cooperation between the northern and southern Sami. An attempt was also made to establish a national body which would be an umbrella organization for all the local Sami associations. But this collapsed in 1921. This was largely due to the fact that the demands made by the Sami organization were not agreed to by the authorities. The work was therefore to all intents and purposes unsuccessful. In the southern Sami area, where pressure on the reindeer herders was greatest, the Sami failed to develop an organizational strategy which could counter the policy of the authorities. After the failure of the attempts to create a national organization, new life was blown into *Waren Sardne.* The paper was published in Røros from 1922–27. But any hopes of an organized Sami movement had disappeared by 1930. Nor were they to be revived in the inter-war period.

What could the Sami do to politicize their interests? In principle there were four possibilities. First, they could try to operate through the traditional party system. Second, they could organize along ethnic lines. Third, they could organize around their economic interests. Fourth, they could form alliances, e.g. with existing political parties. Looked at from a post-Second World War perspective, it is quite clear that it is the ethno-political, and to some extent, the economic strategy that has proved most successful. But one must remember that this success has come about in a period when the political climate for the minorities, has been very different from that which prevailed in 1850–1950.

In contrast to other national movements, it seems that the Sami did not find it necessary to create an identity. It existed already. But it proved difficult to formulate common goals which would unite all of them. In the south the demands were essentially economic, having to do with the reindeer herding. In the north they were cultural. For the northern Sami, who still had a living language, a traditional life-style, and who did not feel that their reindeer herding was under any direct threat, the fight was against assimilation. But in the southern Sami area, assimilation—both in Sweden and in Norway—had gone too far for it to be possible to mobilize against it. What there was left of an ethnic identity was tied to reindeer herding itself and to the campaign against an expanding agricultural society which had the support of the authorities.

Despite these differences it was possible to formulate a number of common aims of both an economic and a cultural nature. One was that both Sami and Norwegians should receive the same treatment. The Sami argued that they should have the same civil rights as Norwegians and that it should not be necessary for them to master another culture before they could get their share of society's benefits. A second demand was for autonomy, specifically that the Sami should be allowed to develop their language and culture on their own terms. The Sami leaders believed that if they could disseminate information about the Sami among the Norwegians, then discrimination and unequal treatment would cease to be so widespread. Additionally they believed that if the Sami could get more education, they would be in a position to exploit the institutions of society, so as to protect their interests and culture.

That the Sami organizations around 1900 became so concerned over the language question was linked to the fact that in the 1880s, nationalism and Social Darwinism provided new ideological support for a policy of compulsory assimilation. Progressive opinion accepted these ideas. The two liberal prime ministers in Norway, Johan Sverdrup and Johannes Steen, were strong supporters of the new view: the norwegianization of the Sami. The cabinet minister Wexelsen—who proved to be Steen's most effective instrument on these questions during the life of both his governments—made frontier outposts of both the school and church in the fight for assimilation. Other methods were also used. Norwegian colonists were encouraged to establish themselves in Troms and Finnmark. State land was only to be sold or rented to people who could speak, read and write Norwegian. A new school law, which applied in areas of mixed language, was made to further both educational and assimilation goals. As early as 1863, Johannes Steen—the Prime Minister—laid the foundations for his assimilation policy when he told the Norwegian parliament *(Storting)* that it was "a misconceived humanity to create and nurture the Sami nationality". And Johan Sverdrup, on the same occasion, added that "the only way to save the Lapps is to absorb them into the Norwegian nation".

Norwegian assimilation policies were directed at the Sami and the Kven in equal measure. The fear of a Finnish or Russian threat against Norway—posed, it was thought, by the Kven immigrants and the loosely assimilated Samis—gave an added impetus to the assimilation policy. As it happened, Kven immigration reached its peak around 1860–65.

Nordkalotten was a sensitive area from a security point of view. It was necessary, therefore, to strengthen the bonds of nationalism. Assimilation was one way of doing this. Proponents of the Sami and Kven languages were often accused of turning the country over to the Russians. Towards the end of the nineteenth century the policy of assimilation had reached the point where it was possible for a priest to declare that the Sami themselves had long since become tired of all the talk about their distinctive qualities, their rights and "suchlike phrases". In the work of assimilation "the interests of religion, education and the nation are as one". This encapsulated the indisputableness of the nationalist case.

Such a view could be expressed, with even greater force, after Social Darwinism, the ideology of the day, gave to the "higher" civilisation a moral right—indeed duty—to raise the "lower" orders. Otherwise the "law of the survival of the fittest" would ensure their extinction. That the reindeer herding nomads should go under was often seen as a natural necessity and as an indication of the dominance of the agriculturalist's culture. Through the work of Herbert Spencer and Thomas Huxley, Darwin's *Origin of Species*, which appeared in 1859, was turned from a theory of natural development into "Social Darwinism". (Indeed the two might be termed the fathers of this liberalistic biological alliance). On the basis of this, they argued that the successful cultures would develop even higher levels of "civilization", while the unsuccessful must succumb. In the 1880s Social Darwinism found expression in legislative ideology, in scientific research and in practical politics. One found here the necessary ideological support for the view that the Sami were an inferior race with an inferior culture who, through the law of the survival of the fittest, were doomed to disappear. The only thing that could "save" them was complete integration.

Agriculture was regarded as the cultural core. If people were farmers they could share in the advancing development of the majority society. From the 1880s farming, recently established in the Sami areas, was clearly given precedence over reindeer herding. Sami areas had also come to be of interest to the outside world for other reasons, not least when vast deposits of iron ore were discovered. This, in turn, led to railway building. An illustration of this comes from the Norwegian ethnographer and historian, Yngvar Nielsen. Travelling in Ofoten in 1899, he reflected on the work being carried out on the new Ofoten railway, work which he was able to observe at first hand. Writing in the Norwegian Tourist Association's Yearbook, he remarked that "it seems to me that the building of the railway will turn out to be a threat to the Lapps' future in these parts". He added that he met "several members of the race in Rombaksbotn, and judging from what he could gather from them, it would seem that they themselves understood that they were doomed, that no longer would the Ofoten mountains be a place for them and their animals. Civilization is merciless. With its steam and its electricity, it strikes down the weaker races regardless. We cannot always understand the whys and the wherefores. It just happens that way."

Assimilation was seen as a way of saving the Sami. There are good grounds here to recall the words of Johan Sverdrup: "The only way to save the Lapps is to absorb them into the Norwegian nation." And assimilation was to be understood in the widest possible sense: way of life, employment, dress etc. As Just Qvigstad, one of Norway's leading authorities on the Sami, put it in 1935: "When the Lapps (...) disappear, it will be because they have adopted Norwegian dress, way of life and language. They have given up speaking the Lapp language. They are reckoned to be Norwegians."[9] Assimilation was also seen as a powerful tool for putting a bit of spirit into "the spineless Finnish youth".

The process of assimilation has, in fact, taken place in many areas, though most of the factors involved have gone unrecognized. For example, one might cite changes in the economy which have gone in the direction of a more diverse and specialised pattern of employment, based on the market. Such changes have not been opposed in any systematic way, nor have alternatives been sought. This is in spite of the fact that they have led to the Sami withdrawing from the outer to the inner districts of Finnmark. The indirect consequences of the market economy and of the products introduced, for example, by traders were recognised by only the few and so no stand could be taken on them. Indeed this whole process, which is of course a form of assimilation, can be characterized as a peaceful form of social change, not one charged with conflict. To some extent, however, one might view the Kautokeino rising of 1852 as an early reaction against the type of development just described.

Changes in two social institutions did lead to a pronounced resistance on the part of the Sami. Here we refer to the church and the school. The growth of the former and the increasing influence of the latter roused the ire of the Sami, as their role in the policy of assimilation was revealed clearly and unambiguously. Formally the solution to the language question was sought through the schools. Here the attempt was made to teach Norwegian to the children while Sami was not used. Much controversy occurred towards the end of the nineteenth century over whether Sami should be used as a pedagogic tool to further the acquisition of Norwegian.

Often in Sami society the school was regarded as an irrelevance. What the children learned there they had no use for. A reaction against the way society was going could originate in the school,

[9] Qvigstad: *De lappiske stedsnavn i Troms fylke,* passim.

given its aims and the lack of importance accorded to them by the Sami. By keeping their children away from school the Sami not only got additional labour but also more opportunity to initiate them into the Sami way of life.

"Norwegianization"—the official Norwegian name for the minority policy in this period—was not unique in Europe, as regards either aims or means. Indeed throughout the continent there was a common ideology and strategy. The Habsburg Monarchy pursued the same policy, as did Germany, the Russians in Finland, the Germans in south Jutland and Alsace. Nevertheless the ideology behind the Norwegian policy does seem to have been marked by a very strong element of conformity and continuity, both as regards aims and means. The idea that society should have a monolithic form was firmly held.

What is the explanation for this? Initially it was not felt that a firm policy would produce the desired results, something the sceptics also pointed out. The Germans had tried this with the Poles in the Ruhr and Alsace. In both cases the result was not assimilation but a powerful ethnic reaction. On the other hand a mild policy in France conducted without precisely formulated goals had led to assimilation. The policy pursued in the USA at this time regarding the "Red Indian" minority falls into the pattern that was generally current. However here a much harder line was taken than in Scandinavia. For example in the 1880s the Indian "nations" were broken up, with the ownership of land and citizenship being tied to the individual: a process usually called "civilizing". From the 1880s to the beginning of the twentieth century the treatment of the Sami in Sweden is thought to have been milder than that pursued in Norway. There are several reasons for this. One cannot, however, ignore the fact that it proved expedient to interpret Social Darwinism differently in the two countries, in order to provide support for quite different policies.[10]

[10] On how Social Darwinism influenced attitudes towards the Sami, see Salvesen: "Tendenser i den historiske sameforskning", pp. 21–52.

In the decade around the turn of the century, one met in Sweden the argument there had a humanitarian obligation towards the weaker and one might say inferior group, as the Sami were seen to be.[11] The official position in Norway was that the reindeer herding Sami would, and ought to, go under. Norway felt it had fulfilled its obligation through a fair-sized payment in the reindeer grazing case, an issue that occurred after the dissolution of the union between Norway and Sweden in 1905 and which led to the grazing convention of 1919. The Swedes found this not only unacceptable but also irrelevant since the question for them was how to maintain, unchanged, the nomadic reindeer-herding way of life. The Swedes constantly used the argument that the Norwegians were lacking in humanity. One might argue that the Swedes' "humanity" argument was a way of exporting their "Sami problem" to Norway, and of using the Sami as a means of exerting a quasi-imperial power over that country. To support such an argument, it is sufficient to look at the result of the negotiations between Norway and Sweden which led to the 1919 convention. That section which dealt with the admission of Swedish Sami to Norwegian grazing areas covered 133 paragraphs; that covering the admittance of the Norwegian Sami to Swedish grazing areas, only 19.[12]

The Post-War Period: The Sami on Their Own Terms

A turnaround in attitudes towards the policy of assimilation did not come until around 1950. But when it came it did so in all Nordic countries. The Soviet Union sought to collectivize the herding of reindeer, in keeping with its general policy for the collectivization of agriculture. The social background to the reorientation of policy in

[11] See Salvesen: "Sørsamene i historisk perspektiv", pp. 27 f. See also Godbolt: "Samar og indianarar", pp. 66–78.

[12] For a further analysis of the differences between the Norwegian and Swedish policies towards the Sami in the ten years around 1900, see Salvesen: "Sørsamene i historisk perspektiv", especially pp. 33–38.

the Nordic countries is, of course, partly the 1948 Declaration of Human Rights and partly the international reaction to the racist ideologies of the 1930s and 1940s and to their results.

In order to understand the new international developments of the post-war period regarding human rights, one needs to start with classical doctrine. That respect for the individual was drawn from respect for his or her country, remained a generally accepted cannon of human rights theory down to the present century. It is true that there were signs, even in the nineteenth century, of a realignment of thinking on this issue, with a direct focus on the protection of the individual as an independent entity. This occurred in connection with the attempt to humanise the conduct of war. There is also a link back to the Treaty of Versailles at the end of the First World War. Here, too, there was a reappraisal of the position of the individual through the body created to protect the rights of minorities, first by the peace treaty itself, and later by the League of Nations. However, it was not until the setting up of the United Nations that the protection of individual human rights was fully and finally accepted. And gradually, as a result of the opinions expressed in various United Nations' bodies being incorporated in a number of conventions, attention came to be directed towards the ethnic minorities. The central decision on the protection of minorities is today to be found in Article 27 of the 1966 United Nations Convention on Civil and Political Rights. The article states, as is well known, that in those countries which contain ethnic, religious or linguistic minorities, the members of such minorities shall not be denied the right, together with other members of their minority group, to confess and practise their own religion or use their own language.

There is no doubt that the Sami in the Nordic countries are a minority group, as understood under the convention. But a convention of this kind is of little value unless it is translated into practical policies and becomes socially acceptable. An attempt to see situations from a Sami point of view, within a more generally problemorientated analysis, is a tendency which has been clearly in evidence in Nordic politics since the Second World War. Part of the explanation for this lies in a recognition of the importance which the preservation of, for example, the farming culture has had for the identity of the majority culture. From this comes an awareness that the Sami culture must have the same value for the Sami. There is also no doubt that Article 27 of the United Nations Convention justifies the demand for *positive discrimination* in order to strengthen the Sami awareness of their own cultural roots, their own identity. Naturally this also requires a thorough investigation into Sami culture. And behind this is the recognition that ignorance of the ethnic minority, on the part of the majority population in the individual countries, has had serious consequences for the Sami situation, in economic and social terms.

The social background to the new direction taken in minority politics is to be found partly in the international reaction against the racialist ideologies of the 1930s, together with their effects, and partly in the general economic growth of the industrialized countries in the post-war years. This growth has resulted in a number of developments of importance for the Sami.

The Scandinavians directed their efforts towards building up welfare states, based on the ideal of equality and with no one suffering want. This resulted in, among other things, "a bad conscience on the part of society as a whole" with regard to the Sami. Furthermore, education was now seen as a benefit for everyone. Several new groups, including the Sami, entered academic circles. This gave them the opportunity of contributing meaningfully to the social debate. All of this proved fertile soil for a new political attitude towards minority groups in general and the Sami in particular. Since the conservation movement has come to the fore, the Sami demands for land use rights and for the protection of the natural habitat they need for their reindeer herding against the building of power stations, has in effect tested the will of the state to take political decisions, and of the courts to decide just how far existing law goes, when it comes to protecting minority rights.

It is, however, an open question as to which of the two strategies, the development of plans with a political outcome in mind or the use of the courts, will lead to the socially most desirable resolution of matters involving the greater society and the minorities. Experience, so far as the Sami are concerned, suggests it is difficult to make progress via the courts. This is to be expected. Current law is the product of how the past wished society to be regulated; and that was a past which, to some extent at least, had different ideals and mental sets than we have today. With so much conflict setting its mark on the way society thought about minority policy during the nineteenth and twentieth centuries, it is hardly surprising that it should also leave its mark on current legal precedent. Only small steps can be achieved through the courts, given their interpretation of these precedents. To make new law is a political act, democratically tested, on the basis of current realities and wishes.

Perhaps the best of all examples of a dispute between the Sami and the greater society which illustrates this is the so-called *Skatte-fjällsmålet*. Here the Sami chose to use the courts to achieve their aims. The background to the case is as follows.

Since the end of the Second World War the Sami, as a matter of principle, have repeatedly raised the issue of their right to land and water. Sami organizations in the Nordic countries have argued that the legal position in these areas is unclear. In order to shed more light on Sami rights, the "Sami Villages" in Sweden brought a lawsuit, on a matter of principle, against the state for increased rights to the old "tax mountains" in Northern Jämtland. Together with the eastern parts of the neighbouring Trøndelag (in Norway), Jämtland is one of the few, if not the only, densely populated highland areas of inland Norden and one that has been so for a long time. Here the farming community and the Sami have lived relatively close to each other. The "tax mountains" were, before the 1880s, well-defined highland areas used by individual Sami. These so-called "tax Sami" *(skattelappar)* paid a tax for this privilege to the Swedish state.

An important question raised during work on the Swedish rein-

deer grazing legislation in the 1880s was whether the "tax mountains" were big enough to meet the needs of the reindeer herders, for
throughout the eighteenth and nineteenth centuries, the expanding
farming community had put ever greater areas under the plough and
taken more and more meadow and grazing land for their animals.
The Sami "tax mountains" and the farms and summer pastures of
the agriculturalists began to overlap, which naturally led to problems
in the fight for resources. To ease these problems the Swedish state,
around 1890, bought up large areas of agricultural land and added
them to the "tax mountains" for the purpose of reindeer grazing.
Gradually legislation limited the rights to individual "tax mountains", partly in favour of the farming community, and partly in favour of the public generally.

The "tax mountain case" (*Skattefjällsmålet*) went through all the
Swedish courts and turned out to be the biggest in Swedish legal history. The courts, the *tingsrätten* (1973) as well as the *hovrätten*
(1976), rejected all the Sami claims. The *Högsta domstolen* did the
same in its judgement of 29 January 1981. The judgement of the
Swedish Supreme Court must nevertheless be seen as increasing the
legal protection given to the economic activities of the Sami—reindeer herding, hunting and fishing—in that the court agreed that the
Sami had a strongly protected user right: "a land use right which is
regulated by the reindeer herding law and is based on the Constitution in the same way as are the land owner rights".

The *Skattefjällsmålet* was, in truth, a dilemma for both the Sami
and the Swedish state. Naturally the general nature of the case was of
great interest for both. But given the way the Sami presented their
case, the Swedish Supreme Court chose not to pronounce on the
possible injuries suffered by the Sami as a people. The case was seen
as a legal dispute about landed property, which should be judged in
accordance with the usual legal norms. The question the court did
pronounce upon was whether the Sami owned the actual land or
had certain rights to it. To declare a property right in certain limited
areas was to direct attention away from the picture of Sami rights as

a whole, and not least, of course, from the rights lost as a result of the regulative activities of past centuries. Viewed in such a perspective, it was naturally of little consequence for the judgement when the Sami argued that much of the legislation enacted around 1900 was characterised by Social Darwinism.

The longterm importance of the *Skattefjällsmålet* lies not in the judgement itself, but in the documents put forward by the Sami to support an ancient and relatively strong right to, among other things, the "tax mountains". Undoubtedly this will have consequences for the drawing up of future legislation. Indeed it was with just this *Skattefjällsmålet* in mind that the 1989 proposals on Swedish Sami Rights urged their strengthening in connection with land and water.

We see that in Norway too, the Sami can lose court cases, but through them achieve a wider hearing, which has resulted in proposals for the political solution of important questions. Thus the campaign against the building of a hydroelectric power station on the Alta-Kautokeino river system at the beginning of the 1980s, must be seen as the direct cause of the setting up of the Norwegian Sami Rights Committee. Its report resulted in an amendment to the Norwegian Constitution which gave the Sami special protection and their own consultative parliament.

Even if the Sami movement is a broad cultural and political force—culturally, identity-seeking; politically, self-assertive—it scarcely has much to gain from the traditional party political system. For that the Sami are too weak a pressure group. Given today's political climate, it would appear easier for them to mobilize a broad political spectrum by focussing on individual matters, where arguments in favour of positive discrimination for their case can be used to achieve rights to exploit natural resources, such as land and water. Success is the more likely when questions can be linked to matters concerning local societies and the environment.

Growing awareness of the Sami identity, and of the demands and political strategies resulting from it, is far from being a phenomenon confined to the Norwegian Sami. It is also marked in Sweden and has come a long way also in Finland. When *glasnost* and *perestroika* became political slogans in the Soviet Union, it was easier to make contact with the Sami of the Kola Peninsula. Here, too, there seems to be a growing sense of identity, as well as an attempt to arouse world opinion over the issue of pollution on the Kola peninsula itself and of the effects of the nuclear tests on Novaja Semlja.

It looks as if minority political action during the 1980s has, in the main, been most successful when it has used extra-parliamentary means, such as demonstrations, boycotts and civil disobedience. On their side the authorities have, generally, placed greater stress on avoiding an explosion of minority politics. Besides this, the state authorities have clearly wished to channel Sami opinion through formal parliamentary organs.

Another aspect of the picture has been a tendency for cooperation and the coordination of policy among the Sami of the Nordic countries. One sees too the outlines of a Sami political strategy which seeks to strengthen the bonds between the Sami and the majority populations. Though it is natural, in this context, to work on organizational cooperation, it is equally important to appeal to the emotions. For solidarity is, in the final instance, a matter of feelings. Here the educational system faces great challenges. To bring about an increased understanding of Sami rights among the majority populations, it is necessary that education to this end should begin in the very first school years. The Sami language, too, must be given an improved status. But the Sami themselves must delineate their own place in Norden. In cooperation with the Sami in all the Nordic countries, they must explain clearly where they want to go.[13]

[13] For further bibliographical information on Nordic minorities' policies and history of the Sami people, see Niemi and Salvesen: "Samene og kvenene/finnene i minoritetspolitisk perspektiv", especially pp. 86–93.

LITERATURE

Aarseth, Bjørn: "Samene", in Gjessing, J. (ed.): *Norges geografi*, Oslo, Bergen, Tromsø 1977

Dahl, Ottar: *Norsk historieforskning i 19. og 20. århundre*, Oslo 1970

Godbolt, James: "Samar og indianarar—felles trekk i møtet mellom to urfolk og storsamfunnet", *Syn og Segn* 2, 1981

Itkonen, E.: "Finnar", in *Kulturhistoriskt lexikon för nordisk medeltid*, Vol. IV, Malmö 1959

Johnsen, Oscar Albert: *Finnmarkens politiske historie aktmæssig fremstillet*, Oslo 1923

Major Peter Schnitlers grenseeksaminasjonsprotokoller, 1742–1745, Vol. III, Oslo 1985

Niemi, Einar and Salvesen, Helge: "Samene og kvenene/finnene i minoritetspolitisk perspektiv", in Karlsson, Gunnar (ed.): *Nasjonale og etniske minoriteter i Norden i 1800- og 1900-tallet. Rapporter til den XX nordiske historikerkongres Reykjavík 1987*, Vol. II, Reykjavík 1987

Norges offentlige utredninger (NOU) 1984:18, Oslo, Bergen, Tromsø 1984

Qvigstad, Just: *De lappiske stedsnavn i Troms fylke*. Instituttet for sammenlignende kulturforskning, Series B, Vol. XXVIII, Oslo 1935

Salvesen, Helge: "Sørsamene i historisk perspektiv", *Jämten* 1981, Östersund 1980

Salvesen, Helge: "Tendenser i den historiske sameforskning—med særlig vekt på politikk og forskning", *Scandia* 1, 1980

Steen, Adolf: *Samenes kristning og finnemisjonen til 1888*, Oslo 1954

Widén, Bill: "Religionsskiftet från hedendom i Nord-Skandinavien", in Baudou, E. and Dahlstedt, K.H. (ed.): *Nord-Skandinaviens historia i tvärvetenskaplig belysning*, Umeå 1980

THE FINNS IN NORTHERN SCANDINAVIA AND MINORITY POLICY

Einar Niemi

Approaches and Concepts

The Finns of Norway and Sweden have a history that goes back several hundred years, in some areas even to the Middle Ages. How this migration and settlement came about in the early Middle Ages is still unclear and subject to controversy. However, from the richer sources of the late Middle Ages we are able to trace a migration northwards and westwards from the heartland of Finnish settlement, in what are today the southern and eastern areas of Finland. It was the Finns who first colonized the great valleys of the rivers which flow into the Gulf of Bothnia. The Lappland *(Lappmarkene, Sami eatnan)* border was crossed in the 1600s; in the 1700s the most northernly valleys of Northern Norway were reached, and in the 1800s they settled on the shores of the Arctic Ocean. Many Finns who moved northwards in the later Middle Ages settled in the towns and cities of central Sweden, especially Stockholm. From the end of the 1500s and throughout the 1600s, the Finns of eastern Finland, in particular people from the landscape of Savolax, colonized the uninhabited western areas of central Sweden, with Värmland as the core area, from which they also migrated into the forest areas of southeastern Norway. The areas of Finnish settlement in southern Scandinavia developed a culture that was markedly different from the Swedish and the Norwegian. This was especially noticeable in agriculture where the distinctive burn-and-clear technique of Savolax was introduced (the *huhta* method).

One can hardly say that in this period the Scandinavian states had a policy for minorities in their own right. However, it is clear that the states tried to incorporate the Finns into their policies. It should be remembered that it was not until the eighteenth and nineteenth centuries that the borders of the states in these areas were formally agreed: Sweden–Norway in 1751, Russia–Norway in 1826. The border between Sweden and Finland in the Torne valley was settled in 1809. Large parts of the interior of *Nordkalotten* (the Northern Cap) were still a *terra nullius* in the late Middle Ages, so far as the states in the area were concerned. Colonization and missionary activities were important tools used by the states in their state-building endeavours in this vast area. The King of Sweden gave privileges and "liberties" to the Finnish farmers colonizing Lappland. The Danish–Norwegian authorities welcomed the Finnish farmers, for here in the far north Finnish agriculture was both an innovatory and stabilizing element in an area long noted for seasonal migration and nomadism. The native population of this district, the Sami never acquired the same economic or political status as the Finns during either the Swedish colonization of Lappland in the sixteenth and seventeenth centuries or in the agrarian politics of the Danish–Norwegian authorities in the eighteenth century. (However both Sami settlements and land use were important factors when it came to drawing state boundaries.) The Finns, however, were regarded positively, right up to the nineteenth century, particularly in the context of national economic politics and more generally in the context of state building.

Thus it was not until the middle of the nineteenth century that the position of the Finns became a matter of debate. This debate formed the basis of a clearly articulated policy with officially stated means and goals. It was really only now that the Finns came to be regarded as an *ethnic minority*, in the first instance from a cultural, social and political viewpoint, yet also more generally as a minority in quantitative terms. This latter was in spite of the fact that in certain areas the Finns actually made up a majority of the population. It was really only at this stage that the situation was ripe for a minority policy. A burgeoning nationalism provided the ideological fodder for the development of national states in the northern areas. Economic and demographic developments resulted in changed relationships between the Finns, the host community and the neighbouring ethnic groups. The articulation of the ethnic identities arose naturally from these relationships. External relations and the authorities' attitudes were thus preconditions for turning the Finns into an ethnic minority.

A comparison of the Swedish and Norwegian minority policies reveals both similarities and differences. To some extent the similarities as regards both the timing and the factors underlying the policies themselves are quite clear. But marked differences emerge in the later phases. In Norway, much more than in Sweden, the policy regarding the Finns became part of a general policy towards minorities. Therefore, it would be of dubious value to distinguish between Norwegian policies towards the Finns and those towards the Sami, at least not until after the Second World War. Sweden, on the other hand, did take a somewhat more differentiated line. It is therefore worth examining the policies of the two countries more closely.

Thus the main concern of this chapter is with the Norwegian and Swedish policies towards the Finnish minorities in their northern territories, i.e. in North Norway and in the county of Norrbotten in Sweden, from the middle of the nineteenth century to about the Second World War. What happened before and after these dates will be examined more briefly. The Finns in the north were the focus of clearly defined minority policies. Those who occupied the areas of earlier settlement in Southern Norway and Sweden received less attention. In the nineteenth century, they were integrated to a much greater extent into the host communities. They received less attention also, in part, because of their geographical position.[1] How then did the minority policies for the northern areas turn out, as regards means and ends? What lay behind their development? Why did they change? What kind of ethnic dimension came to prevail? And what implications did this dimension have for the development of the policies towards the minorities?

The terms used to describe the Finns have varied from one part of Scandinavia to another. So far as Sweden is concerned they have, in general, been named *finnar*, e.g. *värmlandsfinnar* or *tornedalsfinnar*, the latter from the Torne valley in Norrbotten. (We ignore here locally employed dialect forms). However the term *finne* has created problems. It carried overtones of nationality and citizenship, to some extent also among the Swedes. *Tornedalsfinne* (in Finnish *Tornionlaakson suomalainen*) has increasingly been replaced by *tornedaling* (*Tornionlaaksolainen*), especially by the Torne valley Finns themselves, in spite of the fact that the term relates more to a geographical area than to an ethnic or cultural entity. In Finland itself a term such as *Västerbottenfinne* (a Finn from the county of Västerbotten, *Länsipohjan suomalainen*) has continued to be used.[2] The Finns who migrated in the sixteenth and seventeenth centuries to the southeastern parts of Norway, especially to the area around Solør and the so-called *Finnskogen* (Finnish forest) have, together with their descendants, almost always been referred to as Finns. Occasionally, however, in official statistical publications from the nineteenth and twentieth centuries, e.g. in the census of 1930, they have been named *kvener* even though this term was never in general use in southern Norway. On political grounds and also because the lit-

---

[1] On the Finns of southern Scandinavia, and the areas and forests (*finnmarker* and *finnskoger*) which they occupied, see Broberg: "Invandringen från Finland till Sverige före 1700-talet i verkligheten och fiction"; same author in *Fataburen* 1981 and in *Svenska landsmål och svenskt folkliv*; in Huovinen (ed.): *Värmlandsfinnar*; de Geer and Wande: "Finnar", pp. 94–95; Tarkiainen: *Finnarnas historia i Sverige*.

[2] For a discussion of these terms see Wande: "Tornedalen i förändring", pp. 2–4; same author: "Tornedalingar", pp. 439–440.

erature continues for the most part to use the term, we shall refer to the Finns of Sweden and southern Norway as *finner*—Finns.

On the other hand the term *Kven* is generally used in northern Norway both among the local population and by the authorities. The term can be traced in Scandinavian sources to some period before A.D. 900. The earliest source is *Ottar's Account* prepared by the north Norwegian merchant and well-to-do farmer Ottar, and written down by the English King Alfred as an appendix to this translation of Orosius' *World History*.[3] There has, for a long time, been a debate on the etymological and historical origins of the term Kven, a debate not yet ended.[4]

Danish–Norwegian and Swedish sources, from between the late Middle Ages and modern times, give a clear picture of the Kvens as Finnish farmers who settled the Lappland areas suited for agriculture and also traded with the Sami and Norwegians. In the early phases of the colonization they enjoyed certain tax privileges through the so-called *Birkarle* institution.[5]

Many literary sources from the seventeenth and eighteenth centuries confirm this picture of the Kven as Finnish farmers who, step by step, settled Lappland, finally reaching the fjords of the Arctic Ocean. All these accounts draw attention to the key objective criteria of ethnicity, namely origin, language and material culture. *Kven* then became the *official Norwegian term*, in spite of the fact that it has subsequently been hotly debated both from an academic and an ethnopolitical viewpoint.

In this article the term *Kven* will be used of the Finnish migrants to North Norway and their descendants so long as the latter can be eth-

[3] See Holmsen: "Finnskatt og nordmannsskatt", pp. 61–65.

[4] Of newer works see especially Vahtola: *Tornionjoki ja Kemijokilaakson asutuksen synty*, pp. 459–488, 561– 562; Holm: "Kväner, Kvänland och kainulaiset"; Julku: *Kvenland—Kainuunmaa;* Korhonen: "Natur och näringar på platser med G'aino- och Kainu-namn i Sverige".

[5] On the Birkarle institution see especially Vahtola, op.cit., pp. 489–511, 562–563.

nically differentiated. It should be noted, in passing, that the term has definitely been one used by outsiders, though this has changed to some extent in recent years. There have been several in-group terms, which have varied from district to district. But a common term, fully acceptable to both groups, has not emerged. *Finnlender* or *suoma-lainen* could raise political associations in the host society, as could *finne* in Sweden. *Finn* or *finne* was also often used of the Sami in Nor-way, and would therefore create confusion. Furthermore the Kvens neither were nor felt themselves to be Norwegian in every aspect of the term. Nor was the term *norsk-finne* (Norwegian-Finn) acceptable. The term was therefore rarely used, though *norsk-finsk* (Norwegian Finnish) was adopted in linguistic and genealogical contexts.

One result, however, of the ethnic self-awareness and ethnosocial rehabilitation of the 1970s and 1980s has been that the term *Kven* has also come to be accepted by many among the Kvens themselves, in particular by the younger generations. At last, it would appear, the Kvens have got a name that can be used by both the in-group and the out-group without negative associations.[6]

Until the 1960s little was written about the Finns and the Kvens. The relatively few studies that did appear were mostly concerned with linguistics, pedagogy/school history, folk tradition/oral history and general cultural history. However since the second half of the 1960s, and especially since 1970, a broad spectrum of studies have been published, a development that has paralleled the growth of eth-nic self-awareness and ethnopolitical activity. The studies have ap-peared in a number of disciplines including linguistics, the sociology of language, ethnography, historical demography, social and politi-

[6] In recent years a debate about the *Kven* term has blown up again in the areas of Kven settlement, principally in the local press. For an up-to-date academic discussion of the term, viewed from a cultural perspective, see especially Olsen: "Finsk etnisitet", pp. 179–194; Saressalo: "Om etniska stereotyper", pp. 195–211, "Measuring change in culture", "From oicotype (ecotype) to the study of ethnotypes", pp. 3–18; Niemi: "Kven—et omdis-kutert begrep", pp. 120–137.

cal history. A common feature of the newer research, as distinguished from the older, is the greater attention paid to the in-group view of the minority situation.[7]

Areas of Enquiry; Historical Background

The traditional settlement areas of the Kvens in northern Norway and the Finns in the Swedish county of Norrbotten are about equal in size. The majority of the Finns in Norrbotten live in communities in or close to the Torne valley in which the Torne river forms the state border between Finland and Sweden. This is an area of about 50,000 sq. km, or roughly the size of Denmark.

The core areas of Kven settlement are the fjords of the counties of Finnmark and Troms (north of the Lyngen fjord), an area of about 60,000 sq. km. This area, which to the north borders the Arctic Ocean, has traditionally been called *Ruija* by the Finns and the Kvens.

Permanent settlement by the Finns in the Torne valley goes back further than that of the Kven in Ruija. Finnish farms in the late Middle Ages stretched from the coast far up the valley. By 1543 they had reached as far as the village of Pello, about 150 km from the coast. Swedish influence in the area was slight before 1600. The situation changed in the seventeenth and eighteenth centuries with the development of mining. Initially, however, Swedish settlement was confined largely to the mines themselves. Finnish at this time was the dominant language and it appears that the Swedes either used both languages or became Finnish-speaking. Until 1809 the Torne valley was a homogeneous entity, linguistically, culturally and economically. But the Peace of Fredrikshamn between Russia and Sweden in 1809 changed the situation. Finland, which was turned

---

[7] For a historiographical overview see Kalhama (ed.): *Suomalaiset Jäämeren Rannoilla/Finnene ved Nordishavets strender*, especially the articles by Jokipii, pp. 19–71, Onnela, pp. 72–78, Niemi, pp. 119–129, Bratrein, pp. 146–156, Virtaranta, pp. 170–186.

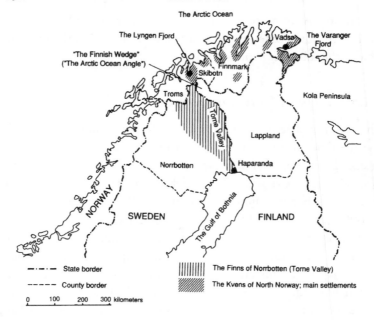

Finnish and Kven Settlement on the Northern Cap (Northern Scandinavia)

into an autonomous Grand Duchy under the Tsar, was separated from Sweden by newly drawn borders splitting the Finnish area of the Torne valley into two parts. The Finns on the Swedish side of the river became a minority. In 1821 they numbered about 7,000. By 1860 their numbers had doubled to nearly 14,000, corresponding to about 20 per cent of the population of the county of Norrbotten.[8]

[8] Recent research on the Torne valley settlement, including its linguistic and cultural history, can be found especially in Tenerz: *Ur Norrbottens Finnbygds historia*; Slunga: *Staten och den finskspråkiga befolkningen i Norrbotten*; Hansegård: *Tvåspråkighet eller halvspråkighet?*; Jaakkola: *Språkgränsen*; Klockare: *Norrbottniska språkstriden*; Wande: "Tornedalingar", pp. 438–449; Hansegård: *Den norrbottniska språkfrågan*.

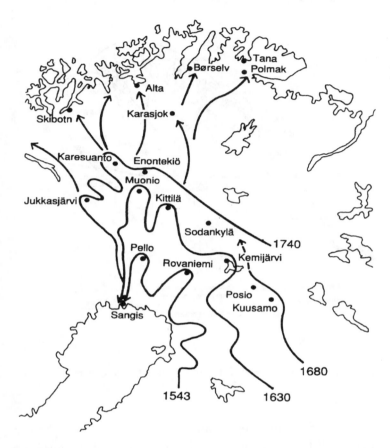

Stages of the Finnish and Kven Migrations and Colonization of
Northern Scandinavia 1500s–1700s

Kven settlement in northern Norway occurred only sporadically
before 1700. Not until the first half of the eighteenth century did a
sustained colonization of the area result from an extension of settlement into the interior of Lappland. From about 1830 the movement
of people from northern Finland and Sweden at times took on the

Einar Niemi

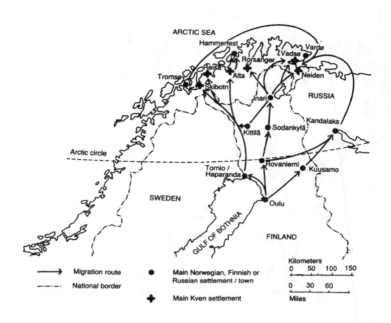

19th Century Kven Migration Routes to the Arctic Coast

character of a mass migration, with labour market forces as the key push and pull factors. Now the main destinations of the migrants were the lower valleys and fjords and, particularly, the coast. For much of the nineteenth century, the area bordering the Arctic Ocean experienced economic growth, with urbanisation and an especially marked expansion of the fishing industry. By contrast the economy of northern Finland witnessed crisis and stagnation, particularly in the agrarian sector. In 1845 the Kvens made up about 13 per cent of the population of Finnmark. By 1875 there were around 3,500 Kvens in Troms (7.6 per cent of the population) and in Finnmark 5,800 (24.2 per cent). The greatest concentration of the Kvens was in the district of Varanger, in eastern Finnmark, near to the border between Russia and Finland, and in Skibotn and Nordreisa in northern Troms, close to the Finnish border area, called "the Arctic Ocean angle" or "the Finnish wedge" (i.e. towards the Arctic Ocean).[9]

To the 1860s: Integration Without Assimilation?

To the extent that any minority policy existed in northern Norway before the middle of the nineteenth century, it was related to cultural matters, especially the Sami language. Two opposing views regarding the fate of the Sami language in the state had been present since the early eighteenth century. The one stood for assimilation, the other for a pluralistic solution.[10] At first neither of these views fully entered the realm of practical politics. However, it is remarkable that for long periods the three states actively involved in the issue—Russia, Sweden and Denmark–Norway—followed a pro-Sami cultural line. The use of the Sami language, both orally and in writing, by the missionaries and the mission schools contributed greatly to this.

Politically the culture of neither the Finns nor the Kvens received the same attention as that of the Sami, probably because, among other things, missionary activity among the Kvens was not on the agenda. Besides, the Finnish language had been firmly established for a long time, in the churches of the Torne valley and to some extent too in the schools. As for North Norway the language question, so far as the Kven were concerned, did not become an issue before the middle of the nineteenth century. It is reasonable to suppose that an important cause of the difference between the two areas lies in the

[9] Niemi: *Oppbrudd og tilpassing,* pp. 21–23; Eriksen and Niemi: *Den finske fare. Sikkerhetsproblemer og minoritetspolitikk,* especially pp. 26–28; Jokipii: "Finsk bosetning i Nord-Norge", pp. 44–48.

[10] Dahl: *Språkpolitikk og skolestell i Finnmark 1814 til 1905,* pp. 1–13.

age and extent of the settlement of the Torne valley on the one hand and of North Norway on the other. That the language question remained outside politics for such a long time was probably also related to the fact that for large sections of these societies, language in practice posed no problems. Here it was common for people to be more or less fluent in two and even three languages. And in a society where the languages were rooted in their respective social worlds, limited to particular social groups and functions, the operation of the society as a whole continued without hindrance. Thus there existed here a bilingual community.[11]

1860–1940: the Assimilation Policy—a Requirement of Integration?

With the 1840s Norway's policy towards the minorities entered a transitional stage. This was to last until the 1860s, when the foundation was laid for a new and, for the first time, clearly articulated minority policy. For the central authorities assimilation became the only acceptable course. With that the political ideology of the secular state came into full conflict for the first time with the age-old policy of the missions. This led, among other things, to the ending of state funding for the missions and the distribution of religious literature written in the Sami language. From now on the missions had to rely on voluntary contributions.

The middle of the nineteenth century also gave rise to a heated debate over the language policy. To some extent this was a reaction against N.V. Stockfleth, the priest and philologist, whose aggressive and, for many, markedly radical views were being pushed in the 1820s and 1830s. Stockfleth and his followers were much influenced by the currents of romantic nationalism that were sweeping across Europe at the time. Stockfleth was the first person who tried to set the Sami and the Kven language question in the same light.

[11] Jaakkola: *Språkgränsen*, p. 38.

Both the Sami and the Kvens, he argued, had the right to use their mother tongue and have it protected. For all that, in practice he paid little attention to the language problems of the Kvens. Rather he took his stand in the battle over the Sami language. Thus there raged a heated debate throughout the northern territories between those who supported Stockfleth and those who opposed him. The latter Stockfleth named the "anti-Sami party". The language question reached the *Storting* (the national assembly) in the sessions of 1848 and 1851. In the former year it was decided, against a substantial minority, that an investigation should be undertaken into the question of teaching the Sami through Norwegian, with the aim of "enlightening this people". The report of the enquiry came before the *Storting* in 1851. Although the government had considerable sympathy for Stockfleth's views, it felt itself under mounting pressure from public opinion. N.F.J. Aars, the vicar of Talvik, a parish in Finnmark with an ethnically heterogeneous congregation, put a proposal before the *Storting* demanding an investigation into the ways and means of introducing teaching through Norwegian. He also proposed that the schoolbooks used by Sami children should have both a Sami and a Norwegian text, to help norwegianize the Sami children. Both proposals gained a majority. This was a final defeat for the Stockfleth anti-norwegianizing policy.[12] This policy was not to be re-activated until well after the Second World War.

The royal decree of 1851, which followed the decision of the *Storting*, was to have far-reaching consequences. The decree provided for an annual grant to be used for a variety of initiatives "with a view to teaching the Sami the Norwegian language". The grant was constantly increased right down to 1921 when it was divided amongst the other budget items of the state funds for education. This grant was known as "the Sami Fund". This became in fact a powerful instrument in the policy of norwegianizing *both* the Sami and the Kvens. In 1853 the break with the Stockfleth line was carried further, when a

[12] Dahl: *Språkpolitikk*, pp. 92–98.

series of supplementary resolutions, aimed at strengthening the hold of the Norwegian language, were set in motion.[13]

The Kven population was not specifically mentioned in the various rules and regulations promulgated on this occasion. It was, however, made perfectly clear, both in local debates and in the Storting, that those who supported a policy of norwegianization viewed both minorities in the same light. In other words the policy was to be applied to both. This also became clear in the practical application of the policy. Nevertheless, the assimilation policy was not articulated with the same precision in the case of the Kvens. One of the main arguments for norwegianizing the Sami was to raise their level of enlightenment, to help "civilize" them. For the Sami were seen as "primitives" still pursuing a nomadic, pre-agrarian way of life. The Kvens could not be viewed in such a light. In the 1860s, however, the policy towards the Kvens was expounded somewhat more clearly, to some extent in public but for the most part behind closed doors.

In Sweden there was no such abrupt shift in policy towards the Sami as in Norway. The Swedish authorities viewed the Sami simply as reindeer herders. The Norwegian authorities, however, also had other Sami groups in mind, not least the Sami who had settled permanently on the coast. The result of this different approach was that in Sweden a policy emerged which was aimed clearly at an economic and ethnic segregation. Throughout the nineteenth century the rules and regulations laid down by the Swedish authorities were far more concerned with the relationship between Sami reindeer herding and Swedish economic activities in the north than was the case in Norway. A good illustration of this is the "agriculture border" (*odlingsgränsen*) drawn in 1867. The thinking behind this was that the different peoples exploited different aspects of the environment. For while the mountain plateaux were not suited to the needs of the Swedish farmers, they did accommodate the wide-ranging economic activities of the Sami, especially their herding of reindeer. By the end

---

[13] Ibid., pp. 115–116.

of the nineteenth century the Swedish policy was moving towards a clear "splitting of the categories" (of economic activities) which ideologically could be summed up in the contemporary expression "let the Sami be Sami", i.e. reindeer herding people.[14] This segregationist ideology certainly did little for the Sami, their ethnic and social status being extremely low. However, it did save them from the threat of a strict assimilation policy to which the Sami in Norway were exposed.

We must go to the Torne valley in order to find a change in the Swedish minority policy analogous to that of Norway. The breakthrough for a clear policy of assimilation towards the Finns occurred here at the same time as in Norway, namely in the 1860s. And the motives appear to have been the same too—security on the one hand and a rising tide of nationalism on the other, epitomised by the slogan "one state, one language". The same arguments for assimilation were used in both Norway and Sweden. Indeed, the parallels are so striking that one wonders if there was not some form of collaboration between the two member states of the Union. So far, however, no documentary evidence of such a development has been found. On the other hand, we do know that Norwegian and Swedish military officers shared a common view of defence policy in the 1880s and 1890s, the root of which could perhaps be traced back to the 1860s. The Torne valley was a "border zone" in which the authorities dared not risk the expanding Finnish population not being Swedish speaking. The debate, initiated by the county governor P.H. Widmark in 1860, on the political problem arising from the language situation in the Torne valley, revolved around this. The Finns were felt to represent a potential danger because their language was the same as that spoken in "the Russian-controlled Grand Duchy of Finland".[15] In the same way the Kven of the "exposed border area" in Finnmark and Troms could be described as potential

[14] Ruong: *Samerna*, pp. 63–64.
[15] Slunga: *Staten och den finskspråkiga befolkningen i Norrbotten*, p. 55.

"fifth columnists" in the event of a conflict between Sweden–Norway and Russia. It was important to act "while there was still time".

The Norwegian fear of Russia was neither so great nor so public as the fear felt by the Swedes, being expressed in Norway for the most part in confidential governmental reports rather than in public debate. There were good grounds for Norway's cautious approach. Russia was her northern neighbour. No buffer zone separated them. The local communities in northern Norway, the White Sea area and the Kola Peninsula had close economic ties. Through the *Pomor* trade northern Norway received important supplies of corn, timber and other products, and Russia was an important market for her fish products, especially those which were not wanted in the European markets.

On the other hand, "the Russian threat" was debated openly both in the *Riksdag* (Sweden's national assembly) and the Swedish press, as a subject in its own right, as well as an element in the new language policy. The fear of Russia also resulted in the formation of new organizations for the defence of the country. In some of these, women were particularly active, e.g. The Swedish womens' association for the defence of the father land.[16] No such dramatic response to "the Russian threat" appeared in Norway, the closest parallel being the Defense Association, a nationwide body formed in 1886.

Research has shown that there was apparently no real justification for the fear of Russian expansion into the northern territories in the nineteenth century.[17] Nor is there any evidence of a real irredentist challenge among either the Finns of the Torne valley or the Kvens of northern Norway. There were, however, a number of factors which account for this fear of Russia. One general underlying factor was the November Treaty of 1855, during the Crimean War.

[16] Lindberg: *Den svenska utrikespolitikens historia*, especially pp. 110–115.

[17] Ibid.; see also the conclusions of Palmstierna: *Sverige, Ryssland och England, 1833–1855*; Erikson: *Svensk diplomati och tidningspress under Krimkriget*; Nielsen: *"Ønsket tsaren seg en isfri havn i nord?"*, pp. 604–621.

This treaty involved a reorientation of Swedish (and Norwegian) security policy, in that Sweden–Norway signed a mutual defense agreement with France and England directed against Russia. The November Treaty created, in terms of security, a general atmosphere of distrust and watchfulness regarding Russia. For example, the Finnish and Russian railway building in the north was seen as militarily offensive.[18] More important were the links made between, on the one hand, the demands of the Finnish nationalists, of which linguistic matters occupied a central place, and, on the other hand, the appraisal of military security. The Swedish authorities feared a cross-border infection. Finnish criticisms of the undervaluing of the Finnish language in the Torne valley were seen as "Finnish provocation". It was feared too that Russia would exploit the Finnish dissatisfaction with the nationalist and linguistic situation by demanding that the Finnish-speaking areas on the Swedish side of the border should be incorporated into Finland.[19]

In Norway old fears of a supposed Russian desire for ice-free harbours on the Atlantic were reawakened. These fears were amazingly long-lived although, as was pointed out repeatedly at the time, the coasts of the Kola Peninsula were as free of ice as those of Finnmark. Rumours were rife of Russian naval personnel, disguised as ordinary fishermen, off the Finnmark coast.

One particular aspect of the Norwegian interpretation of the threat was its link with the Kven spatial pattern. Finnish immigration into northern Norway peaked in the 1860s. It reached its greatest extent in just those supposedly "exposed border areas" of northern Troms and Varanger in particular. Around 1870 the Kven population accounted for about 50 per cent of the total population of the rural districts of the Varanger countryside and some 60 per cent of the town of Vadsø. The town was, not surprisingly, named "the Kven capital of Norway". It was usual to describe this concentration

[18] Slunga, op.cit., pp. 21–22.
[19] Slunga, op. cit., p. 30.

of Kven settlement as "Russia's foothold in western Europe". An additional factor—quite separate from the purely quantitative—which caused the authorities grave concern, was the tendency of the Kvens to live apart from Norwegians, in ghettoes in the towns or in their own villages. The Finnish language was dominant in these areas and it was regularly refreshed by new migrants. It was also noted that in many places linguistic development threatened an about-turn. For while the older generation of Kven had often been bilingual, the younger generation were largely monolingual—the younger Kven often mastering only Finnish. In fact some neighbouring areas originally Norwegian actually became more Finnish.[20]

Thus, in the 1800s, the Kvens, like the Finns of the Torne valley, were seen as a national problem, from both a cultural and a security point of view. There seems little doubt, however, that it was the security aspect that was decisive in the formation of an assimilation policy towards the Finnish and Kven minorities, even though there was always a link between cultural and security policies. The practical application of the assimilation policy in Norway revealed a number of developments that support this thesis. For instance, the policy was approached far more rigorously in the "exposed border areas" and was more obviously directed at the Kven than at the Sami in these areas. Again, "the Sami Fund" was drawn upon for more measures affecting the Kven and the Kven-dominated settlements than for the Sami and their settlements.[21] There is evidence, of a qualitative nature, supporting this hypothesis in the documents in which the various arguments for and against the assimilation policy were presented.

In principle, the policy of assimilation was applied equally to the Sami and the Kvens. And in purely practical terms it was difficult for the authorities to prosecute a one-sided policy. For example, in

[20] Niemi: *Oppbrudd og tilpassing,* pp. 146–148.
[21] Larsson: "Finnefondet. Et fornorskningsinstrument", pp. 65–66 and 83–98.

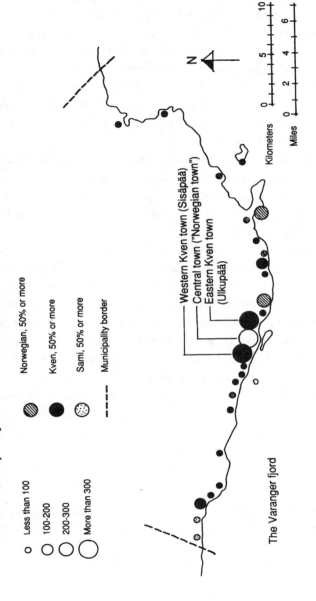

Vadsø municipality, Finnmark. Ethnic spatial pattern 1885

many areas there was the relatively trivial problem of who was who, for the process of cultural integration between the Sami and the Kvens was well under way, especially in the border zones of the interior of Finnmark. Undoubtedly, however, at the outset *intentions* regarding the two groups were different, though here again it must be admitted that the Sami living in frontier areas eventually also came to be seen as posing a threat to security. There is thus no doubt that the norwegianizing policy, applied to the Sami, was both comprehensive and pursued with vigour. But the actual measures taken towards the Sami were primarily cultural and educational, while those applied to the Kvens stretched across a broader spectrum. Indeed it would not be unreasonable to pose the counter-factual hypothesis that without the Kvens, the assimilation policy towards the Sami would not have been so strict.[22]

Throughout the second half of the nineteenth century Norwegian nationalism was yet another factor moulding the policy of assimilation. Nationalist feeling in Norway was strengthened by the campaign for the dissolution of the union with Sweden. A markedly aggressive conformist ideology emerged, which in the northern areas provided an important contribution to legitimizing the policy of assimilation. Here in the north the matter rested upon a clear desire to create a society based on the notion of the nation state.[23] As the century neared its end, economic factors came more to the fore with the desire to secure for the state the newly discovered resources of land, timber and, not least, minerals.[24] As for racial theories and the ideology of Social Darwinism, they played a legitimizing role in the policy towards the Sami rather than in that directed at the Kvens.

Finally one ought to draw in the European perspective. For there

[22] Eriksen and Niemi: *Den finske fare. Sikkerhetsproblemer og minoritetspolitikk*, pp. 331–333 and Eriksen and Niemi: "Kirka og minoritetspolitikken i nord", pp. 141–142.

[23] Eriksen and Niemi: *Den finske fare. Sikkerhetsproblemer og minoritetspolitikk*, pp. 324–331.

[24] Otnes: *Den samiske nasjon*, pp. 89–107.

were many parallels in Europe to the Swedish and Norwegian assimilation policies. There was, to a certain extent, throughout Europe a common ideology and a common strategy. For example, we find many similarities between what was happening in Sweden and Norway and the minority policies pursued in parts of the Habsburg Monarchy and in Germany, especially with regard to the schools.[25]

Concrete measures aimed at assimilation were not long in coming. For example, teaching through Finnish in the primary schools of the Torne valley was ended, little by little, after 1870. The same policy was applied in the teachers' training college of Haparanda (in the Torne valley) just after the turn of the century. Teachers who could show good results from their Swedish language lessons were given bonuses. The same policy was carried out in Norway, this being one of the uses to which "the Sami Fund" was put. In 1899 the People's High School of the Torne valley was established; its purpose was "to cultivate Swedish language and culture". The school's library was explicitly charged with giving the population a chance "to become acquainted with good literature in the Swedish language".[26]

Norway's assimilation policy can be examined under three heads: the assessment of the threat, strategy, and tactics.[27] Towards the end of the nineteenth century a supposed "Finnish threat" loomed up, usually in combination with that from Russia. This originated in part from the Finnish nationalist demand for a Greater Finland. Such ideas were, to some degree, actively propagated in the Kven settlements, and sometimes linked with the Laestadian evangelical movement. Laestadianism was—and is to this day—a fundamentalist, pietistical movement which found both the Sami and the Kvens a rich source of recruits. A key feature of the movement was pre-

[25] ESF Project "Comparative Studies on Governments and Non-dominant Ethnic Groups in Europe".

[26] Cf. Jaakkola: *Språkgränsen*, p. 45.

[27] Eriksen and Niemi: *Den finske fare. Sikkerhetsproblemer og minoritetspolitikk*, passim.

aching through the mother tongue; thus for the Kvens the Finnish language became a *lingua sacra*, as did the Sami language for the Sami people. In the period just after the Russian October Revolution in 1917 and Finland's declaration of independence in December of the same year, the notion of a double threat from Finland and Russia dominated the attention of the Norwegian authorities. Throughout the interwar years "the Finnish threat" came more and more to the fore as a supposed danger in its own right—and a much more serious one than previously—nurtured by the resurgence, at that time, of the idea of a Great Finland.[28]

To a certain extent the detailed tactics of the assimilation policy reflected changes in the assessment of the threat. In the *first phase* of the policy, down to the end of the nineteenth century, cultural matters were dominant, in particular those relating to schools and the language. This phase also saw the introduction of measures in agriculture and other economic activities by which Norwegian-speaking colonists were given precedence over the Kven settlers. From about 1870 to the 1930s three extensive land settlement projects were carried out as part of the norwegianization programme, all of them in that "exposed border zone" *par excellence*, namely the area south of the Varanger fjord. In the *second phase*, from the turn of the century down to 1918, a series of measures which had been tried out earlier were firmed up and carried through. An attempt was also made— not entirely successfully—to coordinate the various measures taken by the military and by the educational and other civil authorities. Also in this phase national symbolism was used in the frontier areas, especially in architecture with, among other things, the use of the Norwegian wood dragon style. It was also a great period for building "cultural border fortresses" in the form of churches and state-run boarding schools. In the *third and final phase*—the interwar years—a coordination of all the various measures was at last accomplished, with the military authorities playing an especially important role. In-

---

[28] Nygård: *Suur-Suomi vai lähiheimolaisten auttaminen.*

ternally, intelligence-gathering and surveillance, together with measures aimed at bringing to a fruitful conclusion the efforts directed at nation building, continued to be of importance. Externally a diplomatic offensive was attempted, aimed at both Russia and Finland, with a view to pushing back the border in eastern Finmark and northern Troms, thus keeping Finland further from the sea. When this strategy failed, one of reducing and controlling contacts and communications with Finland was introduced. The border was not to be hermetically sealed, but movement and trade were to be kept to a minimum.

It has been pointed out already that the Norwegian and Swedish policies towards the Sami went partly in different directions. On the other hand, the policies towards the Finns of the Torne valley and the Kvens of North Norway ran parallel, as regards origins, aims and measures, at least down to the end of the nineteenth century. But did they continue to run parallel thereafter?

Even though "the Russian threat" was, around 1900, still painted in strong colours by a section of the press and in certain literary circles, e.g. when the Finnish press headlined a suggestion that Russia wanted the Torne valley in exchange for the Åland Islands,[29] it seems clear that the responsible authorities in Sweden now began to play it down. Any separate threat from Finland seems never to have been taken seriously in Sweden in the 1900s. This prepared the ground for a more receptive attitude towards the strong criticism levelled at the linguistic policy in the Torne valley, which was by degrees now being heard in Sweden too. The League of Nations' work on minority rights in the interwar period was no doubt also of some importance in this context. One can speak of a thaw in the 1930s. For instance the *Riksdag* decided in 1935 to change course. It was agreed that in the Torne valley the Finnish language should be offered as a voluntary subject in the secondary schools and the Grammar School at Haparanda. This policy of linguistic détente, together

[29] Slunga: *Staten och den finskspråkiga befolkningen*, pp. 84–85.

with better relations generally between Finland and Sweden in the north, was consolidated by a meeting in the Torne valley in 1937 of the Swedish and Finnish foreign ministers. At the meeting both ministers stressed the importance of the mother tongue and the values of bilingualism.[30] Thus the policy of assimilation was modified in Sweden, but it was not fully abandoned. Down to the Second World War—and indeed longer—many of the old cultural policies were continued, and old attitudes regarding cultural and linguistic matters remained alive in many circles.[31]

No such change occured in Norway before the Second World War. Both the strength and continuity of Norway's policies towards its minorities were remarkable. The policies survived three governmental regimes, in 1884, 1905 and 1935. A government's political colour seems to have been of no significance. Though Norway played an active role in the work of the League of Nations on minorities, this seemed not to be reflected on the government's home front. Criticisms of the policy from Sami spokesmen and from the tiny numbers (mostly academics) who spoke out on behalf of the Kvens seem also to have had no effect.

The Sami did manage to organize an opposition body with clear ethnopolitical goals around the turn of the century. But the body all but collapsed in the interwar years. This was due partly to internal divisions arising from frustration at the lack of progress, and partly to economic and social matters overshadowing the ethnopolitical. And when it came to social and economic affairs, the burgeoning labour political movement was seen to be in a better position to do something than a purely Sami ethnopolitical organisation.[32]

The Kvens never managed to organize themselves on an ethnopolitical basis. There were too many risks of sanctions from

[30] Jaakkola: *Språkgränsen,* pp. 47–48.
[31] Hansegård: *Den norrbottniska språkfrågan,* pp. 22–35.
[32] Jernsletten: "Samebevegelsen i Norge", passim; Minde: "Samebevegelsen, Det norske arbeiderparti og samiske rettigheter", pp. 97–99.

the wider society, and the uneasiness felt towards the host society was too great. For the Kvens were *immigrants*—and were repeatedly told so by the authorities—not, like the Sami, an indigenous people. Clear evidence of loyalty to the host society was demanded, and most Kvens felt it necessary to accede to such demands. Utilitarian and social needs were added to the political. Anxiety and a feeling of ethnic inferiority often resulted.

It was in factors such as these that one finds the explanation why the minority policies of Sweden and Norway partly went their separate ways. The nationalism of the two countries took a different form too in the twentieth century. As late as the 1930s a rather aggressive Norwegian nationalism took many forms, e.g. with imperialistic moves in the Arctic Ocean, where one finds several attempts made to expand Norway's territory in areas where Norway claimed historic rights through her hunting and fishing activities.[33]

In a markedly nationalistic society the pressure for conformity was especially strong, the goal being that of a monolithic homogeneity. Differences in the foreign policies of Norway and Sweden after the turn of the century, together with differences in their diplomatic traditions, also go some way to account for the divergence in their minority policies. Norway was a young nation without its own direct experience of foreign affairs. As such, it easily became apprehensive in security and foreign policy matters. Finally one should take account of the differences in the two countries' military forces and potential. In this area Norway lay a long way behind Sweden. Indeed, up to the Second World War Norway's defences hardly amounted to very much from a security point of view.

Although the development of Sweden's policies towards the minorities was different from that of Norway, this did not mean that the Torne valley Finns were quickly reconciled to living in a united, yet culturally and linguistically pluralistic, society. Old prejudices among the Swedes died hard, as mentioned above. The Torne valley

---

[33] Dahl: *Norge mellom krigene*, passim.

Finns were often themselves—as a result of the assimilation policy—of two minds about their mother tongue. It was a love-hate situation which frequently produced a sense of inferiority,[34] as it had among the Kvens.

After the Second World War: From Non-Policy to Integrated Pluralism?

The attitude of the authorities to Sami culture has changed dramatically in all three Nordic countries since the war. A common feature has been the acceptance of Sami cultural and social life as a responsibility of the state, with the concomitant duty to protect and coordinate activities centrally, while at the same time delegating tasks to specifically Sami organisations. Admittedly this has happened somewhat differently in the different countries. Not all aspects of the course of events, ideological development and the nature and extent of the measures taken have been researched. Nevertheless it is possible to identify certain characteristics.

For one thing paternalism continued for quite a long time after the war. For another, during many of the postwar years, the policy measures were dominated by individual initiatives. There was no co-ordinated policy based upon a thorough assessment of the situation as a whole, with the possible exception of certain measures in the Norwegian school sector in the 1940s. A comprehensive Norwegian report on the Sami minority situation, published in 1959, including the recommendation of new policy measures was received positively by the central authorities. However, little of practical value came out of it, probably because of party political opposition in the north, both at the local and regional level.[35] Not until the 1980s did a

[34] Hansegård: *Den norrbottniska språkfrågan*, p. 32.

[35] Minde: "Samebevegelsen", pp. 102–105; Eidheim: *Aspects of the Lappish Minority Situation*, pp. 18–20; Paine: "Norwegians and Saami", pp. 228–232.

pluralistic minority policy towards the Sami in Norway make a complete breakthrough, largely as the result of the massive ethnopolitical mobilization aroused by the issues raised over the damming of the Alta-Kautokeino river.[36]

Since the war the minority policies directed at the Finns and the Kvens have differed from those directed at the Sami in several ways. There were differences too in the treatment of the Finns in the Torne valley and the Kvens in Norway, stemming, no doubt, from the different course policy had taken already before the war. Policy towards the Torne valley Finns must also be seen in the light of the heavy migration of Finns to Sweden since the war, especially to the south of the country. Problems of language and integration were highlighted and hotly debated, and this forced the authorities to articulate new and moderate positions.

The war itself marked no turning point in the Torne valley as regards either official attitudes or actions. The work that had begun in the schools before the war continued, though initially with little input by the state. But, beginning in the 1960s, one finds a change in both attitudes and measures. In 1958 the old prohibition against speaking Finnish during school play-time was formally abolished. In 1970 experiments in the school with Finnish as the first language started. In 1987 the Finns of the Torne valley (together with the Sami and the gypsies of Sweden) were given "partial minority status".[37]

Local and regional factors also played a role here, in addition to the more general changes in minority policies. The people of the Torne valley developed a strong sense of self-awareness, the origins of which can be traced to the school environment, which, integrated into the local community movement, emphasized the values and

[36] See the official reports NOU 1984:18, NOU 1985:14, NOU 1987:34; Paine: "Ethnodrama and the Fourth World", passim.

[37] Wande: "Tornedalingar", pp. 442–443; same author: "Tornedalen i förändring", pp. 7–8.

uniqueness of the area. The movement received strong support from individual national figures, such as the highly respected politician and county governor Ragnar Lassinantti in Norrbotten. Key elements in this ethnic revitalisation were the language and culture of the local community. Perhaps the most important single factor in the efforts of the Torne valley Finns to create and preserve a cultural identity during recent decades has been the "our language" movement *(meän kieli)* through which the schools have obtained the right—and the means—to promote the Finnish language of the region.[38] Svenska Tornedalingars Riksförbund (Tornionlaaksolaiset), a national body to promote the language and culture of the Torne valley, was founded in 1981. An Academy of the Torne Valley was established in 1988, and a cultural journal, *Met* ("We") has appeared. In spite of these and other initiatives, the process of assimilating the Torne valley Finns into the greater Swedish society has continued.[39]

Although, in principle, the Kvens and the Sami suffered the same treatment at the hands of Norway's minority policy before the Second World War, their fate after the war has been markedly different. Even though the political measures affecting the Sami have long been relatively moderate and the product more of *ad hoc* solutions to particular problems rather than of a holistic policy, there has been an open debate on a new policy for the Sami people throughout the entire postwar period.

The Kven question, on the other hand, has for much of the postwar period been made invisible. The authorities have shown scarcely any initiative. Nor have they been pressured either by public opinion or at least, not until recently by Kven lobbying. This lack of ethnopolitical activity by the Kvens must, for the most part, be explained as the result of the strict assimilation policy carried out over several generations. This has produced results in the postwar period, not least at the psychological level. The Kvens in the late interwar period

[38] Wande: "Tornedalen i förändring", pp. 12–13.
[39] Ibid., pp. 6–7.

and in the early postwar years can be seen as a sort of lost generation. They had not been completely assimilated either socially, politically or culturally. Yet their sense of identity and cultural awareness had been weakened. They did not want their own trauma and frustration to be passed on to the next generation, a feeling, as we have seen, that was shared in part by the Torne valley Finns. A conscious attempt was in fact made *not* to pass on the language and culture, e.g. by Kven parents choosing to use Norwegian in the home even though they themselves had Finnish as their mother tongue.

Even though Finland's fate during the Second World War produced a wave of sympathy in Norway, there are several indications that the memory of the supposed "Finnish threat" continued to survive in military and security circles for some time after the war. The Kven settlements were, to some degree, still not regarded as completely "housetrained". However, the old overt assimilation line was now politically impossible. Yet it was still not considered desirable, from a security and defence point of view, to back a policy of ethnic and cultural revitalization among the Kvens or to meet the challenge presented by the fact that, in spite of heavy odds, several thousand Kvens continued to use Finnish as their everyday language. The result was, at least until the 1960s, a non-policy.[40]

The general reawakening of interest in ethnicity and local culture in the 1960s and 1970s also touched the Kvens. The first organisational signs of this can be seen in the Norwegian–Finnish associations that were formed to encourage friendly contacts between the two countries and an interest in their culture and folklore. This was paralleled in time by a marked increase of interest in history (especially family history) amongst the Kvens themselves, many of whom had by now been in Norway for three or four generations. But what

[40] Eriksen and Niemi: *Den finske fare. Sikkerhetsproblemer og minoritetspolitikk,* p. 350; Niemi: "Finsk språk og kultur i Nord-Norge". On the development of language amongst the Kvens see especially Aikio: "The Kven and Cultural Linguistic Pluralism".

really brought the Kvens into the limelight was an upsurge of interest in them amongst researchers. The academic world rediscovered Kven culture and history. There was still a great deal of material to get one's teeth into, both physical and linguistic.

As a result of all this, Kven organisations took on a more pronounced ethnopolitical form, especially on educational and language questions. In the mid-1970s there appeared the first official report, with recommendations, on Kven conditions in North Norway.[41] After a heated debate, Finnish was recognized as a voluntary subject in primary schools and as a third choice of foreign language in the Grammar Schools.

The 1980s witnessed a sharp increase in the organisation of Kven interests. Norske kveners forbund ("the Association of the Norwegian Kvens") was set up in 1987 with its own newsletter *Met ruijassa* ("We the people of Ruija"). In addition, the new Finnish immigrants have their own organization. This recent migration of a Finnish labour force (especially to the northern Norwegian fishing industry during the 1960s and 1970s) undoubtedly contributed to the awakening of interest in the Kven culture. Norske kveners forbund has so far concerned itself mainly with school matters, partly inspired by the "our language" movement of the Torne valley. It will probably, however, be a long time before Finnish occupies the same position in the schools of North Norway as it does in the Torne valley, if it ever does. A victory for the Kven did, however, occur in 1990. Finnish was recognized by the Norwegian Ministry of Education as an alternative to the second Norwegian official language, *nynorsk* (rooted in the old Norwegian rural dialects), for use in the primary schools in areas of Kven settlement.

In 1977 the Kven Monument (also named the Immigrants' Monument) was unveiled in the centre of Vadsø, the old Kven "capital" of Norway. The monument, in bronze, was the creation of the Finnish sculptor Ensio Seppänen. King Olav of Norway, King

---

[41] *Norsk–finske kulturforhold*, passim.

Carl Gustav of Sweden and Finland's President Urho Kekkonen were present at the unveiling ceremony. The event was seen as a final Nordic recognition of the Kven culture and as an expression of a Nordic desire for cooperation over minorities. Among other things it was noted that the term "Kven" was consistently used during the ceremony and the subsequent festivities, not least by the heads of state present. For many the monument has proved an inspiration for the work of cultural preservation and revitalization. For others it has become a symbol of a culture of the past.

Although it would seem, in principle at least, that the authorities are now in the process of adopting a culturally pluralistic position on the Kvens, in practice they have taken very much a wait-and-see line right up to the present day.[42] A true culturally pluralistic policy demands a lot of resources and is built on fundamental ideological beliefs. The authorities still seem to be uncertain what these are. Many of the Kvens, too, have ambivalent attitudes, while at the same time their mother tongue is losing ground. Just as in the Torne valley, the old assimilation policy still casts long shadows.

However, the situation for the Sami, culturally and politically, is to a large extent clear and full of promise. There is today a close cooperation between the Sami organisations and the authorities on all levels. The rights of the Sami people as an ethnic indigenous group in Norway have recently been set forth in constitutional terms. Laws and regulations provide measures within a wide range of fields. The establishment in 1989 of a Sami representative body, the Sami Parliament (*Sametinget*), opened by King Olav of Norway, meant that Norwegian authorities have recognised, within limits, a form of Sami autonomy. Without doubt, the Sami organisational success has been an inspiration to the younger generation of Kvens.

---

[42] Søndergaard: *Finskundervisning i Nord-Norge.*

176   *Einar Niemi*

LITERATURE

Aikio, M.: "The Kven and Cultural Linguistic Pluralism", *Acta Borealia,* 1989

Bratrein, H.D.: "Folkekultur", in Kalhama, M.-L. (ed.): *Suomalaiset Jäämeren Rannoilla/Finnene ved Nordishavets strender,* Turku 1982

Broberg, R.: "Finsk invandring till mellersta Sverige", in *Svenska landsmål och svenskt folkliv,* 1988

Broberg, R.: "Invandringen från Finland till Sverige före 1700-talet i verkligheten och fiction", *Nordisk utredningsserie* 14/70, 1981

Dahl, H.F.: *Norge mellom krigene. Det norske samfunn i krise og konflikt 1918–1940,* Oslo 1971

Dahl, H.: *Språkpolitikk og skolestell i Finnmark 1814 til 1905,* Oslo 1957

De Geer, E. and Wande, E.: "Finnar", in Svanberg, I. and Runblom, H. (ed.): *Det mångkulturella Sverige. En handbok om etniska grupper och minoriteter,* Stockholm 1988

Eidheim, H.: *Aspects of the Lappish Minority Situation.* Oslo 1971

Eriksen, K.E. and Niemi, E.: "'Den finske fare'—grenseproblemer og minoritetspolitikk i nord (1870–1940)", in Kalhama, M.-L. (ed.): *Suomalaiset Jäämeren Rannoilla/Finnene ved Nordishavets strender,* Turku 1982

Eriksen, K.E. and Niemi, E.: *Den finske fare. Sikkerhetsproblemer og minoritetspolitikk i nord 1860–1940,* Universitetsforlaget 1981

Eriksen, K.E. and Niemi, E.: "Kirka og minoritetspolitikken i nord—lojalitet overfor Gud eller Keiser?", *Heimen,* 1982

Erikson, S.: *Svensk diplomati och tidningspress under Krimkriget,* Stockholm 1939

Hansegård, N.-E.: *Den norrbottniska språkfrågan. En återblick på halvspråkighetsdebatten,* Uppsala 1990

Hansegård, N.-E.: *Tvåspråkighet eller halvspråkighet?,* Stockholm 1968

Holm, G.: "Kväner, Kvänland og kainulaiset", in *Språkhistoria och språkkontakt i Finland och Nord-Skandinavien.* Kungl. Skytteanska Samfundets handlingar 26/1982, Umeå 1982

Holmsen, A.: "Finnskatt og nordmannsskatt", in Bergsland, K. (ed.): *Samenes og sameområdenes rettslige stilling historisk belyst,* Universitetsforlaget 1977

The Finns in Northern Scandinavia and Minority Policy   177

Huovinen, S. (ed.): *Värmlandsfinnar. Om finnskogens historia och kultur*, Stockholm 1986

Jaakkola, M.: *Språkgränsen. En studie i tvåspråkighetens sociologi*, Malmö 1973

Jernsletten, R.: "Samebevegelsen i Norge. Idé og strategi 1900–1940". Graduate thesis in history, University of Tromsø 1986

Jokipii, M.: "Finsk bosetning i Nord-Norge—historiske hovedlinjer", in Kalhama, M.-L. (ed.): *Suomalaiset Jäämeren Rannoilla/Finnene ved Nordishavets strender*, Turku 1982

Julku, K.: *Kvenland—Kainuunmaa*, Jyväskylä 1986

Klockare, S.: *Norrbottniska språkstriden 1888–1958*, Föreningen Norden, Stockholm 1982

Korhonen, O.: "Natur och näringar på platser med G'aino- och Kainunamn i Sverige", in Julku, K. (ed.): *Nordkalotten i en skiftande värld— kulturer utan gränser och stater över gränser*, Studia Historica Septentrionalia 14:2, Rovaniemi 1987

Larsson, B.: "Finnefondet. Et fornorskningsinstrument". Graduate thesis in history, University of Tromsø 1989

Lindberg, F.: *Den svenska utrikespolitikens historia III:4, 1872–1914*, Stockholm 1958

Minde, H.: "Samebevegelsen, Det norske arbeiderparti og samiske rettigheter", in Thuen, T. (ed.): *Samene—urbefolkning og minoritet*, Universitetsforlaget 1980

Nielsen, J. P.: "Ønsket tsaren seg en isfri havn i nord?", (Norwegian) *Historisk tidsskrift* 4, 1991

Niemi, E.: "Finsk språk og kultur i Nord-Norge", in *Suomi prohjoismaisena kielenä/Finskan som språk i Norden*, Helsinki 1983

Niemi, E.: "Kven—et omdiskutert begrep", in *Varanger. Årbok 1991*, Vadsø 1991

Niemi, E.: "Kvensk kulturforskning og vernearbeid", in Kalhama, M.L. (ed.): *Suomalaiset Jäämeren Rannoilla/Finnene ved Nordishavets strender*, Turku 1982

Niemi, E.: *Oppbrudd og tilpassing. Den finske flyttingen til Vadsø 1845–1885*, Vadsø 1977

Norsk-finske kulturforhold, Norsk kulturråd, Oslo 1976

NOU 1984:18; *NOU* 1985:14; *NOU* 1987:34

178   *Einar Niemi*

Nygård, T.: *Suur-Suomi vai lähiheimolaisten auttaminen*, Keurun 1978

Olsen, V.: "Finsk etnisitet mellom norsk storsamfunn og samisk minoritet belyst ut fra begrepet etnonym", in Sandnes, J. et al. (ed.): *Folk og ressurser i nord*, Trondheim 1983

Onnela, S.: "Om den finske kvenforskning", in Kalhama, M.-L. (ed.): *Suomalaiset Jäämeren Rannoilla/Finnene ved Nordishavets strender*, Turku 1982

Otnes, P.: *Den samiske nasjon*, Oslo 1970

Paine, R.: "Ethnodrama and the Fourth World: The Saami Action Group in Norway 1979–1981", in Dyck, N. (ed.): *Indigenous Peoples and the Nation-State: Fourth World Politics in Canada, Australia and Norway*, Newfoundland: St. John's 1985

Paine, R.: "Norwegians and Saami: Nation-State and Fourth World", in Gold, G.L. (ed.): *Minorities and Mother Country Language*, Newfoundland: St. John's 1984

Palmstierna, C.F.: *Sverige, Ryssland och England 1833–1855*, Stockholm 1932

Ruong, I.: *Samerna*, Stockholm 1975

Saressalo, L.: "From oicotype (ecotype) to the study of ethnotypes", *Acta Borealia* 1986

Saressalo, L.: "Measuring change in culture", *Nord nytt* 1985

Saressalo, L.: "Om etniska stereotyper", in Sandnes, J. et al. (eds.): *Folk og ressurser i nord*, Trondheim 1983

Slunga, N.: *Staten och den finskspråkiga befolkningen i Norrbotten*, Luleå 1965

Søndergaard, B.: *Finskundervisning i Nord-Norge. Muligheder og begrænsninger*, Tønder 1989

Tarkiainen, K.: *Finnarnas historia i Sverige, vol. 1. Innflyttarna från Finland under det gemensamma rikets tid*, SHS/Helsinki 1990

Tenerz, H.: *Ur Norrbottens finnbygds historia*, Uppsala 1962

Vahtola, J.: *Tornionjoki ja Kemijokilaakson asutuksen synty*, Rovaniemi 1980

Virtaranta, P.: "Om kvenenes språk", in Kalhama, M.-L. (ed.): *Suomalaiset Jäämeren Rannoilla/Finnene ved Nordishavets strender*, Turku 1982

Wande, E.: "Tornedalen i förändring", *Nordisk tidsskrift*, 1990

Wande, E.: "Tornedalingar", in Svanberg, I. and Runblom, H. (eds.): *Det mångkulturella Sverige. En handbok om etniska grupper och minoriteter*, Stockholm 1988

FINNS AND SWEDES
IN FINLAND

Max Engman

Relations between Finns and Swedes in Finland in modern times have been formed by nation building and state making within the Russian Empire in 1809–1917, which laid the foundation of the independent republic of Finland. During this process the Swedish kingdom's Finnish-speaking minority became the dominant majority and the Swedish-speaking group, consisting of both the upper class and common people, a minority, some of whom formed the autonomous region of Åland. Finnish evolved from being one of the Swedish kingdom's regional minority languages, chiefly used in oral communication and in church, into a modern majority language, which achieved this position even before the outcome of the First World War paved the way for new states in which new groups became dominant.

Finland as Part of the Kingdom of Sweden

Finland became part of the Swedish kingdom in the early Middle Ages. The Swedish conquest of the areas populated by western Finnish-speaking tribes was followed by the immigration of Swedish colonists who settled in the coastal areas. As a result of migration, Swedish settlement areas evolved, as did a language boundary between Swedish and Finnish which remained fairly constant over the centuries up until the second half of the 19th century, when the Swedish districts began to shrink because of an increase in Finnish migration to the coastal areas. Up to that point, migrants across the language boundary had been assimilated by the local majority.[1]

Finland was incorporated into the kingdom of Sweden as an integral part. It was not a province like the Baltic provinces or Ingria (Ingermanland); its inhabitants had the same obligations and rights as the inhabitants of Sweden, among them, representation in the Swedish Parliament.

The question of Finland's position and the existence of a separate Finnish identity within the Swedish kingdom are among the most controversial questions in Finnish historical research. Sweden as a great power was a multinational empire with a hierarchy of regional and local identities. It has been pointed out that Finland occupied a special position in having some separate institutions, a frontier position to the east and the Finnish language. Finland thus formed a bishopric—the Åbo (Turku) diocese, which was divided up in 1555 when the diocese of Viborg (Viipuri) was founded—and a superior court district (1624–1775). For short periods Finland was administered separately by a Governor General. These administrative regions, however, had different and varied boundaries, and no clear and stable concept of Finland existed. Regional Finnish awareness, however, was strengthened in the 18th century by research activities at the University of Åbo, the Russian occupations in 1710–1721 and 1741–1743, the special Finnish deputations for the "improvement" of the region and the officers' opposition against Gustavus III during the war of 1789–1790.

The Finnish language was a feature that distinguished Finland from the rest of the Swedish realm, but this was not a clear-cut criterion, since there was Swedish settlement in Finland and considerable Finnish settlement in Sweden (Tornedalen and Värmland). With the publication of Mikael Agricola's *ABC book* (1540), and the translation of the New Testament (1548) Finnish became a written

---

[1] Christiansen: *The Northern Crusades: the Baltic and the Catholic Frontier 1100–1525;* Meinander: "Om svenskarnes inflyttningar till Finland"; Wallén: *Språkgränsen och minoriteterna i Finlands svenskbygder omkr. 1600–1865*; Klövekorn: *Die sprachliche Struktur Finnlands 1880–1950*.

language, principally based on the western dialects. In the centuries that followed, literature chiefly of a religious nature was published in Finnish; the whole Bible in Finnish came out in 1642. There were also translations of laws, and for example the Law Code of 1734 appeared in Finnish translation (1759). The government and the church endeavoured to ensure that officials and clergy knew the language of the country.

In the 17th and 18th centuries, a number of projects were planned in order to make the population of Finland more Swedish, the aim being to make the kingdom more uniform. However, it was social development which helped to oust Finnish. The administrative unification and centralisation of the 17th century put an end to distinctive local features; at the same time the switch to an administration which mainly functioned in writing automatically pushed Finnish aside, although it was used in oral communication and in the church, in administrative functions and in the courts of law. All higher education was conducted in Latin or in Swedish, and the role of Swedish increased, e.g. at the University of Åbo in the 18th century when it partially replaced Latin. A knowledge of Swedish was a *sine qua non* for social advancement.

Finland as an Autonomous State

Regardless of what importance one attaches to Finnish national awareness before the 1808–1809 war, Finland's inclusion in the Russian Empire was a drastic change both for the country and for its language groups. Finland was not incorporated into the Russian Empire, but was allowed to retain its own laws, and became one of the many separately administered areas in Russia. Although Finland's position was not clearly defined and became the subject of constitutional conflicts at the turn of the century, it was crucial that Finnish autonomy created an unambiguously demarcated political and administrative Finland, which, moreover, was expanded northwards when the frontier was moved from the western boundary of

Åbo diocese on the Kemi river to the Torne river. When Viborg county, conquered by Russia in 1721 and 1743, was united with the Grand Duchy in 1812, the boundaries then drawn up remained in existence more or less until 1940.

Tsar Alexander I announced at the Borgå Diet in 1809 that he had "elevated Finland to be numbered among the nations", but in reality he had only created the conditions necessary to enable a nation to develop. In many ways the Grand Duchy was a framework without content, but the Finns gained what the autonomist nationalism of small nations struggled in vain to achieve in most parts of Europe before the First World War: a state of their own, with its own central administration. During the first decades of the autonomy the administration really constituted Finland. Defending the autonomy gradually became the central issue in Finnish politics. In Finland, then, there evolved a kind of nationalism that mixed features of the form of nationalism customary in western Europe, nationalism as a "civic religion", i.e. support of the existing state, with the form of nationalism customary in eastern Europe, which aimed at liberation from the multinational empires and from a ruling class which spoke another language.[2]

At the beginning of the 19th century the Finnish-speaking proportion of Sweden's population was approximately 22%. After the union of Viborg county, Finnish speakers constituted about 87% of the Grand Duchy's population. The radically changed language conditions, however, did not acquire political importance immediately. The clergy and the peasant estates thus requested at the Borgå Diet in 1809 that Swedish should be retained as the official language.

The administrative class carried on a policy that has been called the bureaucratic-patriotic line, based on protecting Finnish autonomy and, if possible, extending it by loyalty to the Emperor.[3] Ideo-

[2] Cf. Alapuro: *State and Revolution in Finland,* pp. 89–100.

[3] Jussila: *Maakunnasta valtioksi. Suomen valtion synty,* Tommila:

logically, it was a matter of Finland's shaking off Swedish influence and having the Grand Duchy form closer ties with Russia, while at the same time avoiding integration. In a way, the policy was the result of a process of elimination, which was summed up in an apocryphal phrase attributed to A. I. Arwidsson: "Swedes we are not, Russians we will not be, so let us be Finns." In the eyes of the bureaucratic-patriotic faction, however, it was a question of creating "political Finnishness", not of a nationality programme, although they had nothing against "ethnographic nationalism" which was expressed in studies of the country's language, ancient monuments, folk culture and history. The Emperor thus looked favorably upon the founding of the Finnish Literature Society in 1831 and promoted the development of Finnish. The line for this patronage was clearly drawn at political activity, as was shown in the aftermath of the 1848 revolution when publication of texts in Finnish other than religious and administrative ones was prohibited for a brief period in 1850. The ban was levelled against the distribution of subversive literature to the people, not against Finnish as such, as is indicated by the fact that a professorship in Finnish was established at the university the same year.[4]

The policy of extending autonomy by means of loyalty may be said to dominate a large part of the 19th century—Finland remained peaceful when Poland revolted; furthermore, it succeeded. In Finland, from the 1860s onwards, major reforms were carried out and the Grand Duchy got a Diet (1863) that met regularly, its own coinage (1865) and even a separate, conscripted army (1878–1903).

The upper class that had led the Grand Duchy during the first part of the autonomy consisted of the nobility and officials. Although the largest estates were in the hands of the aristocracy, peasants owned about 90% of the land. The power élite in Finland was not an exten-

Suomen autonomian synty 1808–1819.

[4] Klinge: *Från lojalism till rysshat* and *Let Us Be Finns—Essays on History.*

sion of the Empire's power élite, like for example German officials in Bohemia or the Magyars in Transylvania and Slovakia. The nobility and upper class in Finland thus had no independent position of power but were dependent on posts in Finland's newly-created central administration. They were therefore prepared to defend it against the Empire by looking for support inside the country and by responding favorably to demands from below.

One decisive factor in Finland's development was the fact that the Grand Duchy was allowed to evolve undisturbed for a long time. Customs autonomy and access to the Russian market brought economic progress. Whereas the Grand Duchy's regions had earlier been oriented towards Stockholm or St Petersburg, economic development and improved communications caused integration centred on Helsingfors (Helsinki), which grew into a capital city in the modern sense. At the same time, a Finnish civic society developed with national institutions and symbols. J. L. Runeberg wrote patriotic literature, and Elias Lönnrot produced *Kalevala*, the first edition in 1835 receiving an enormous response. A national epic signified that the nation had a great past and was worthy of a place among the nations; *Kalevala* became "Finland's passport into the family of civilized nations".[5]

The growth of separate Finnish institutions had—unnoticed—produced a modern state right on St Petersburg's doorstep. When Russian nationalists realized at the end of the century what had happened, and the central government, under pressure from public opinion but mainly for military reasons, began to take measures to limit Finnish autonomy at the turn of the century, this move aroused strong opposition. As a result of the nation building and mobilization of the people for national ends that had taken place, the opposition was quite effective. Both language groups were characterized by a patriotic adherence to the Finnish state.

---

[5] Wilson: *Folklore and Nationalism in Modern Finland*, pp. 58, 75–76.

The Finnish Nationalist Movement

The roots of the Finnish nationalist movement lay both in the uncertainty that the divorce from Sweden had created and in the Romantic concept of language as an expression of the deepest identity
of a nation. In order to maintain the rather fragile construction that
was Finland's autonomy, it was not sufficient merely to base the national existence of the Grand Duchy on the Swedish-speaking administrative class. It was necessary to mobilize the vast majority of
the people. Drawing on Herder's and Hegel's doctrines, the philoso-
pher J. V. Snellman worked out his nationality theory, which was
further developed by the historian G. Z. Yrjö-Koskinen. Both of
them wanted to strengthen Finland's position by creating a united
Finnish nation. To both of them, the nation rather than specific institutions was the whole point, to strengthen the nation and in this
way give it power to survive pressure from Russia.[6]

The only way to strengthen the nation was to bridge the gap between the upper class and the people by the upper class becoming
Finnish. Snellman, who himself wrote in Swedish, envisaged a long
transitional period of bilingualism, during which the Swedish-speaking educated class who learnt Finnish would constitute a bridge to a
united Finnish nation. Yrjö-Koskinen, who had learnt Finnish with
some difficulty, wanted to hasten the process by recruiting a new
educated Finnish class from among the ranks of the people by means
of regulations about official languages and a rapid expansion of
Finnish schools.

In Nicholas I's bureaucratic state, political demands by the Finnish movement were looked upon as opposition and an incursion
into areas that did not concern ordinary citizens. Consequently,
Snellman did not obtain a post at the university, and his critical
newspaper *Saima* was banned by the censor. During the liberalisa-

[6] On the Finnish movement, see the new but partly very traditionally
conceived Tommila (ed.): *Herää Suomi. Suomalaisuusliikkeen historia.*

tion period following the Crimean War, the situation changed, and
when the Diet met in 1863 after an interval of fifty years, new opportunities opened up for the Finnish movement to take political action. Snellman himself was made a senator in 1863.

On the Emperor's visit to Finland in 1863, Snellman drew up a
language rescript which pledged that Finnish would be on an equal
footing with Swedish as an official language inside twenty years. The
rescript was the basis for a long series of administrative regulations
concerning language, extending the domain in which Finnish was
used. In 1902 Finnish achieved equal status with Swedish as an official language, but Russian was also being introduced as an official
language to an ever-increasing extent.

Initially, the Finnish Movement did not attempt to be a party or
build up a field organisation, chiefly because they considered they
represented the whole people and no particular interests. Only with
the Diet of 1877–1878 did the movement present an explicit programme, emerging during the following decade as a political party.
Snellman's and Yrjö-Koskinen's ideas started out from Hegel, and
were not based on relations between the individual and society but
on the preconditions necessary for a nation's existence. The key
point was not institutions or even the state, which could be sup-
pressed by the stronger side. The key was the nation: it might loose
its political existence but all was not lost as long as a national identity could be maintained.

In Yrjö-Koskinen's conception of history, the Swedish element
was alien: the Swedish-speaking upper class was either foreign or
made up of Finns forced to become Swedicized and who ought to
revert to their true nationality as soon as possible. The Swedish
population along the coast consisted of Swedish immigrants, who
would be allowed to keep their local language. Yrjö-Koskinen's goal
was not to change the structure of society, but the branch of "Fen-
nomania" he headed espoused conservative and patriarchal values.
Its objective was rather to conquer the bureaucracy and hence the
state machinery by means of a new upper class which, in language

and ways of thinking, would be at one with the people, and by means of education conducted in Finnish.[7]

The younger generation, however, thought quite differently on crucial points, although they too referred to Snellman and put forward a Finnish nationalist programme that was at least as radical. They no longer relied on Hegel, but were instead influenced by Anglo-Saxon social philosophy and liberalism and by social radicalism. They considered that it was possible to distinguish between nationality and language. Language demands were equated with demands for justice: the language question was one social reform among others, albeit the most urgent one. Yrjö-Koskinen and his adherents "turned against the ruling class because it was Swedish-speaking, while the younger generation turned against Swedish speakers because they represented the upper class".[8]

However, the final break between the groups, known as the Old and the Young Finns, was caused by Russian policy. The language question and Russian policy were the first crucial cleavages constituting parties, and the Finnish party system acquired its main traits before the First World War through the class-aligned Social Democratic Party (1899) and the Agrarian Union (1908).

Yrjö-Koskinen had entered into cooperation with the Governor General as early as the 1880s in order to force through the Finnish demands. He was well aware that this cooperation was hazardous since the aim of the Governor General and the Russian authorities was to force Swedish out in order to make way for Russian. As Russian pressure increased in the 1890s, Yrjö-Koskinen and the Old Finns shifted ground, orienting themselves to the political line which has been dubbed appeasement. In accordance with his basic philosophy, it meant that institutions might be sacrificed to the long-term goal of preserving the nation. The Old Finns' line was, then, that by conceding to Russian demands they would save as

[7] Tommila (ed.): *Herää Suomi*, p. 85.
[8] Klinge: *Runebergs två fosterland*, pp. 183–232.

much as possible and keep the administrative offices in the hands of Finns. As Russian pressure intensified, the Old Finns, following their aim of fortifying the nation, went in for a harsher Finnish policy with fierce conflict as a result.[9]

The Young Finns, on the other hand, moved in the direction of a line of action which emphasized the sanctity of the constitution, the law and institutions. Only by standing firmly by them could the resistance of the people be maintained. The Swedish party as a whole took this line, which was called passive resistance. The Young Finns and the Swedish Party then set up a constitutional front which, despite controversy on the language question, lasted until independence. The differences between the two Finnish parties were crystallized in discussions of a language law in 1907. The Old Finns accepted the presence of a Swedish-speaking settlement area but not the principle of a bilingual country. The Young Finns' stance, which contained many of the principles that were to be included in the 1922 language law, accepted bilingualism.

The Development and Expansion of Finnish

After a period of conflict concerning which dialects of Finnish were to be the basis of the written language, and a long period in which language use vacillated, the language evolved very rapidly. In the middle of the 19th century, however, the written language was still inadequate for the needs of a developed societal life because of gaps in the basic vocabulary, and variation in syntax and orthography. Language researchers consider 1870 to be the watershed between early modern and modern Finnish.[10]

Literature in Finnish was very modest for a long time. In the

---

[9] Rommi: *Yrjö-Koskisen linja. Myöntyvyyssuunnan hahmottuminen suomalaisen puolueen toimintalinjaksi.*

[10] Pulkkinen: "Suomen kielestä täysipainoinen sivistyskieli", pp. 307–326; Lind: *Mellem "venska" og "vinska".*

period 1809–1855 only 425 titles in Finnish were published, but in the 1870s there were already more Finnish than Swedish titles in Finland (because of book imports from Sweden, the figures are not entirely comparable). Finnish was used early on in official publications; the statute book began to be issued in a complete parallel edition in Finnish in 1860, the official yearbook in 1869, Diet documents in 1872.

The first Finnish language newspaper came out as early as 1776 for one year, but the second did not appear until 1820. Not until 1844 were Finnish language newspapers published regularly, but by 1878 there were more Finnish than Swedish ones. Development was equally swift in the school world. In 1841 Finnish was introduced as an extra school subject, and the first Finnish school was founded in Jyväskylä in 1858. As a result of the rapid development of school education, in the beginning through private schools, in 1889 for the first time more students from Finnish-speaking schools than from Swedish-speaking ones were enrolled at the university. The number of Swedish-speaking students subsequently increased slowly until the 1920s, while the number of Finnish-speaking schools tripled and the number of students rose fivefold in 1900–1940.

In 1906 the Finnish Union (Suomalaisuuden Liitto) was founded: it drew together Finnish enthusiasts from all parties, and its aim was to promote Finnishness and Finnish literature. In 1906, too, to commemorate the centenary of Snellman's birth, the Union organized a campaign that resulted in over 100,000 people Finnicizing their family names in one year.[11] Similar campaigns were organized later, although the activity of the Union decreased, only to be intensified again at the end of the 1980s.

[11] Jussila: "Suomalaisuusliike Venäjän paineessa vuosina 1890–1917", pp. 156–157.

The Period of Bilingualism

In spite of, or perhaps rather because of, the language conflict, Finland was characterized by very widespread bilingualism at the turn of the century. Swedish was still necessary for social advancement and was needed in many contexts, whereas from the 1870s onwards Finnish was becoming so with the expansion of Finnish culture and the school system, and with the effects of self-awareness of the majority of the population, who were being drawn into the economy and the society in a new way.

What is remarkable is that some of the élite made a point of becoming Finnish in language and political outlook. But at all events, individual language changes remained relatively rare; a Finnish-speaking élite emerged, more because of the next generation's schooling; but changing one's language created a Finnish-speaking élite more quickly than schooling alone would have done. Language divided families because some of the family chose Finnish. It also happened that some of the children were sent to a Finnish school and some to a Swedish school. Likewise, it happened that Swedish speakers sent their children to Finnish schools, and, up until the turn of the century often vice versa as well. In changing languages, of course, people still had their knowledge of the other language, and it was often just as difficult for contemporaries as for later researchers to assign people to simply one or the other language group.[12]

Bilingualism was not only a phenomenon among the élite, but was also common in towns. In the working-class districts of Helsinki where the language groups at the turn of the century were of approximately equal size, the classic Helsinki slang developed; it was a mixture, a kind of "working-class-district Esperanto".[13]

[12] Jutikkala: "Suomalaisuus yhteiskunnassa", pp. 253–278.

[13] Paunonen: "Från Sörkka till kulturspråk. Iakttagelser om Helsingforsslangen som språklig och kulturell företeelse", pp. 585–622.

The Finland Swedes

Finnish nationalism gave rise to Swedish nationalism; the Swedish national movement was a reaction to the Finnish-speaking one. Finland Swedes, both as a concept and as a quite clearly defined group, first emerged at the end of the 19th century. Previously the upper class, the residents of towns and the agrarian population had had very little to do with each other, and had not felt any sense of affinity on the basis of language. One sign of this, too, is that not until the beginning of the 20th century was the word "Finland Swede" coined and used. After a fairly long debate, above all among Swedish university students, it came to be used instead of other designations from the 1910s onwards. The debate had to do with discussion of the terms "Finn" and "Finlander", which resulted in Swedish speakers—with varying degrees of acceptance by Finnish speakers—introducing the term "Finlandish/Finlander" as a collective designation for people and circumstances in a national context and independent of language, whereas "Finn" and "Finland Swede" were used in contexts in which people wanted to assert their adherence to a particular language. The terminological question is complicated by the fact that "Finnish/Finn" has a historical tradition and is also used in many contexts in legal language (e.g. Finnish citizen).[14]

Evidence of the subordinate role previously played by language is that there are no systematic data in official statistics about the size of the language groups before 1880. All previous information is based on estimates and is rather unreliable. According to official statistics (somewhat corrected) the number of Swedish-speaking people was greatest in 1940, but during the period 1910–1950 it remained fairly constant (Table 1). In relative figures their percentage of the total population, however, has decreased continuously during the period covered by statistics from 14% to 6%.

[14] Mustelin: """Finlandssvensk"—kring ett begrepps historia", pp. 50–70.

Table 1. Number of Finland Swedes and Their Share of the Total Population in the Respective Counties 1880–1982 According to Official Statistics.

Year	All Finland	Cities	Other Residential Areas	Nyland County	Åbo-Bj.borg County	Åland	Vasa County	Other Counties
			Finland Swedes (x1,000)					
1880	294.9	65.7	229.2	101.9	38.3	20.2	117.8	16.7
1890	322.6	78.5	244.1	114.7	42.5	21.9	126.4	17.1
1900	349.7	97.3	252.5	134.1	43.2	24.1	131.1	17.3
1910	339.0	108.0	231.0	149.2	43.0	20.5	111.1	15.2
1920	341.0	114.0	226.9	157.8	41.2	20.4	109.3	12.2
1930	342.9	121.5	221.5	164.0	39.4	19.0	108.5	12.0
1940	354.0	139.0	215.0	176.9	36.9	20.3	109.1	10.9
1950	348.3	148.3	200.0	168.4	36.7	20.9	112.8	9.5
1960	330.5	148.9	181.7	163.0	33.3	20.3	106.2	7.7
1970	303.4	160.1	143.4	149.7	28.8	19.9	99.0	5.9
1980	300.5	181.9	118.6	145.0	28.0	21.7	99.6	6.0
1982	300.1	180.5	119.6	143.5	27.8	22.1	100.5	5.9
			Finland Swedes as % of Total Population in the Area					
1880	14.3	37.9	12.1	50.3	11.1	98.6	32.9	1.8
1890	13.6	33.4	11.4	47.9	11.4	98.9	30.3	1.7
1900	12.9	28.6	10.6	45.5	10.3	96.9	28.5	1.1
1910	11.6	25.3	9.3	41.0	9.4	96.2	25.3	0.93
1920	11.0	23.1	8.7	37.3	8.8	96.7	24.0	0.74
1930	10.1	19.3	8.0	33.3	7.9	96.7	22.5	0.63
1940	9.6	16.1	7.6	29.8	7.2	95.7	21.1	0.53
1950	8.6	11.4	7.3	25.2	5.8	96.2	18.6	0.45
1960	7.4	8.7	6.6	19.6	5.0	96.5	23.9	0.31
1970	6.6	6.8	6.3	14.9	4.3	96.3	23.5	0.24
1980	6.3	6.3	6.2	12.8	4.0	95.2	23.0	0.26
1982	6.2	6.2	6.2	12.5	3.9	94.9	22.9	0.26

There is reason to emphasize that language legislation and census criteria are based on the fact that the individual can and must state which language group he belongs to. Thus, it is not possible to register oneself as bilingual. Formerly the question in the census asked for "main language"; when this was changed in 1950 to "mother tongue", the number of Swedish speakers increased by approximately 6,000, according to one estimate. However, what is more important is that this method of counting Swedish speakers is a minimum method distinguished from cantonal or regional systems in which everyone living in a particular area is classed as belonging to the language group in question (as e.g. in Switzerland) or calculations based on origin. Many European minorities would more or less disappear if they were calculated according to the same principles: of the Basque population, for instance, only 15% know Basque.[15]

The drop in the Swedish-speaking percentage and, from the 1940s, in absolute numbers too, may chiefly be attributed to lower fertility, changing languages ("Finnization") and high emigration. All these factors have a connection with Swedish-speaking settlement areas and relative positions. Fertility has apparently long been lower in the coastal areas and in the towns than farther inland.[16]

Investigations have shown that language shifts were surprisingly common but that the net results were relatively small. On the other hand, the effect of "mixed marriages", i.e. those across language boundaries, was to reduce the natural growth among Finland Swedes by a good 3%. The proportion of linguistically mixed marriages—at least since the 1930s—has been on the increase; according to a survey of marriages contracted between 1941 and 1950, 21% of

[15] Allardt & Starck: *Språkgränser och samhällsstruktur. Finlandssvenskarna i ett jämförande perspektiv*, pp. 58–61.

[16] Cf. Fougstedt: "Finlandssvenskarna under 100 år", in Engman & Stenius (eds.): *Svenskt i Finland 2. Demografiska och socialhistoriska studier*, pp. 19–35 and other essays in the volume. Finnäs: *Den finlandssvenska befolkningsutvecklingen 1950–1980*. For the most recent data, see *Finlandssvenskarna 1990. En statistisk översikt*.

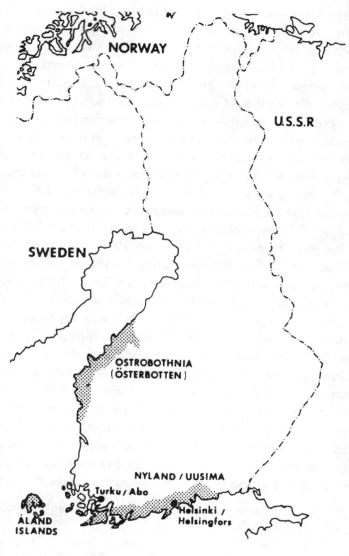

NORWAY

U.S.S.R

SWEDEN

OSTROBOTHNIA
(ÖSTERBOTTEN)

NYLAND / UUSIMA

Turku / Abo

ÅLAND
ISLANDS

Helsinki /
Helsingfors

FINLAND   Swedish speaking areas

Swedish men and 14% of women had married Finnish partners. Today half of Swedish men in towns marry Finnish women, and in Helsinki the proportion is higher. Previously, among children of mixed marriages, approximately 40% became Swedish-speaking. In recent years the proportion has risen to over half, which underlines the increasing importance of bilinguals for the position of Swedish in Finland.[17]

Swedish speakers have been over-represented in some of the great waves of emigration. The Swedish-speaking group made up a fifth of emigrants to America (about 80,000 people). It has been calculated that between a fourth and a fifth of immigrants to Sweden from Finland in the 1970s were Finland Swedes (60–70,000 people). The higher inclination to emigrate among Finland Swedes is not only due to language factors, but rather to the Swedish speakers having lived in areas where foreign contacts, naturally also made easier by a knowledge of Swedish, were livelier and the inclination to emigrate was generally higher.

The Swedish-speaking population resides principally in three counties and on Åland. Of these the importance of Nyland in particular has grown on account of migration. In 1880 a good third of the Swedish speakers lived in Nyland (35%) but by 1960 the proportion had risen to almost half (49%). Although the Swedish speakers only constituted in round figures a tenth of the country's population, they made up about a quarter of the population in regions where they were mainly resident. Thus, in 1880, 86% of Swedish speakers lived in municipalities with a Swedish-speaking majority (Table 2). On account of the Swedish-speaking population living largely in regions (particularly on the south coast, the districts round Helsinki and Åbo/Turku) where economic development and population growth have been rapid and immigration high, this proportion has fallen steeply, especially in Nyland county. In the coun-

---

[17] The percentage was 57% in 1991, *Hufvudstadsbladet* 19 Nov. and 28 Dec. 1992.

Max Engman

Table 2. The Share of Finland Swedes in Settlements with Swedish Majority, 1880–1980

Year	Nyland County	Åbo-Bj. County	Åland	Vasa County	Other Counties	Whole of Finland
1880	94.8	55.1	100.0	96.5	9.4	85.9
1910	62.2	59.1	100.0	98.6	-	73.0
1930	50.9	62.7	100.0	87.8	-	64.9
1950	43.6	63.0	100.0	83.9	-	60.8
1960	44.1	62.6	100.0	83.0	-	60.8
1970	34.9	61.8	100.0	75.1	-	54.2
1980	21.8	59.3	100.0	76.5	-	48.6

Note: Åland has been reported separately also during the years when the territory was part of Åbo-Björneborg county.

ties of Åbo and Björneborg, where a large number of the Swedish-speaking population live in the archipelago, and in Vasa county, the changes have not been as dramatic.

Since the towns in Finland were situated mainly on the coast, the Swedish element in the urban population was traditionally important, 38% in 1880, for example. Due to migration, there has been a considerable levelling out, and today the proportion of Swedish speakers in urban areas is as large as in the rural population (in 1980, 6.3% and 6.2%, respectively).

Structural changes (urbanization, migration, industrialization) have thus exercised a profound influence on the Swedish population areas and hence on living conditions for the Finland Swedes. The end result is that the Swedish areas, regions with a clear Swedish majority, have shrunk considerably, especially in southern Finland, and that half of the Swedes occupy a minority position in their home municipality, often as a relatively small and dispersed minority. In Ostrobothnia, about three-quarters still live in municipalities with a

Swedish majority, which paves the way for regional tensions among the Swedish-speaking population in decisions concerning matters such as regional location policy.[18]

The small Swedish-speaking upper class played a dominant role during the early decades of the Grand Duchy, and Swedish speakers had an important role in the administration and commercial life for a long time afterwards, but this has tended to over-emphasize the social differences between the language groups as a whole. After some of the upper class had become Finnish and the Finnish-speaking school system had been built up at the end of the 19th century, the language groups have had more or less the same social structure. The most crucial difference has been rather that the Swedish speakers have a larger lower middle-class element and, to a corresponding degree, a smaller working-class element.

The ordinary people in the towns, craftsmen, small shopkeepers, and others, were mainly Swedish-speaking before large scale urbanization, since a large proportion of the urban population were Swedish-speaking. When the major migration to the towns began, the fact that Swedish speakers were "first on the spot" as it were—along with the status, advantages, and identification patterns attaching to the language—started to have some importance. There was a Swedish-speaking working class in the towns, some having also arrived fairly recently, but it was usual that Swedish speakers occupied higher positions as foremen, craftsmen, skilled workers, clerks, and so on, rather than the equivalent Finnish group. The number of Swedish-speaking workers has been reduced more through "Finnization" than have other social groups among the Swedish speakers, both because a knowledge of Swedish did not have the same importance in the working class and because the Swedish network of voluntary associations,

---

[18] Johansson: "Varieties of Conflict Development: Ethnic Relations and Societal Change in Belgium, Finland and Switzerland". Johansson brings out the regional aspect, but in a way overlooks other dimensions.

for both social and political reasons, has not been able to reach this group.[19]

From Liberalism to Swedishness

At the end of the 1850s, in the Nyland student corporation at the university, a group came into existence round the future Professor of Swedish Language A. O. Freudenthal, who asserted that Swedish speakers constituted a separate people, even though politically they formed one nation with the Finns. The decline of Swedish nationality and its integration with Finnish nationality was not desirable, but should be opposed, in order also to maintain Finland's contacts with the other Nordic countries.

Up until the 1880s, however, the majority of the Swedish-speaking educated class formed a liberal group. The liberals looked on language as a question to be decided *ad hoc*, and put the main emphasis on a liberalization of society and an underpinning of Finland's constitutional position in the empire. Attempts to form a genuine Liberal Party failed in 1881, and the majority of liberals joined forces with the Swedish Nationalists, creating the Swedish Party which took distinctive shape in the 1890s.

The two groups forming the Swedish Party—the Constitutionalists and the Swedish Nationalists—can be discerned later on in two approaches which have been labelled the Swedish cultural policy *(kultursvenskhet)* and the Swedish regional policy *(bygdesvenskhet)*. The former stressed Swedish as the bearer of a Western cultural and legal heritage and consequently as a second national language in the administration and culture. The Swedish regionalists again tended to emphasize the Swedish settlement areas and their culture, i.e. a policy of emphasizing the borderline against the Finns. These two approaches have existed like intertwined threads in Swedish non-socialist politics in Finland. After the introduction of universal and

[19] Allardt & Starck, op.cit., passim.

equal suffrage in 1907, the Swedish Party was reconstructed as the Swedish Peoples Party, which became a broad language party. The so-called "Swedish coalition movement" meant an "aggregation of interests" between the different Swedish population groups, which can be described as successful.[20] Since 1907 the party has gained about 70% of the Swedish votes. One consequence of the broad spectrum of the party was that it had several factions, only two of which, however, formed breakaway parties. In the interwar years, as a result of the constitutional conflict in which a majority of the party advocated a monarchy, a Swedish non-socialist left-wing group was started and at the beginning of the 1970s, a right-wing group broke away. Neither of them has had more than two Swedish members of parliament.[21]

The Swedish Peoples Party thus dominated Swedish politics in Finland, and its principal rivals were the bilingual parties, mainly the Social Democratic Party. There were plans to set up a Swedish Labour Party at the beginning of the century, but they were shelved when the Social Democratic Party officially declared in 1906 that it was trilingual (Finnish, Swedish, Russian). Inside the party the Finland Swedish Workers' Union has formed a party district.[22]

Development around the turn of the century entailed a drastic reduction of the political influence of the Swedish speakers. While the Swedish Party dominated two estates (the nobility and the bourgeoisie) out of four, the Swedish Peoples Party was reduced in 1907 to a medium-sized party with 24 representatives out of 200. The Russification measures again struck a blow at Swedish speakers'

---

[20] The term was coined by Axel Lille: *Den svenska nationalitetens i Finland samlingsrörelse;* Allardt & Starck, op.cit., pp. 200–224.

[21] Lidman: *Män och idéer,* pp.127–159; *Svenska folkpartiet I–III* (Helsingfors 1956–1992); Sundberg: *Svenskhetens dilemma i Finland.*

[22] Hentilä: "Arbetarrörelsen och finlandssvenskarna i storstrejkens Finland", pp. 147–165; Bondestam & Helsing: *Som en stubbe i en stubbåker. Finlands Svenska Arbetarförbund 1899–1974.*

positions in the administration, since they were usually constitutionalists and were thus forced to resign.

As a result of the changed situation and under the influence of
the Germanistic currents of the time, there was a wave of Swedish
nationalism, especially among students, in the 1910s. This line emphasized cultural and in some cases racial differences from the Finnish majority, an attitude of superiority which was insulting to the
Finns, but quite apart from this it meant an attempt to create separate organizations as far as possible. A division of different associations according to language had been going on since the mid-19th
century and was now taken much further.[23]

Autonomy or Equality?

In many respects, Finland's independence ought to have meant a fa-
vorable starting position for Finland Swedes. The majority of them
had supported resistance to Russia, and Swedish speakers were over-
represented on the winning White side in the Civil War of 1918.[24]
Following the impact of the political changes arose the idea of creating guarantees for the social order and for Swedishness. The former
were sought mainly in the form of a monarchic constitution, while
language guarantees were sought in two mutually conflicting ways.
One group emphasized equality between the languages in accordance
with the practice that had developed through the language legislation
in the 19th century. Another group looked for protection of the minority in regional autonomy, following the provincial Swedish line
and the radicalized Swedish movement of the 1910s.

The plans for self-government aimed at comprehensive regional
self-government, either for the Swedish-speaking provinces separately or for a union of provinces, Swedish-Finland, under one gov-

---

[23] Klinge: *Från lojalism till rysshat*, pp. 220–234.

[24] Hamalainen: *In Time of Storm. Revolution, Civil War, and the Ethnolinguistic Issue in Finland.*

ernor *(ståthållare).* Further demands included cultural autonomy within the church and in education, and a Swedish military unit. In order to lend force to and provide a broader base for the Swedish demands, an assembly of representatives, appointed by general election, was convened, the "*Svenska Finlands folkting*" in 1919. Its representativeness was rather diminished, however, because the Ålanders and the Social Democrats did not take part in the election. Since Swedish opinion was divided, and Finnish opinion consistently rejected the plans for regional self-government, the regional demands could not be realized. On the other hand, limited cultural autonomy was created through the establishment of a Swedish diocese, which included all the Swedish congregations in the whole country, and a Swedish department at the Board of Education.[25]

The idea of regional self-government was thus defeated, while the demands for equality were realized in the constitution of 1919 which decreed that Finnish and Swedish were the national languages of the Republic and that the authorities were to satisfy the cultural and economic needs of both language groups on the "same basis". The language law of 1922 regulated the rights of citizens to use their mother tongue in their contacts with the authorities, the demands on civil servants' knowledge of languages, as well as the criteria for considering municipalities monolingual or bilingual. The limit for identifying a municipality as bilingual was originally set at 10%, but after revisions the rule today is that a municipality is bilingual if the minority (Swedish, Finnish or Sami) amounts to 8% or at least 3,000 people.[26]

One important factor in the struggles concerning self-government, the constitution, and language legislation was that the nationality conflict on the mainland was never made international. There were opinions among the Swedish-speaking population that they should turn to the

[25] von Bonsdorff: *Självstyrelsetanken i finlandssvensk politik åren 1917–23;* Klemets: *Samling genom separation. Den svenska kyrkliga samlingsrörelsens i Finland uppkomst, utformning och verkningar åren 1917–1918.*

[26] Modeen: *Finlandssvenskarnas nationella grundlagsskydd I;* Törnudd: *Svenska språkets ställning i Finland.*

Paris Peace Conference or appeal officially to Sweden, but the struggle was carried on inside Finland. A measure of the position of Swedish speakers was that they were not interested in the treaties on protection of minorities drawn up at the Peace Conference and within the framework of the League of Nations, since they were considered inadequate and inappropriate to Finnish conditions.

Åland

One background factor in the discussion of language laws and self-government was the Åland question. In relation to Sweden, the League of Nations and international opinion, it was important for Finland to show that the country was not oppressing the Swedish-speaking population there.

The Åland Islands had belonged to the Åbo diocese since the Middle Ages, and administratively to the county of Åbo and Björneborg. The population of the islands, which numbered more than 19,000 in 1918, was Swedish-speaking, apart from small groups of immigrant Finnish workers. In 1809, Sweden was interested in keeping the islands for strategic reasons, or having them demilitarized, but was forced to give them up together with the rest of Åbo and Björneborg county by the Peace of Fredrikshamn. After the Crimean War, the islands were demilitarized on Sweden's initiative by the Treaty of Paris in 1856.[27]

At the outbreak of the First World War, Russia infringed the convention of Åland by fortifying the islands and placing a garrison there. In the final phase of the war, Åland was the scene of both the dissolution of the Russian garrison, battles between White and Red Finns, and Swedish and German landings. At the end of 1917, the so-called Åland Movement was formed; over 7,000 signatures (more than 95% of the adult population) were collected for a petition re-

[27] Söderhjelm: *Démilitarisation et neutralisation des Iles d'Aland en 1856 et 1921.*

questing association with Sweden. The spokesmen of the movement maintained that it embodied an ancient wish for "reunion with the motherland", but the main reasons lay in a fear of Russian anarchy and the strong Finnish nationalist and socialist movements on the mainland, as well as uncertainty about the future of an independent Finland. Similar feelings were present among the Swedish-speaking population on the mainland, but the Ålanders saw a feasible alternative. Many Ålanders looked upon themselves initially as parts of the Swedish population and culture in Finland and only emphasized a separate identity for Åland while the struggle was in progress. The attempts of the Ålanders to liberate themselves reveal features similar to those of Vorarlberg to associate itself with Switzerland at the same time.[28] Although, in its background, the Åland Movement was part of the nationality conflict in Finland, it became an international question because of the Ålanders' goal of union with Sweden.[29]

The Swedish Government, and in particular the King , were eager to support the Ålanders, and during the Civil War in Finland sent an expeditionary force to Åland in February 1918; its objective was said to be to maintain law and order but the intention was to create a *fait accompli* and safeguard Sweden's strategic interests.

The Ålanders and Sweden, referring to the right of self-determination, tried to have the question taken up in international arenas and demanded a plebiscite. Finland originally intended to treat the islands as an integral part of its territory, and disputed the fact that the 1856 convention concluded by Russia was binding on Finland. The government categorically opposed a referendum on the grounds that sovereignty over the islands could not be questioned and that it was thus an internal matter for Finland. Finnish opinion was quite unanimous on this point, although within the Social Democratic

[28] Bondestam: *Åland vintern 1918*; Rystad: "'Återförening med moderlandet'. Ålandsrörelsens uppkomst"; Gullberg: "Åland och Vorarlberg. Nationell självbestämmanderätt efter första världskriget".

[29] Cf. Barros: *The Åland Island Question. Its Settlement by the League of Nations* and Modeen: "The Åland Islands Question", pp. 153–168.

Party and among the left-wing Socialists there were different opinions, especially as Finland was demanding national self-government or a plebiscite for eastern Karelia and Ingria. For the Finland Swedes, the question was awkward since, on the one hand, they wanted to safeguard the integrity of state territory, while on the other hand they were working for self-government. Initially, most Finland Swedish politicians tended to see the Ålanders as part of the Swedish population in Finland. A number of Finland Swedes were prepared to use the Ålanders as a lever to prepare the way for self-government on the mainland.[30]

The Paris Peace Conference referred the Åland question to the League of Nations. Following a proposal of a commission of inquiry, the League of Nations stated in 1921 that the islands should go to Finland and recommended that Finland and Sweden between them should come to an agreement about further guarantees for Swedish nationality and neutral status for the islands.

By this time, the Finnish Government, under pressure from abroad, had already granted Åland autonomy by a law of 1920. In consequence of the Sweden-Finland accord of 1921, the new guarantees were incorporated into a law on self-government in 1922. The neutralization of the islands was carried out through the 1921 Geneva convention concerning the non-fortification of Åland and its neutralization; it was signed by all the Baltic states except Soviet Russia. By a treaty between Finland and the Soviet Union after the Winter War (1940) and again in 1948, Finland undertook to demilitarize the Åland islands, which had been fortified during the Second World War.[31]

[30] Rystad: "'Särställning under Finland.' Finlandssvenskarna och Ålandsfrågan"; Hyytiä: *Puolueettomuuden ja rauhan linja*, pp. 198–205, 215–217, 222.

[31] Cf. Modeen: *De folkrättsliga garantierna för bevarandet av Ålandsöarnas nationella karaktär* and "Völkerrechtliche Probleme der Åland-Inseln"; Söderhjelm, op.cit., passim; Björkholm & Rosas: *Ålandsöarnas demilitarisering och neutralisering*.

The Åland question led to sharp polemical exchanges in public, in which the country's leading historians, among others, involved themselves in order to prove their country's right to the islands. The question weighed heavily on the relations between countries and the relations between Åland and the Republic for a long time afterwards. In Finland the Swedish intervention in Åland was regarded as a stab in the back in a critical situation. The final decision satisfied none of the parties involved. Sweden was disappointed and showed no interest in Åland until it was decided that Finland and Sweden would jointly fortify the islands before the Second World War (the Stockholm plan). The plan was dropped because of resistance from the Soviet Union. Finland had granted autonomy in response to external pressure. It was duly observed, but unenthusiastically. No government in the interwar years submitted any proposals affecting Åland's self-government. The Ålanders themselves were discontented at not having achieved their maximum goals and were inclined to disparage their autonomy. One sign that self-government worked satisfactorily, however, was that none of the parties made any complaint to the League of Nations.

The self-government laws gave Åland quite generous self-governing powers. The law of 1920 gave the self-governing parliament, the *Landsting,* wide powers concerning planning, fire prevention, public order and security, social security, schools, agriculture, fishing, etc. Taken together with the extensive local self-government in Finland, this gave the Ålanders command over most local questions. The self-government laws of 1922 extended their autonomy on certain important points. Swedish was the only language permitted in schools. By means of special measures, it was ensured that the land would remain in the hands of Ålanders. The new self-government law of 1951 introduced Åland domiciliary rights, i.e. in practice a separate Åland "citizenship", which presupposes Finnish citizenship and which immigrants can acquire by a "naturalisation" process that requires five years' residence (and, beginning in 1993, a knowledge of Swedish).

Max Engman

The government is represented in Åland by a Governor. Since 1948, Åland is a constituency sending one member to the Finnish Parliament. Demilitarisation means that there are no Finnish military installations on the islands, and that Ålanders are exempt from military service.

Åland's self-government has expanded considerably due to extensive revisions of the postwar self-government laws and a reform which comes into force in 1993. In both cases powers have been transferred to the province. The revisions have not given rise to any conflicts, although in connection with the most recent amendments there was disagreement about the size of the government grant to be allocated to the province. Åland received far-reaching rights regarding its own budget within the framework of 0.45% of the State's revenue, and at present it is investigating the possibility of introducing its own taxation. Finland's EEA agreement contains special clauses concerning Åland, and the province has demanded that demilitarization, self-government and monolingualism should be guaranteed if Finland becomes a member of the EC. The criticism heard on occasion about Åland's special position in Finland has often been levelled at the status of the Finnish language. On the whole, however, criticism of Åland has consisted of populist outbursts from the political fringe.

Åland's self-government has been extended on the symbolic level by an increased use of the Åland flag and having postage stamps of its own. Åland's participation in Nordic and international contexts has also worked in the same direction. Within the framework of self-government, Åland's identity and self-esteem have been strengthened, and in this process, its standing as an autonomous and demilitarized area now plays an important role, especially as Åland is often held up as an example of international conflict-solving and protection of minority interests. Its special position in Finland has guaranteed Åland development on its own terms, whereas annexation by Sweden would probably have led to the province becoming a peripheral part of the Stockholm region.

If one can say that the involuntary break with Sweden and the administrative autonomy after 1809 resulted in the creation of Finland, then one might claim that enforced autonomy from 1920/1922 created Åland. It is striking, for example, that the call for reunion with Sweden has died away, while there is a small but vociferous group claiming independence.

The Language Struggle during the Interwar Years

The Swedish-speaking nationalism of the 1910s and after independence gave rise to a reaction from the Finns. The endeavours of Swedish speakers to build up organizational structures and self-governing regions of their own were looked upon as attempts at isolation, while Germanistic attitudes antagonized the Finns. The increase in Finnish nationalistic feelings however, was not primarily due to what Finland-Swedish politicians did, but was largely the result of attempts to strengthen the identity of the young republic. National pride, insecurity and hypersensitivity to what was conceived as Swedish (Swedish or Finland-Swedish) superiority contributed to the demands that Finnish should be made the principal language of the country and the majority be given rightful control in their own country. The aim was to create a strong national state, and the Finland Swedes appeared to be an alien element and a security risk. From this seedbed grew the so-called "true Finns", a movement that got its name from a True Finn Club founded in Helsinki in 1923.

The goals of the True Finns were to abolish the official bilingualism of the country and reduce Swedish to a regional minority language. They at least wanted to cut down on higher education and the cultural grants given by the state to a level that corresponded to the percentage of the population that were Swedish-speaking. The language conflict of the interwar years centered to a great extent on the language situation at the University of Helsinki. The True Finns did not want to accept the fact that the state supported university teaching in Swedish at all, and particularly not at the country's only state university.[32]

The True Finns won support mainly among university students. Of the political parties, the Agrarian Party was the first to put the question on its political programme, and later the extreme right-wing party IKL (Fatherland Popular Movement), which obliged the other non-socialist parties to support "true Finnishness" to some extent. The Social Democrats, however, stuck to bilingualism and considered the language question to be "a sixth-rate issue", as the party leader Väinö Tanner expressed it. This meant that the two outsiders in the political arena, the conservative Swedish People's Party and the Social Democrats, gradually found themselves tactically collaborating to prevent extensive changes in language legislation.

The language conflict aroused a storm of excitement among the public in the interwar years, but its peaceful character must be stressed: it did not cause any major violence except for street fights in Helsinki on two occasions at the beginning of the thirties. The focus of the language conflict on educational issues resulted among other things in the founding of a Swedish and a Finnish private university in Åbo/Turku after 1917. The failure of organized boycotts of firms that were considered Swedish is also a sign that the battle was far from being a head-on collision between two clearly distinct ethnic groups.

On the Swedish-speaking side, there was an appeal to opinion in Sweden, for example on the university question, and sympathy was indeed expressed, but the language struggle was not taken up on the international level in such a way as to make Sweden a party to the issue. In this respect the situation was different from that in countries with German and Magyar minorities. International considerations, on the other hand, helped to soothe the language conflict in

---

[32] Hämäläinen: *Nationalitetskampen och språkstriden i Finland 1917–1939* is based on his unpublished dissertation, *The nationality struggle between the Finns and the Swedish-speaking minority in Finland, 1917–1939*; Uino: "Kielitaistelu ja 'uusi suomalaisuusliike' 1918–1939", pp. 177–249.

Finland at the end of the 1930s. In view of the international situation, the government adopted a Nordic orientation in foreign policy, wanting to settle a divisive controversy and do away with a source of irritation in relations with Sweden.

The war and wartime unity contributed a great deal to eliminating the language question as a political issue; the "True Finn" organisations had adopted positions so far to the right that they were either discredited or prohibited. The discussion about colonizing the evacuated Karelians in Swedish-speaking districts was a last burst of the interwar language debate. After the war, the Finns saw themselves as a nation that spoke two languages.

The Language Climate Today

Today's opinion among the Swedish-speaking population reveals tendencies which in some respects can be seen as a continuation of the differences in emphasis between the cultural and provincial Swedish factions, but there is also regional contention, especially between Helsinki and Ostrobothnia. In day-to-day politics the "cultural Swedish attitude" stresses the need for contributions at the centre, for Swedish speakers being represented in the centres of power and cultural life, for the equality of the two languages, and for bilingualism. This line has also strongly emphasized the role of Swedish today as a window on Europe and the Nordic countries.

The Swedish provincialists have emphasized that Swedish stands and falls by thriving, more or less unilingual Swedish districts; they have drawn their strength primarily from the regions—the fringes— and their culture. Provincial Swedish policy has thus implicitly and sometimes explicitly advocated a distancing from the attempt to maintain positions in the centre and contributions at the national level in favour of consolidating the regions and finding "autonomistic" solutions. It might be said that it is a matter of affirming the minority position in word and deed, with the aim of safeguarding a majority position in the Swedish-speaking regions.

It is obvious that this dichotomy is embedded in the different historical components of the Swedish-speaking population, but interestingly it does not coincide with a division into political left and right. Instead, the two dichotomies rather form a field in which there are "provincial Swedish" People's Democrats, Social Democrats oriented towards national politics, non-socialist regional politicians and bilingual right-wing Helsinki politicians, as well as a number of other combinations. Recently there has also been a debate concerning earlier concepts that were taken for granted, such as "Finland Swede" and "Swedish Finland".

Today's situation shows certain contradictory tendencies. Finnish plays a totally dominant role today in society. It is more and more difficult to get services in Swedish, and Finnish dominates public life. Because of the relatively small size of the group, it is also more difficult to create or maintain Finland-Swedish popular culture in highly internationalized or commercial sectors. Similarly, it seems that the economic crisis in the 1990s is likely to strike a severe blow at the small administrative and educational Swedish units.

In some respects, the position of Swedish has improved in the country as a whole. When the comprehensive school was introduced in 1967, Swedish became a compulsory language. The vast majority of children choose English as their first modern language after their mother tongue, but the change means that all Finns attending compulsory school will study at least some Swedish. Several opinion polls have also revealed an awareness of the importance of knowing Swedish. A Canadian study in 1983 showed that 55% of the Finnish-speaking population considered it "very important" or "quite important" for Finland to retain bilingualism, while 76% viewed a knowledge of Swedish as "quite important" or "very important". Similarly, surveys have shown that Swedish is the language (after Finnish) that is needed most in business and commerce.[33]

Studies in self-assessed knowledge of languages reveal an increase

---

[33] Herberts: *Detta svenskatalande bättre folk*, pp. 3–7.

in people's knowledge of Swedish. In a survey in 1988 of the Finnish-speaking adult population in the whole country except Åland, 42% reported that they considered they could speak at least passable Swedish. No corresponding survey had been made since the 1950 census when the equivalent figure was 8%. The figures are not quite comparable, but indicate a clear increase at any rate.[34]

Language debates and discussions of the relative positions of the languages are natural in a bilingual society where setting boundary lines is a constantly ongoing process, both in everyday intercourse and in administrative practice, university entrance, programmes in the media, etc. At the end of the 1980s, several language debates were conducted in the major newspapers both in editorials and in "Letters to the Editor". Most of them were spontaneous, while some were the direct consequence of a radical group taking over leadership of the Finnish Union and initiating a deliberate campaign against the "privileges" of Finland Swedes. Their goal was to cut down Finland Swedes' representation, funds etc. until they corresponded to the percentage share. The Union argued among other things that Sweden takes no account of Finnish immigrants' linguistic and educational needs.

A summary of the contributions shows that the Finnish newspapers in the capital treated language questions in a fairly balanced way. The editorial material (editorials, features, articles by regular staff) reveals a clear tendency to defend the position of Swedish and to repel attacks on the Swedish language and Finland Swedes' rights, whereas denunciations occur mainly in Letters to the Editor, often anonymously.

It would seem that the most important watershed in opinion is the Finnish Movement's old, cardinal question whether Finland should be monolingual or bilingual, and its attitude to the surrounding world in general. Those who attacked Swedish described Finland Swedes in very traditional terms as an alien upper class, a leftover from the days of Sweden as a great power. In their opinion, Finland ought

[34] Sandlund: *Svenska i Finland.*

to be monolingual and get rid of Swedish which is a burden, representing the influence of a foreign power. In overseas contacts, including those with the other Nordic countries, English should be used. Those who defended Swedish asserted that Finland, in keeping with tradition and its constitution, is bilingual, and that the Swedish language and the Finland Swedish population are natural elements of Finnish society and life.

The debate showed that it is hardly possible to talk of a massive, aggressive attitude among the majority; on the other hand, there are concrete questions which annoy Finns: the share of Swedish programmes on television, recruitment to institutions of higher learning, and above all, the position of Swedish as a compulsory language at school. There was lively public debate on the subject when the cultural committee of the Finnish parliament proposed in 1990 that the comprehensive school should only have one compulsory language. The discussion revealed some resistance to Swedish and opinions for making the choice of languages voluntary, but also strong support for compulsory instruction in Swedish. Parliament decided the question by a clear majority (159—28) according to former customary practice, i.e. that the second native language would be compulsory as a first or second language in the comprehensive school— but the discussion is still going on.[35]

Considering the degree of integration of both language groups in society and the low level of conflict, "the Finnish model" has been rather successful. In spite of the ongoing debates, it has allowed the minority to maintain its language and institutions and channelled tensions into competition in the cultural and educational arena. As such it may serve as an example of peaceful coexistence, even if it has to be admitted that in many respects the historical circumstances were favourable.

[35] Herberts & Landgärds: *Tvång eller privilegium? Debatten om obligatorisk svenskundervisning i den finska grundskolan; Helsingin Sanomat* 15 Dec. 1992; *Hufvudstadsbladet* 16 and 18 Dec. 1992.

LITERATURE

Alapuro, Risto: *State and Revolution in Finland*, Berkeley, Cal. 1988

Allardt, Erik & Starck, Christian: *Språkgränser och samhällsstruktur. Finlandssvenskarna i ett jämförande perspektiv*, Stockholm 1981

Barros, James: *The Åland Island Question. Its Settlement by the League of Nations*, New Haven 1968

Björkholm, Michaela & Rosas, Allan: *Ålandsöarnas demilitarisering och neutralisering*, Meddelanden från Ålands kulturstiftelse 3, Mariehamn 1989

Bondestam, Anna: *Åland vintern 1918*, Skrifter utgivna av Ålands kulturstiftelse VI, Mariehamn 1972

Bondestam, Anna & Helsing, Alf-Erik: *Som en stubbe i en stubbåker. Finlands Svenska Arbetarförbund 1899–1974*, Helsingfors 1978

Bonsdorff, Göran, von: *Självstyrelsetanken i finlandssvensk politik åren 1917–23*, Bidrag till kännedom av Finlands natur och folk 94, Helsingfors 1950

Christiansen, Eric: *The Northern Crusades: the Baltic and the Catholic Frontier 1100–1525*, London 1980

Finlandssvenskarna 1990. En statistisk översikt, Finlandssvensk rapport 20, Helsingfors 1992

Finnäs, Fjalar: *Den finlandssvenska befolkningsutvecklingen 1950–1980. En analys av en folkgrupps demografiska utveckling och effekten av blandäktenskap*, Skrifter utgivna av Svenska litteratursällskapet i Finland 533, Helsingfors 1986

Fougstedt, Gunnar: "Finlandssvenskarna under 100 år", in Engman, Max & Stenius, Henrik (ed.): *Svenskt i Finland 2. Demografiska och socialhistoriska studier*, Skrifter utgivna av Svenska litteratursällskapet i Finland 519, Helsingfors 1984

Gullberg, Tom: "Åland och Vorarlberg. Nationell självbestämmanderätt efter första världskriget", *Historisk Tidskrift för Finland* 1991

Hamalainen, Pekka Kalevi: *In Time of Storm. Revolution, Civil War, and the Ethnolinguistic Issue in Finland*, Albany, N.Y. 1979

Hämäläinen, Pekka Kalevi: *Nationalitetskampen och språkstriden i Finland 1917–1939*, Helsingfors 1969

Helsingin Sanomat (newspaper) 15 Dec 1992

Hentilä, Seppo: "Arbetarrörelsen och finlandssvenskarna i storstrejkens

Finland", in Engman, Max & Stenius, Henrik (eds.): *Svenskt i Finland 1. Studier i språk och nationalitet efter 1860*, Skrifter utgivna av Svenska litteratursällskapet i Finland 511, Helsingfors 1983

Herberts, Kjell: *Detta svenskatalande bättre folk … En dokumenterande innehållsanalys av språkdebatter i finsk huvudstadspress under åren 1984– 1988*, Institutet för finlandssvensk samhällsforskning, forskningsrapporter 7, Vasa 1988

Herberts, Kjell & Landgärds, Ann-Sofi: *Tvång eller privilegium? Debatten om obligatorisk svenskundervisning i den finska grundskolan*, Institutet för finlandssvensk samhällsforskning, forskningsrapporter 17, Vasa 1992

Hufvudstadsbladet (newspaper) 19 Nov, 16, 18 and 28 Dec 1992.

Hyytiä, Osmo: *Puolueettomuuden ja rauhan linja. SDP:n suhtautuminen Suomen ulkopolitiikkaan ja turvallisuuskysymyksiin. Toukokuu 1918– toukokuu 1922*, Historiallisia tutkimuksia 137, Helsinki 1986

Johansson, Rune: "Varieties of Conflict Development: Ethnic Relations and Societal Change in Belgium, Finland and Switzerland", in Tägil, Sven (ed.): *Regions in Upheaval. Ethnic Conflict and Political Mobilization*, Lund Studies in International History 22, Lund 1984

Jussila, Osmo: *Maakunnasta valtioksi. Suomen valtion synty*, Helsinki 1987

Jussila, Osmo: "Suomalaisuusliike Venäjän paineessa vuosina 1890–1917", in Tommila, Päivö (ed.): *Herää Suomi*

Jutikkala, Eino: "Suomalaisuus yhteiskunnassa", in Tommila, Päiviö (ed.): *Herää Suomi*

Klemets, Bengt: *Samling genom separation. Den svenska kyrkliga samlingsrörelsens i Finland uppkomst, utformning och verkningar åren 1917–1918*, Meddelanden från stiftelsens för Åbo Akademi forskningsinstitut 113, Åbo 1986

Klinge, Matti: *Från lojalism till rysshat*, Helsingfors 1988

Klinge, Matti: *Let Us Be Finns—Essays on History*, Helsinki 1990

Klinge, Matti: *Runebergs två fosterland*, Helsingfors 1983

Klövekorn, Martin: *Die sprachliche Struktur Finnlands 1880–1950. Veränderungen im sprachlichen Charakter der finnlandschwedischen Gebiete und deren bevölkerungs- wirtschafts- und sozialgeographische Ursachen*, Bidrag till kännedom av Finlands natur och folk 105, Helsingfors 1960

Lidman, Sven: *Män och idéer. Historiska uppsatser*, Meddelanden från Stiftelsens för Åbo Akademi forskningsinstitut 61, Åbo 1981

Lille, Axel: *Den svenska nationalitetens i Finland samlingsrörelse*, Helsingfors 1921

Lind, John: *Mellem "venska" og "vinska". Finsk fra almuesprog til statsbærende kultursprog*, Finsk afdelnings skrifter 3, København 1989

Meinander, Carl-Fredrik: "Om svenskarnes inflyttningar till Finland", *Historisk Tidskrift för Finland* 1983

Modeen, Tore: *De folkrättsliga garantierna för bevarandet av Ålandsöarnas nationella karaktär*, Mariehamn 1973

Modeen, Tore: *Finlandssvenskarnas nationella grundlagsskydd I*, Acta Academiae Aboensis A 54:3, Åbo 1977

Modeen, Tore: "The Åland Islands Question", in Smith, Paul (ed.): *Ethnic Groups in International Relations*, Comparative Studies on Governments and Non-dominant Ethnic Groups in Europe, 1850–1940 V, Strasbourg 1991

Modeen, Tore: "Völkerrechtliche Probleme der Åland-Inseln", *Zeitschrift für ausländisches öffentliches Recht und Völkerrecht* 37, 1977

Mustelin, Olof: "'Finlandssvensk'—kring ett begrepps historia", in Engman, Max & Stenius, Henrik (eds.): *Svenskt i Finland 1. Studier i språk och nationalitet efter 1860*, Skrifter utgivna av Svenska litteratursällskapet i Finland 511, Helsingfors 1983

Paunonen, Heikki: "Från Sörkka till kulturspråk. Iakttagelser om Helsingforsslangen som språklig och kulturell företeelse", *Historisk Tidskrift för Finland* 1989

Pulkkinen, Paavo: "Suomen kielestä täysipainoinen sivistyskieli", in Tommila, Päiviö (ed.): *Herää Suomi*

Rommi, Pirkko: *Yrjö-Koskisen linja. Myöntyvyyssuunnan hahmottuminen suomalaisen puolueen toimintalinjaksi*, Lahti 1964

Rystad, Göran: "'Återförening med moderlandet.' Ålandsrörelsens uppkomst", *Scandia* 38, 1972

Rystad, Göran: "'Särställning under Finland.' Finlandssvenskarna och Ålandsfrågan", *Åländsk Odling* 1980

Sandlund, Tom: *Svenska i Finland*, Finlandssvensk rapport 13, Helsingfors 1988

Söderhjelm, J.O.: *Démilitarisation et neutralisation des Iles d'Aland en 1856 et 1921*, Helsinki 1928

Sundberg, Jan: *Svenskhetens dilemma i Finland. Finlandssvenskarnas samling och splittring under 1900-talet,* Bidrag till kännedom av Finlands natur och folk 133, Helsingfors 1985

Svenska folkpartiet I–III, Helsingfors 1956–1992

Tommila, Päiviö (ed.): *Herää Suomi. Suomalaisuusliikkeen historia,* Kuopio 1989

Tommila, Päiviö: *Suomen autonomian synty 1808–1819,* Helsinki 1984

Törnudd, Klaus: *Svenska språkets ställning i Finland,* Helsingfors 1978

Uino, Ari: "Kielitaistelu ja 'uusi suomalaisuusliike' 1918–1939", in Tommila (ed.): *Herää Suomi*

Wallén, Holger: *Språkgränsen och minoriteterna i Finlands svenskbygder omkr. 1600–1865,* Åbo 1932

Wilson, William A.: *Folklore and Nationalism in Modern Finland,* Bloomington, Ind. 1976

KARELIANS BETWEEN EAST AND WEST

Max Engman

The Karelians are one of those peoples whose area of settlement has been divided by a national border. Whereas Karelians and their home area have been regarded as Finnish in the west, they have been considered Russian in the east. Hence, like Macedonia or Bessarabia, for example, Karelia has become a transitional area claimed by several states, which has left little scope for political initiatives of her own. As a people on the border, Karelians have been exposed to Finnization as well as Russification: they have literally found themselves between the sword and the scimitar, the two weapons that adorn the arms of Karelia[1]

The Division of Karelia

Karelians constituted one of the northern Finno–Ugrian tribes. Karelian, which is sometimes also called Karelian–Olonetsic (or Karelian and Olonetsic), belongs to the Baltic–Finnish group of the Finno–Ugrian languages. Karelian is characterized by large dialectal differences and displays a considerable Russian influence in the south (Olonets or Aunus Karelia) as well as a more original variety in the north (White Sea or Viena Karelia), where the language is fairly close to Finnish; in periods of Finnish expansionism, in connection with the World Wars, for example, there has been a tendency to re-

---

[1] For a brief account of Karelia in the history of Finland see Sihvo: "Karelia: Battlefield, Bridge, Myth"; Aminoff: *Mellan svärdet och kroksabeln* (Between the Sword and the Scimitar).

gard Karelian as one, or several, "east Karelian" dialects of Finnish. In the Grand Duchy (1809–1917) and in the Republic of Finland (1917–), Karelian was only spoken in a small area in the easternmost parts north of Lake Ladoga.

Around A.D. 700, Karelians inhabited an area south and southeast of Lake Ladoga, from which, in a fan-like pattern, they spread to the west into today's Finland and to the north towards the White Sea. The fundamental division between the east and the west was first formalized in the Peace treaty of Nöteborg in 1323, which divided the Karelian tribal area in the south between Sweden and Novgorod. The Swedish crusades to Finland had caused the area west of the Nöteborg border to be incorporated into the western church, while the area east of the border was incorporated into the Orthodox church by means of peaceful missionary work. This was a slow process, and happened in a way that made it possible for Finno–Ugrian folk traditions to survive in a form that was to constitute the foundation of the Finnish national epic, *Kalevala*, in the 19th century.

Whereas in the early Middle Ages Karelians were an important element (*Votskaya pyatina*, the Votic fifth) in the city republic of Novgorod, where Karelian magnates were able to rise to the ruling class, the increasing influence of Moscow made Karelia a peripheral area. At the same time, Russian acquired a strong position at an early stage, partly due to the immigration of Russians, especially in the southern parts of the area (Olonets–Karelia), but above all due to its complete dominance in the church, the administration, the army, and later also in the modern sectors of the economy. In the 17th century, the Lutheran as well as the Orthodox church created ecclesiastical texts with Cyrillic letters, but the Karelian dialects remained spoken varieties. While Finnish became a written language through the Reformation, it was only in the 20th century that the first serious attempts to create a Karelian written language were made.

The balance between the Lutheran and the Orthodox was disturbed when the Swedish realm achieved its furthermost expansion to the east in the peace treaty of Stolbova in 1617. For the first time, a large number of Orthodox Karelians came under Swedish rule.

The Swedish crown's harsh religious and taxation policies caused a considerable number of Karelians to emigrate. Instead, Finns migrated from the west, both to the Swedish parts of Karelia, where this Finnish-speaking Lutheran population were named Karelians after the province, and to Ingria (Ingermanland), where the immigrants from Savolax and the Karelian Isthmus formed the Ingrian population.

The 17th-century population shifts created two kinds of Karelians. This division gave rise to the basic dividing line between Swedish, later Finnish, Karelia and Russian Karelia. To the west of the border created by the Stolbova peace treaty there mainly lived Lutheran Karelians, who spoke the eastern Finnish dialects called Karelian. To the east of the border lived Orthodox Karelians, who spoke different dialects of the Karelian language.

The emigration, however, also gave rise to a third kind of Karelia. The majority of the Karelians who emigrated settled in the Tver area, where they have lived in a few connected areas up to the present time. Earlier estimates put them at approximately 200,000, but today, in spite of considerable Russification, about 30,000 are likely to have preserved their Karelian language.[2]

Old Finland and the Viborg Province

A completely new situation arose with the Great Nordic War (1700–1721) and the foundation of St Petersburg in 1703, which thoroughly changed the geopolitical constellations. The border of the Russian realm was moved west, initially, in 1721, to the so-called border of Peter the Great (by and large identical with the eastern border of present-day Finland), and, in 1743, to the Kymmene

---

[2] Virtaranta: "Om karelarna i det forna Tverska guvernementet" (On the Karelians in the Former Tver *Guberniya*), pp. 83–131.

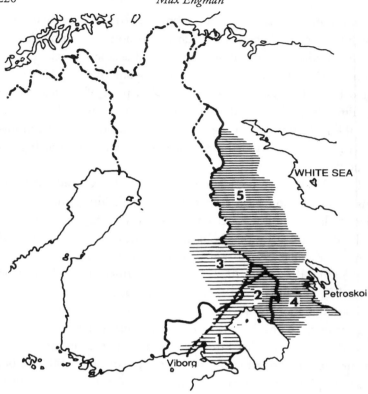

Karelia

This map shows the historic Finnish province of Karelia, which consists of the Karelian Isthmus (1), Frontier or Ladoga Karelia (2) and North Karelia (3). The unbroken line running to the west of Viborg/Viipuri/Vyborg marks the 1743 frontier. The Karelian Isthmus and Frontier Karelia formed the *guberniya* of Viborg in the eighteenth century, but was united with the Grand Duchy in 1812 and constituted the province of Viborg until the Second World War. The part of the province (west of the broken line) which remained to Finland after the war was made into the province of Kymi, while North Karelia became a separate province in 1960. The area to the east of the 1812 frontier (East Karelia) was divided between the *gubernii* of Olonets (4) and Archangel (5). Both districts also embraced large regions that were purely Russian. The narrowly shaded area denotes Orthodox population.

river (see Map). In 1812, Old Finland merged with the Grand Duchy of Finland and was integrated into its administrative structure. The province of Viborg, however, long enjoyed a special status in the Grand Duchy and the Republic of Finland, not least for being part of St Petersburg's field of influence for two centuries.[3]

Around 1900, Karelia came into the foreground in unprecedented fashion. The occasion can be described as a Finnish–Russian struggle about Karelia by cultural means.

The inspiration of Romanticism, notably Celtic Romanticism, and the general interest in folk epics became the incentives to treat Karelian topics. Some of the foremost results were Runeberg's *Elgskyttarne* and Lönnrot's *Kalevala*, of which the latter was to have an impact on the image of Karelia for many years to come. In the folkloric-ethnological period of Karelianism, *Kalevala* was seen as a source for the history, religion and mythology of the original Finns, as well as a literary and political inspiration and a bedrock for the future.[4]

It is striking how little Karelianism in Finland actually had to do with Karelia itself. It was inspired by international or Finnish models and was seen in a purely Finnish perspective. Finnish artists and scholars were looking for an original Finnish paradise and found the last traces of it in Eastern Karelia. The national-romantic currents of ideas that may have been given their most pregnant expressions in connection with Karelia played an important part in building the nation in Finland, and also in making Karelia a kind of Promised Land to Finns.[5]

[3] See also the articles in the special issue on Old Finland, *Historisk Tidskrift för Finland* 1, 1982. Kallio: *Viipurin läänin järjestäminen muun Suomen yhteyteen*; Klinge: *Runebergs två fosterland*, pp. 88–124. Engman: *S:t Petersburg och Finland.*

[4] On Karelianism, see Sihvo: *Karjalan kuva. Karelianismin taustaa ja vaiheita autonomian aikana.* On the use of folklore, see Wilson: *Folklore and Nationalism in Modern Finland.*

[5] Wilson, op.cit., pp. 141–142, 148–155.

Russification and Finnization of Karelians in Finland

Although the Orthodox Karelians in the Grand Duchy held an intermediate position between Finland and Russia, they were increasingly integrated in Finland in the 19th century. At the same time, the low educational level and poor literacy in the wilderness parishes of eastern Finland made the issue of expanding the educational system a national one. In the mid-1800s, there were requests for Orthodox clergymen who knew Finnish, and a large number of Karelians were swept along by the national revival in Finland, although there were also Russian-oriented circles.

From a Russian perspective, the Finnish interest in Karelia and the "pan-Finnish propaganda", which was also connected with the process of Lutheranization, seemed alarming. Karelians in Finland, especially the Orthodox ones, were regarded as natural allies of Russia, as "potential Russians" who had been exposed to Finnization and economic integration through the union of Old Finland. It was important to counteract Great Finland and Lutheran propaganda that attempted to disturb Karelians' loyalty to Russia, and even penetrate into Eastern Karelia. This resulted in the Russians' paying more attention to Finnish Karelia, which, among other things, manifested itself in the foundation of a Finnish Orthodox diocese in 1892. At its foundation, the diocese comprised 23 parishes with approximately 47,000 parishioners (including Russians). In the majority of these parishes, services were held in Finnish.[6]

The real battle, however, was fought over the conditions of education in Karelia on both sides of the border after the turn of the century. The Russian authorities stopped any attempt to open Finnish schools in Eastern Karelia and carefully controlled any activity that might be considered as Finnization of the Orthodox population

---

[6] Luntinen: "Karjalaiset suomalaisuuden ja venäläisyyden rajalla", pp. 125–159; Merikoski: *Taistelu Karjalasta;* Koukkunen: *Suomen valtiovalta ja kreikkalaiskatoliset 1881–1897.*

in Finland. Another Russian strategy was to found Russian schools not subject to the Finnish school authorities in borderland Karelia. Services were held in Russian instead of in Finnish or Church Slavic. This programme may be seen as a manifestation of the unification policy of the Russian government at the turn of the century. Ethnic Russification was only one of the manifestations of this policy in the borderland areas of the realm, but it was the central element of the policy conducted against Orthodox Karelians. We can discern a parallel in the struggle against Polish and Catholic influence in western Russia.[7]

At the time of the February Revolution, the inhabitants in many places spontaneously closed the Russian schools and expelled some of the clergy, although there was also a body of opinion that wished to keep those schools. After 1917 the schools were placed under the aegis of the Finnish school board, and henceforth instruction in Russian was available only to the Russian minority in Finland. In the 1920s, other measures were taken by Finnish authorities in order to raise the national consciousness of the population in the borderland areas by means of schools, libraries, lectures and the Finnization of names.[8]

When independence was achieved, the Orthodox church was compromised by its part in the Russification policy. Therefore, for national and security reasons, the Finnish government took steps to nationalise the church by founding an independent church communion, requiring that clergymen and monks be Finnish citizens, introducing Finnish as the administrative language, changing over to the Gregorian calendar and, finally, liberating themselves from the patriarchate in Moscow. *Autocephaly*, i.e. a totally independent church, could not be achieved, but in 1923 the church became subject to the

[7] Thaden (ed.): *Russification in the Baltic Provinces and Finland, 1855–1914.*

[8] Merikoski, op.cit., pp. 338–353. Tarasti: *Suomalaisuuden liitto 1906–1966*, pp. 47–49.

Ecumenical Patriarchate in Constantinople, which was not accepted
by the Patriarch in Moscow until 1957.[9]

National Awakening, Finnish Irredentism and
Aspirations for Independence in Eastern Karelia

At the turn of the century, there were slightly more than 87,000
Karelians and a somewhat larger number of Russians in Eastern
Karelia. The two groups led fairly separate lives; the Karelians were
dispersed in the countryside, whereas the Russians lived in densely
populated areas. By and large, the slow process of Russification was
conducted through migration as well as through the educational
system and the church. Grain was imported into the area, where the
standard of living was among the lowest in Russia. Only 15–25% of
the population were literate. Extensive house-to-house peddling in
Finland and Northern Russia was one of the most important liveli-
hoods of the Eastern Karelians, wich was also a means of getting in
touch with the outside world.[10]

The violent political upheavals of 1917–1920 afflicted an area
that was economically and socially backward, but that had gone
through a national awakening in northern Eastern Karelia around
the turn of the century. Before the Revolution, there had been no
real aspirations for autonomy nor any attempts at approaching Finland, even though an expansion of the right to trade with the west
was desired. In 1906, Eastern Karelians in Finland founded Vienan
Karjalaisten Liitto (The Association of White Sea Karelians), which
later developed into Karjalan Sivistysseura (The Karelian Cultural
Association). A private Finnish-speaking school had been closed by
the authorities in 1889, but shortly afterwards new schools, reading
rooms and a newspaper were founded by the Association. Among

[9] Setälä: *Kansallisen ortodoksisen kirkkokunnan perustamiskysymys
Suomen politiikassa 1917–1925.*
[10] Naakka-Korhonen & Keynäs: *Halpa hinta, pitkä mitta.*

other things, this newspaper made propaganda for the Finnization of Russian names (Karelian names that had gradually been converted into Russian forms), a suggestion which was connected with a massive, contemporary campaign for the Finnization of names in Finland.[11] Following the Stolypin reaction, the Association could only function in Finland, and its schools were closed as a result of the same Russian and Orthodox counterattack that had struck Finnish Karelia. At the same time, the number of Russian schools was doubled in White Sea Karelia.

After the February revolution, many advocates of the old order, such as police officers and clergymen, were spontaneously expelled. The political developments of 1917 resulted in a majority of the population orienting themselves towards the social revolutionaries; only a minority directed their interest towards Finland. The concept of autonomy was most strongly embraced in the north. At a meeting in Uhtua in White Sea Karelia in July 1917, a proposal for a constitution for a Karelian autonomy based on that of the soviets was adopted. The Karelian language was to be employed in the administration and educational system, and a Karelian diocese was to be established. Other demands were those for an agrarian reform and the transfer of the Crown's forests to the municipalities. The programme was a radical break with the past. Eastern Karelians refused to regard themselves and behave as Russians; rather than a Finnish national consciousness, there was a tendency towards a Karelian awareness. The Finnish expansion programme was never wholeheartedly embraced; even those Eastern Karelians who approved of a union with Finland demanded a special status, almost autonomy within Finland.[12]

In 1918, it was felt in Finland that the time had come to implement the cultural mission behind the eastern border. Between 1918

[11] Sihvo: "Polemiikkia karjalan kielestä karjalaislehdistössä ja -kirjallisuudessa", pp. 393–394.

[12] Churchill: *Itä-Karjalan kohtalo 1917–1922*, which enlarges on the author's PhD thesis (London), *The East Karelian autonomy question in Finnish–Soviet relations, 1917–1922* (1967).

and 1919, Finland attempted to have her demands met by supporting expeditions of volunteers that were, officially, independent of the state of Finland. In practice, and unofficially, however, they were cautiously supported by the Government, which tried to win over Eastern Karelia with diplomatic and military assistance, first from Germany and later from the Entente. The Finnish expansion was based on the idea that the population of Eastern Karelia wanted to be liberated and incorporated into Finland.[13]

Between 1918 and 1920, a complex military and political game was played involving the Bolsheviks, the White Government in Arkangelsk, the British, Eastern Karelians and White and Red Finns. A conflict soon arose between the Eastern Karelians and the Arkangelsk Government, which disapproved of any kind of Karelian particularism and wished to incorporate Karelians into their troops. Although the Eastern Karelian movement lasted longer than the government of Northern Russia, it was not able to resist the Red Army, which occupied the northern parts of Eastern Karelia in the spring of 1920.[14]

The Bolsheviks were suspicious of the Karelian movement for autonomy, regarding it as an agent of Finnish aspirations. Consequently they refused to discuss the demands for independence that had again been raised at a meeting in White Sea Karelia in March 1920. Since the Russian population was indifferent to these aspirations, the Bolsheviks were soon able to achieve military control. The occupation, the establishment of a Karelian department at the People's Commissariat of Nationalities and the eventual foundation of the Karelian Workers' Commune in June 1920, all proved that the Soviet Government was not prepared to give up the area but was indeed, to some extent, prepared to pay attention to the Karelian aspirations for autonomy.

---

[13] Jääskeläinen: *Die ostkarelische Frage*; Vahtola: *"Suomi suureksi—Viena vapaaksi"*.

[14] Polvinen: *Venäjän vallankumous ja Suomi 1917–1920 2*; Nevakivi: *Muurmannin legioona*.

At the peace negotiations at Dorpat in 1920, the Soviet Government refused to go further than a declaration of the right of the Karelian population to autonomy—already granted by the founding of the Commune—and to the use of their own language. Finland brought up the issue repeatedly in diplomatic contexts, and appealed to the League of Nations and the International Court in the Hague, but it had limited possibilities to exert an influence on the issue since every attempt was rejected by the Soviet Government as an interference in the internal affairs of Soviet Russia.

During the revolt against the Bolshevik rule that took place in White Sea Karelia in 1921–1922, all Finland could do was to deliver notes of protest, and she also had to receive more than 10,000 refugees from Eastern Karelia, the majority of whom returned after an amnesty issued by the Soviet Government in 1923. The Academic Karelian Society (AKS) was founded in order to assist the refugees in Finland; however, it rapidly developed into an irredentist student organization that grew increasingly Fascist in character. That organization dominated student politics in the interwar period and saw to it that Karelia remained a topical issue in an irredentist and vigorously anti-Soviet spirit.[15]

Soviet Karelia in the Interwar Period

In view of the opposition caused by the Finnish expansionist aspirations in Eastern Karelia, it is paradoxical that the Red Finnish refugees from the Civil War in 1918 should leave a pronouncedly Finnish mark on Soviet Karelia in the interwar period. Within the Finnish Communist Party, a future union between Karelia and Finland under the aegis of Communism was envisaged.[16]

[15] Nygård: *Itä-Karjalan pakolaiset 1917–1922,* and *Suur-Suomi vai lähiheimolaisten auttaminen;* Alapuro: *Akateeminen Karjala- seura.*

[16] Hakalehto: "De finska kommunisternas planer på en skandinavisk sovjetrepublik" (The Finnish Communists' Plans for a Scandinavian Soviet Republic).

The foundation of the Karelian Workers' Commune was opposed by local Bolsheviks, who preferred to see it as a temporary diplomatic trick before the peace negotiations with Finland, and who denied the existence of a Karelian culture and language. The local Russians would have preferred a demarcation of the border according to the ethnic dividing line, but instead a more economically viable unit was created, with a border from Lake Ladoga along the Svir and the Onega as far as the White Sea, i.e. what is traditionally seen as Eastern Karelia. In 1923, the Commune was transformed into the Karelian Autonomous Socialist Soviet Republic, incorporating large areas to the east of the Onega with a totally Russian population.[17]

The Karelian ASSR has had a solid Russian majority, further strengthened as a result of World War II. The population groups were still clearly separated; Karelians constituted over 80% of the population in half of the districts of the Republic. In absolute numbers, the Karelian population increased up to the war, but its share of the total population has continuously decreased. The Finnish population increased up to the 1930s, but decreased by the end of the decade, only to start increasing again. The area received considerable additions of Finnish groups through the Red refugees in 1918 and the so-called "defectors", i.e. some 15,000 unemployed Finns who crossed the Soviet border illegally in the interwar period. The 1930s saw another increase in the Finnish population through the recruiting of some 6,000 Finnish Americans, including large groups of lumberjacks who brought capital and professional skills.[18]

The Finnish Communists were to have an impact on Eastern Karelia that far exceeded their numerical strength, partly because

[17] Kauppala: "Die qualvolle Geburt und das kurze Aufblühen des autonomen Sowjet–Karelien. Ost-Karelien 1917–1930".

[18] Kero: *Neuvosto-Karjalaa rakentamassa. Pohjois-Amerikan suomalaiset tekniikan tuojina 1930-luvun Neuvosto-Karjalassa*, and "The Canadian Finns in Soviet Karelia in the 1930s"; Kostiainen: *Loikkarit. Suuren lamakauden laiton siirtolaisuus Neuvostoliittoon*.

they were needed by the Bolsheviks to administer the area. Up to the mid-1930s, the leading posts in the Republic were almost exclusively occupied by Finns. Edvard Gylling was chairman of the Council of People's Commissars (Prime Minister) between 1923 and 1935. Finns were clearly overrepresented in the party and most of its prominent bodies, whereas Karelians and Russians were underrepresented.[19]

The Finns pursued what was called a Karelianization policy. In 1922, Finnish and Karelian became official languages, and in the 1930s they were made compulsory subjects at school for both language groups. The Karelian population were allowed to use their dialects in schools and civil service departments, but "real" Finnish served as the written language. The Finnish educational system was expanded, even at the expense of the Russian one. In 1932, Finnish was used as the language of instruction in more than half (278) of the schools in the Republic. Finnish culture thrived thanks to theatres, 13 newspapers and periodicals and an extensive publishing business.

In 1935, two great anniversaries were celebrated in the Karelian Soviet Republic. The first was the centenary of *Kalevala* which was considered the national epic of Soviet Karelia and "the cultural heritage of the workers". The motto of Finnish-speaking cultural activities was emphasized: "socialist in content, national in form". In the summer of 1935, the 15th anniversary of the foundation of the Karelian Workers' Commune was celebrated. It was pointed out that impressive progress had been made in the economic and cultural fields; by adhering to the Leninist-Stalinist national policy, Great Russian chauvinism and local nationalism had been com-

---

[19] On the nationality issue, see Kostiainen: "Dominating Finnish Minority? On the Background of the Nationality Problem in Soviet Karelia in the 1930's", pp. 341–366; Vihavainen: "Internationalists' Ordeal. The Peculiar Story of the Red Finns in Soviet Russia", pp. 55–74; Hodgson: *Communism in Finland*, pp. 147–173.

230   *Max Engman*

batted, and a firm policy of national self-determination had been created.[20]

At this time, the Finns were already in a precarious situation. Soviet Karelia with its nationality policies was the creation of the internationalist stage of the history of the Soviet Union and in many ways was an example of the New Economic Policy. Stalin's buildup of Socialism in one country accommodated only one national order. In 1935, the regional committee of the Communist Party in Leningrad criticized the leaders of the Republic for their lack of internationalism and for bourgeois nationalism. That criticism resulted in leading Finnish communists losing their positions and in purges; in all, 3,000–3,500 people, most of whom were accused of espionage for Finland, are likely to have been executed or put in prison camps. To some extent, those purges also affected Karelians, but above all it was the Finns who suffered.[21]

In 1937, shortly after a regulation concerning three official languages (Russian, Finnish and Karelian) had been adopted in the Karelian constitution, all publications in Finnish were proscribed in the Soviet Union. Instead, a Karelian written language was introduced in Karelia; it had been developed in 1931 for the Tver Karelians and was written in Latin letters until 1937, when all minority languages began to be written in the Cyrillic alphabet. Developing written languages for the ethnic minorities was part of the Leninist national policy and literacy campaign.[22] Suddenly, in 1940, this experiment was abandoned as well. At the beginning of the Winter

[20] Account given in Renvall: "Neuvosto-Karjalan suomalaisuuden kriisin alkuvaiheista", pp. 77–84.

[21] Kero: "The Role of Finnish Settlers from North America in the Nationality Question in Soviet Karelia in the 1930s", pp. 229–241; Takala: "Gyllingin-Rovion juttu", pp. 129–147.

[22] Vihavainen, op.cit., pp. 69–71; Uimonen: "Neuvosto-Karjalan karjalankielisen kirjallisuuden kielitausta vuosina 1920–1936", pp. 128–141. The Eastern Karelians in exile in Finland were generally favourable to the use of Finnish as the written language, Sihvo: "Polemiikkia", pp. 390–397.

War between Finland and the Soviet Union in 1939–1940, the world was informed that the Soviet government had realized the century-old dream of the Finnish people by ceding Eastern Karelia to O.V. Kuusinen's Terijoki government, to be incorporated into Finland when that country had been conquered by Kuusinen's People's Army, which was supported by the Red Army. In 1940, a Finnish-Karelian Soviet Republic was founded with Kuusinen as head of state. The Republic received the areas ceded by Finland, and Finnish was introduced as a second official language, for example at the newly-established university in Petrosavodsk, while the Karelian written language discreetly disappeared. In 1944, the Karelian Isthmus was merged with the Leningrad region, and in 1956 Karelia lost its status as a Soviet Republic and became an autonomous Soviet republic within the Russian Federation. At the same time, the "national" (Finnish–Karelian) schools were abolished. Not until 1963 was Finnish reintroduced as a subject in Karelian schools.

Finnish Irredentism 1941–1944

The Continuation War in 1941–1944 opened up new opportunities for Finnish politics; the starting-point was a return to the borders of 1939, since the Moscow Peace of 1940 was considered both unfair and unreasonably demanding for Finland. The rapid advance into Eastern Karelia and the German victories gave rise to the idea of territorial expansion. When the Finnish leadership realized that Germany intended to crush the Soviet Union, the Government gradually began to express wishes for modifications of the border of 1939. According to the maximum alternative, the new border was supposed to have run from the Kola Peninsula, all of which would have gone to Finland, via the White Sea to the Onega, further south of the Svir to Lake Ladoga and—depending on the future destiny of Leningrad—along the Neva or the former border to the Gulf of Finland. To avoid schisms, the Government did not publicize these plans, but public opinion was manipulated in that direction. At the beginning of 1943, however, the most Finland could hope for was a negotiated peace based on the borders of 1939 and for Eastern Karelia to be granted autonomy, which would result in a buffer area between Finland and the Soviet Union.[23]

During the Finnish occupation, Eastern Karelia was under a military administration in which former AKS members played an important part. After the evacuation of most of the population of the ASSR, only about 30 per cent of the population, mainly women, children and elderly people remained. The military administration worked out plans for a Finnization of the population and began to implement them. Comprehensive resettlement of the population was planned; the Russian population was placed in internment and concentration camps, pending its replacement after the war with a population of Finno–Ugric origin from other parts of the Soviet Union. The planners were working with the aim of a Great Finland, the home of people of Finnish origin. Hence their idea was to create a "pure" Finno–Ugrian population; as colonizers they envisaged Finnish veterans as well as people from Ingria. The policy of Finnization, as manifested by elementary schools and the support of the Lutheran church (the Orthodox church was considered to be too strongly rooted in Russian traditions) was not very successful; an active desire to join Finland never arose among the population of Eastern Karelia.[24]

The Evacuation of Finnish Karelians

The peace treaties of 1940 and 1944 made more than 400,000 Finns homeless. Finland lost about 12% of its area, 30% of its energy sources, 22% of its forest reserves and 20% of its railway

---

[23] Manninen: *Suur-Suomen ääriviivat.*

[24] On the administration during the occupation, see Laine: *Suur-Suomen kahdet kasvot.*

system. Approximately 12% of the population were to be resettled in new circumstances.[25]

The Karelians from the areas ceded were not refugees in the usual sense of the word, since they were Finnish citizens and were relocated within their own country; they belonged rather to the category called "displaced persons" or "expellees" after the war. The people evacuated from Karelia came from an area which was comparatively homogeneous both economically and politically. There were, however, large cultural and social differences between the city of Viborg with its Swedish, German and Russian minorities and the Isthmus with its Lutheran population and its many voluntary associations, on the one hand, and borderland Karelia with its Orthodox population and cultural isolation on the other.

The province of Viborg had gone through a very rapid development in the interwar years, thanks partly to land reforms and a land clearance policy. Despite intensive regional industrialization, the areas ceded were agrarian in character. Small-scale farming dominated on the Karelian Isthmus and north of the Lake Ladoga; to the west of the lake, the farms were somewhat larger, but large-scale farming were extremely rare.

The problems caused by the evacuation were reinforced by the fact that it was carried out twice. The reconquest in 1941 of the areas lost in 1940 gave rise to some uncertainty about their legal status. Some jurists thought that they should be treated as conquered areas, whereas others felt that they were areas that had been restored to the realm. The latter opinion prevailed, which resulted in Finnish law and previous legal and real property conditions becoming operative again in 1941.

Those who had been evacuated had a strong desire to return, and it was difficult for the authorities to slow down a process of remigra-

[25] For further information on this section, see Engman: "De förflyttade karelarna—evakuering och integrering" (The Relocated Karelians—Evacuation and Integration), and the references cited there.

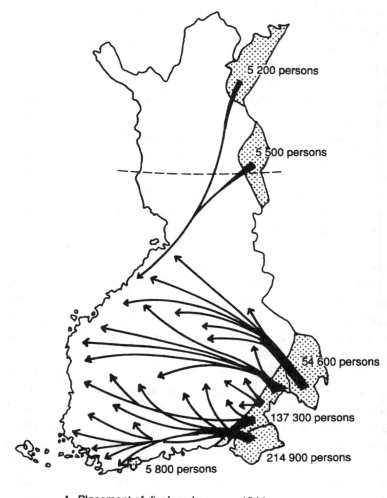

5 200 persons

5 500 persons

54 600 persons

137 300 persons

214 900 persons

5 800 persons

Placement of displaced persons 1944

Finland: Ceded Territories and Displaced Persons, 1944

tion that they considered premature in view of the war being still in progress and the fact that the area had been severely devastated by the war. Due to the difficult supply situation, however, they were interested in exploiting the resources of the area. As early as the end of June 1942, almost half of the population, or 195,000 people, had returned to the province of Viborg.

Even though the reconquest of Karelia had been a generally espoused goal of the war in 1941, resistance to giving up the area again was naturally strongest among Karelians, who were categorically against a peace on those terms. This limited the Government's room for manoeuvre, and made it impossible for them to start evacuating the population before the massive offensive of the Soviet forces in June 1944 created a situation which did not offer them any choice.

When the evacuees were settled, the important decision was made that they should not be put in camps but accommodated with the population of the rest of Finland, and also that they should be given an opportunity to practise their old occupations by means of various temporary arrangements.

The losses suffered by the state and by private citizens in the ceded areas represented total amounts exceeding the war indemnity Finland was obliged to pay the Soviet Union. During the first few years after the war, compensation constituted one of the Government's largest expenses, next to the war indemnity.

In order to integrate those who had been moved, it was important to give as many of them as possible an opportunity to pursue their previous occupations. Since there was a great demand for labour after the war, it was comparatively easy for town-dwellers and industrial workers to find employment, but harder for such groups as entrepreneurs and fishermen. The great problem that had to be rapidly solved was the agricultural population, which was allotted land by means of the Rapid Colonization Law of 1940 and the Land Acquisition Law of 1945. Even though there was general agreement on the principle, its implementation was controversial, since it was obvious that the evacuees would not be able to purchase the necessary 40,000 farms on the open market and that some kinds of coercive measures would be required. It was very important for the Karelians that they should manage to maintain a united front and look after their interests by means of a well-developed network of organizations with the Karelian Union as the umbrella organization.

One crucially important factor was the agrarian reforms during the interwar period, including legislation and preparedness for colonization. When the question of locating a large agricultural population arose, that tradition was reinvoked, and thus the solutions of 1940 and 1944 took on the appearance of a land reform.[26] In the late 1940s, during the most intense period of colonization, more than 120,000 new farm units were created, 38% of which were allotted to the relocated population, 50% to the veterans and their families, and 12% to other groups. Those who had been relocated were likely to have received at least two-thirds of the actual cultivation lots; only 5% of their applications were rejected. The colonization process proceeded rapidly; by the end of 1948, a mere 4% of those relocated had not been placed. Furthermore, it was a very thorough process, involving some 600,000 people simply in their capacity as recipients of land.

In the post-war years, the placement and integration of the relocated Karelians became one of the major social issues in Finland and the subject of extremely lively debate. The issue to which the general public paid most attention was the colonization in the Swedish-speaking areas of the country. Concern about the linguistic consequences of the Rapid Colonization Law led to the convocation in 1941 of Svenska Finlands folkting, an unofficial body representing the Swedish-speaking population which had not been convened since 1919. In practice, the policy was to try to create better opportunities and more time for the inhabitants in the Swedish municipalities to acquire compensatory land for Karelians on the other side of the language border rather than colonize their own municipality.

[26] Hietanen: *Siirtoväen pika-asutuslaki 1940.*

If that could be achieved, it would have been an economic burden rather than a transfer of land. This was considered necessary by Swedes in order to preserve language conditions intact, whereas Finns saw it as a way of selfishly escaping responsibility.[27]

The final outcome was that Åland was exempted from colonization, and that the principle was established that the placement of Karelians was not to increase the share of the Finnish-speaking population in Swedish-speaking or bilingual municipalities by more than 2%.

The colonization was a success in so far as the economic goals that had been set up were achieved. On the farms created by the Land Acquisition Law, almost 150,000 hectares of new arable land were cleared, and about the same amount on already existing farms. This resulted in an expansion of the arable land in the country by more than the area that had been lost in Karelia. The Karelian colonization contributed to the violent structural change in Finland after the war, and created many small farms; therefore it has sometimes, in retrospect as well as at the time, been characterized as a misguided venture. Nevertheless, given current public opinion and economic conditions, it is hard to imagine any other practicable solution.

Since the evacuated Karelians were distributed among the rest of the population, the natural unity of their culture and environment disappeared in the process. No ready channels for maintaining unity existed, but traditions were passed on within the framework of families and formal organizations, notably the large number of Karelian Associations. Although some Karelian cultural features have been preserved up to our time, generations born after the 1940s have mostly abandoned their parents' dialect.

---

[27] Kulha: *Karjalaisen siirtoväen asuttamisesta käyty julkinen keskustelu vuosina 1944–1948.*

Should the Ceded Karelia Be Restored?

In the 1980s, it seemed as if Karelia would only survive in Finland in the form of Karelian nostalgia, the so-called "tribal therapy of the last Karelians", where the Karelia of memories has been described in an extensive literature. Since most of the area was off limits to foreigners, the Karelia of the interwar years was seen in a mythical light; hence the Soviet emphasis on Viborg being "an ancient Russian town" felt all the more bitter.[28]

The evacuated Karelians still retain a well-developed and well functioning organizational structure. The Karelian Union has more than 500 member organizations and some 73,000 members, which implies that the younger generations are also involved in the activities. The annual Karelian days arranged by the Association attract thousands of Karelians.

In 1977, the Karelian Union adopted a cultural programme whose primary aim is to emphasize the unity of Karelian culture, which also includes Karelians in the (former) Soviet Union, i.e. the Eastern Karelian and the Tver Karelian cultures. On another level, similar ideas are being stressed in the cooperation between the Universities of Joensuu and Petrosavodsk.

The 1980s witnessed a general Karelian renaissance. Even though some of its manifestations have been regarded as vulgarizations and commercializations of Karelian traditions, they do, nevertheless, display the vitality of Karelians and their special place in Finnish culture. To some extent, this renaissance was inspired by the traditions of the ceded areas, but it was also based on a new Karelian identity in today's northern Karelia, the area around Joensuu and the parts of southern Karelia inside the Finnish border. This Karelian renaiss-

[28] Sihvo: "Karjala kirjallisuudessa", pp. 127–147; Lehtonen: "Kadotettu Karjala Suomen kirjallisuudessa", pp. 216–220; Kuujo: "'Viborg – en urgammal rysk stad' – Karelens förflutna ur sovjetisk synvinkel" ("'Viborg—an ancient Russian city'—The Karelian Past from the Soviet Point of View"), pp. 137–140.

ance stressed the importance of Karelia as a bridge between East and West, a bridge which had facilitated a large amount of cooperation in the fields of science, culture and tourism even before the stage when borders in Europe were opened.

The Finnish Government explored the possibility of repossessing the ceded areas on a few occasions in the 1940s and 50s. In 1956, when the Karelian Union adopted a resolution in the hope that the Government would ask the Soviet Union to agree on a redrawing of the border, the Soviet press categorically dismissed all such plans. After that, the issue was not publicly discussed for three decades, but the Soviet reform policy under Gorbachev and the dissolution of the Soviet Union meant that the issue of the ceded areas once again became topical. Previously, it had been very difficult for foreign citizens to visit the area, but it was rapidly opened to tourists in the late 1980s. In 1991 some of the associations for preserving the traditions of the ceded parishes were able to arrange local folklore festivals in their former home parishes.

Since 1989, there has at times been a quite intensive debate in Finland as to whether Finland should attempt to repossess the areas ceded in Karelia. The Soviet and, later, the Russian leaders have consistently adopted a negative stance. On his visit to Finland in August 1989, Minister of Defence Dmitri Yazov announced that it was inappropriate to discuss that issue and that redrawing borders was a dangerous matter: "In principle, we don't redraw borders; if we were to start redrawing borders established after World War II, it would lead to more warfare." They did not want to create a precedent, and when the Soviet Republics had gone their separate ways, Russian leaders again expressed the same opinion. On a visit to Finland in July 1992, Boris Yeltsin maintained that there was no Karelian issue, and that reopening borderland problems in Europe would only result in chaos.[29]

The Finnish Government has consistently been restrained and,

[29] *Hufvudstadsbladet* 18.8.1989 and 6.7.1992.

for example, did not bring up the issue when a new agreement between Finland and Russia was negotiated. At the same time, it was observed that, according to the principles of the Conference on Security and Cooperation in Europe, it is possible to adjust borders by peaceful means, given that there is a willingness on both sides. In 1991, President Mauno Koivisto declared that Finland had lost Karelia in two wars, and that the outcome had been laid down in three peace treaties. In his view cooperation across the border was more important than the border as such.[30]

The debate in the press was characterized by a general agreement that the Soviet attack on Finland in 1939 was unjustified and that the loss of Karelia was unwarranted; it was also generally agreed that the interest of the evacuees in their home areas was natural, and that the economic and cultural cooperation with the ceded areas should be expanded. Nevertheless, the main body of opinion was against repossessing Karelia. Their arguments were partly the same as those adduced by the Government, namely that pursuing the issue would be economically unjustified, politically unwise, and would go against the grain of the main orientation of Finnish post-war foreign policy. Among other things, they pointed out that Finland would have acquired a Russian minority almost the size of the Finland–Swedish population.[31]

Their opponents wanted to see the repossession as a historic opportunity and as a question of justice. Consequently, repossession would be the prerequisite for genuine friendship between the two countries. It has also been suggested that the ceded areas might function as a buffer zone between the countries, possibly with a demilitarized status comparable to that of Åland.

[30] *Hufvudstadsbladet* 23.9.1991 and 3.3.1992.

[31] Signed contributions to *Suomen Kuvalehti* 18.8.1989 (Jukka Tarkka), *Helsingin Sanomat* 15.9.1991 (Max Jakobsson), 30.9.1991 (Erkki Pennanen) and 26.4.1992 (Risto Penttilä), *Hufvudstadsbladet* 14.9.1991 (Sture Gadd) and 25.9.1991 (Bo Stenström). Interview with the commander of the General Staff, General Gustav Hägglund. *Åbo Underrättelser* 7.3.1992.

The issue has been pursued by activists in the Karelian Union, among others. The populist Rural Party is the only political party that has committed itself to the issue, and opinion polls seem to indicate that citizens are inclined to support the policy of the Government. In the autumn of 1992, 68% of the citizens of Finland were opposed to negotiations with Russia about the ceded areas.[32]

National Awakening in Eastern Karelia

It was not only in Finland that the question of Karelia arose. In 1988, in connection with *perestroika* and *glasnost*, there were also increased demands in Eastern Karelia for expanded tourism, commerce across the border and aid from Finland. People also wanted more instruction in Finnish and closer relations to Finland at various levels. In 1991, some kind of affiliation with Finland was even suggested.

In the censuses of 1970 and 1979, Karelians constituted 11.8 and 11.1% of the population of the Republic, respectively. In the census of 1989, 79,000 of the inhabitants of the Republic considered themselves to be Karelian, but a mere half of them (51.5%) named Karelian as their mother tongue, the rest of them naming Russian. The process of assimilation has been accelerated by urbanization, migration and the disappearance of the traditional Karelian villages.[33]

The new situation has made the old question of the written language topical again, and in certain respects the discussion has continued where it was interrupted in the 1930s. Some people have ad-

[32] For example, *Helsingin Sanomat* 16.9.1991 (Martti Valkonen), 5.10.1991 (Pentti Virrankoski), *Iltasanomat* 23.9.1991 (Rauno Meriö) and 2.10.1992, *Hufvudstadsbladet* 18.2. and 2.10.1992.

[33] Lallukka: *Suomalais-ugrilaiset kansat Neuvostoliiton uusimpien väestönlaskentojen valossa*, p. 22; Klementjev: "Karjalaiset. Vuoden 1989 väestönlaskenta", p. 163.

vocated creating two Karelian written varieties.[34] At a meeting of delegates in June 1991, demands were raised that Karelian should be an official language along with Russian, and that instruction in Karelian should be available to those who desire it; the extent of assimilation, however, was demonstrated by the fact that not all of the participants spoke Karelian and that the minutes were taken in Russian. The journal of the Society of Karelian Authors, which changed its name in 1991 from *Punalippu* (The Red Flag) to *Carelia*, has continued to use Finnish, whereas such new periodicals as *Oma Mua* (Our Own Country) are published in Karelian, every author writing in his or her dialect. The meeting of delegates appointed a committee that is to represent Karelians with the authorities, and suggested that Karelia should be a republic of its own within the federal union.

The present uncertainty about the future of Karelia reflects the ambiguities of its history. Squeezed in between East and West, Karelians have held their own, but history has not made it possible for them to develop and implement a national consciousness. Throughout their history, they have lived under the double pressure of their language being related to Finnish and having a common religion and history with the Russians. The West has mainly subjected them to the mission of the sword, whereas Russian has had a strong impact by dominating the church, the school system and the modern sectors of the economy. Most of the time, Karelians have been compelled to opt for either "exit" or "loyalty".[35]

The Swedish expansion to the east led to the emergence of the Lutheran Karelians in the 17th century. They came under Russian rule in the 18th century, and in 1940–1944 they had to resettle in a diminished Finland where they have tended to merge into the ma-

[34] Jalava: *Kansallisuus kadoksissa*, pp. 156, 170. *Helsingin Sanomat* 2. and 30.6.1991.

[35] Cf. above p. 30.

jority of the population. This process, however, is not yet completed, as is shown for example by the discussion about repossessing Karelia.

LITERATURE

Alapuro, Risto: *Akateeminen Karjala-seura. Ylioppilasliike ja kausa 1920- ja 1930-luvulla,* Helsinki 1973

Aminoff, Torsten G.: *Mellan svärdet och kroksabeln. 700 års kamp om karelarnas land* (Between the Sword and the Scimitar; 700 Years of Dispute over the Land of the Karelians), Helsingfors 1943

Churchill, Stacy: *Itä-Karjalan kohtalo 1917–1922. Itä-Karjalan itsehallintokysymys Suomen ja Neuvosto-Venäjän välisissä suhteissa 1917–1922,* Helsinki 1970

Engman, Max: "De förflyttade karelarna—evakuering och integrering" (The Relocated Karelians—Evacuation and Integration), in Johansson, R. & Persson H-Å. (eds.): *Nordisk flyktingpolitik i världskrigens epok* (Nordic Refugee Policy in the World War Epoch), CESIC Studies in International Conflict 1, Lund 1989

Engman, Max: *S:t Petersburg och Finland. Migration och influens 1703–1917.* Bidrag till kännedom om Finlands natur och folk 130, Helsingfors 1983

Hakalehto, Ilkka: "De finska kommunisternas planer på en skandinavisk sovjetrepublik" (The Finnish Communists' Plans for a Scandinavian Soviet Republic), *Historiallinen Arkisto* 63, 1968

Hietanen, Silvo: *Siirtoväen pika-asutuslaki 1940. Asutuspoliittinen tausta ja sisältö sekä toimeenpano.* Historiallisia tutkimuksia 117, Helsinki 1982

Historisk Tidskrift för Finland 1, 1982. Special issue on Old Finland.

Hodgson, John H.: *Communism in Finland. A History and Interpretation,* Princeton, N.J. 1967

Jääskeläinen, Mauno: *Die ostkarelische Frage. Die Entstehung eines nationalen Expansionsprogramms und die Versuche zu seiner Verwirklichung in der Aussenpolitik Finnlands in den Jahren 1918–1920,* Studia Historica 6, Helsinki 1965

Jalava, Aulikki: *Kansallisuus kadoksissa. Neuvosto-Karjalan suomenkielisen epiikan kehitys,* Suomalaisen Kirjallisuuden Seuran toimituksia 537, Helsinki 1990

Kallio, O.A.: *Viipurin läänin järjestäminen muun Suomen yhteyteen,* Helsinki 1901

Kauppala, Pekka: "Die qualvolle Geburt und das kurze Aufblühen des autonomen Sowjet-Karelien. Ost-Karelien 1917–1930", in Hösch, Edgar (ed.): *Finnland-Studien,* Veröffentlichungen des Osteuropa-Instituts München 59, Wiesbaden 1990

Kero, Reino: *Neuvosto-Karjalaa rakentamassa, Pohjois-Amerikan suomalaiset tekniikan tuojina 1930-luvun Neuvosto-Karjalassa,* Historiallisia tutkimuksia 122, Helsinki 1983

Kero, Reino: "The Canadian Finns in Soviet Karelia in the 1930s", in Karni, Michael G. (ed.): *Finnish Diaspora I,* Toronto 1981

Kero, Reino: "The Role of Finnish Settlers from North America in the Nationality Question in Soviet Karelia in the 1930s", *Scandinavian Journal of History* 6, 1981

Klementjev, Jevgeni: "Karjalaiset. Vuoden 1989 väestönlaskenta", *Carelia* 6, 1991

Klinge, Matti: *Runebergs två fosterland,* Helsingfors 1983

Kostiainen, Auvo: "Dominating Finnish Minority? On the Background of the Nationality Problem in Soviet Karelia in the 1930's", *Faravid* 9, 1985

Kostiainen, Auvo: *Loikkarit. Suuren lamakauden laiton siirtolaisuus Neuvostoliittoon,* Helsinki 1988

Koukkunen, Heikki: *Suomen valtiovalta ja kreikkalaiskatoliset 1881–1897.* Joensuun korkeakoulun julkaisuja A 7, Joensuu 1977

Kulha, Keijo K.: *Karjalaisen siirtoväen asuttamisesta käyty julkinen keskustelu vuosina 1944–1948,* Studia Historica Jyväskyläensia 7, Jyväskylä 1969

Kuujo, Erkki: "'Viborg—en urgammal rysk stad'—Karelens förflutna ur sovjetisk synvinkel" ("'Viborg—an ancient Russian city'—The Karelian Past from the Soviet Point of View"), *Historisk Tidskrift för Finland* 1982

Laine, Antti: *Suur-Suomen kahdet kasvot. Itä-Karjalan siiviiliväestön asema suomalaisessa miehityshallinnossa 1941–1944,* Helsinki 1982

Lallukka, Seppo: *Suomalais-ugrilaiset kansat Neuvostoliiton uusimpien väestönlaskentojen valossa,* Neuvostoliittoinstituutin julkaisusarja A 11, Helsinki 1982

Lehtonen, Maija: "Kadotettu Karjala Suomen kirjallisuudessa", *Kanava* 1981

Luntinen, Pertti: "Karjalaiset suomalaisuuden ja venäläisyyden rajalla", *Historiallinen Arkisto* 83, 1984

Manninen, Ohto: *Suur-Suomen ääriviivat. Kysymys tulevaisuudesta ja turvallisuudesta Suomen Saksan-politiikassa 1941*, Helsinki 1980

Merikoski, K.: *Taistelu Karjalasta. Piirteitä venäläistämistyöstä Rajakarjalassa tsaarinvallan aikoina*, Helsinki 1939

Naakka-Korhonen, Mervi & Keynäs, Maiju: *Halpa hinta, pitkä mitta. Vienankarjalainen laukkukauppa*. Suomalaisen Kirjallisuuden Seuran toimituksia 491, Helsinki 1988

Nevakivi, Jukka: *Muurmannin legioona. Suomalaiset ja liittoutuneiden interventio Pohjois-Venäjällä 1918–1919*, Helsinki 1970

Nygård, Toivo: *Itä-Karjalan pakolaiset 1917–1922*, Studia Historica Jyväskyläensia 19, Jyväskylä 1980

Nygård, Toivo: *Suur-Suomi vai lähiheimolaisten auttaminen. Aatteellinen heimotyö itsenäisessä Suomessa*, Helsinki 1978

Polvinen, Tuomo: *Venäjän vallankumous ja Suomi 1917–1920 2*, Helsinki 1971

Renvall, Pentti: "Neuvosto-Karjalan suomalaisuuden kriisin alkuvaiheista", *Historiallinen Aikakauskirja* 1944

Setälä, U.V.J.: *Kansallisen ortodoksisen kirkkokunnan perustamiskysymys Suomen politiikassa 1917–1925*, Porvoo 1966

Sihvo, Hannes: "Karelia: Battlefield, Bridge, Myth", in Engman, M. & Kirby, D. (ed.): *Finland. People. Nation. State*, London 1989

Sihvo, Hannes: "Karjala kirjallisuudessa", *Karjala* 1, Hämeenlinna 1981

Sihvo, Hannes: *Karjalan kuva. Karelianismin taustaa ja vaiheita autonomian aikana*. Suomalaisen Kirjallisuuden Seuran toimituksia 314, Helsinki 1973

Sihvo, Hannes: "Polemiikkia karjalan kielestä karjalaislehdistössä ja -kirjallisuudessa", *Virittäjä* 1968

Takala, Irina: "Gyllingin-Rovion juttu", *Carelia* 9, 1991

Tarasti, Kari: *Suomalaisuuden liitto 1906–1966*, Helsinki 1966

Thaden, Edward C. (ed.): *Russification in the Baltic Provinces and Finland, 1855–1914*, Princeton N.J. 1981

Uimonen, Jorma: "Neuvosto-Karjalan karjalankielisen kirjallisuuden kielitausta vuosina 1920–1936", *Punalippu* 4, 1989

Vahtola, Jouko: *"Suomi suureksi—Viena vapaaksi". Valkoisen Suomen pyrki-*

mykset Itä-Karjalan valtaamiseksi vuonna 1918, Studia Historica Septentrionalia 17, Rovaniemi 1988

Vihavainen, Timo: "Internationalists' Ordeal. The Peculiar Story of the Red Finns in Soviet Russia", *Scandinavian Journal of History* 10, 1985

Virtaranta, Pertti: "Om karelarna i det forna Tverska guvernementet" (On the Karelians in the Former Tver Guberniya), *Saga och sed. Kungl. Gustav Adolfs Akademiens årsbok* 1980

Wilson, William A.: *Folklore and Nationalism in Modern Finland*, Bloomington, Ind. 1976

NEWSPAPERS:
Åbo Underrättelser 7.3. 1992
Helsingin Sanomat 2.6, 30.6, 15.9, 16.9, 30.9, 5.10. 1991, 26.4. 1992
Hufvudstadsbladet 18.8. 1989, 14.9, 23.9, 25.9. 1991, 18.2, 3.3, 6.7, 2.10. 1992
Iltasanomat 23.9. 1991, 2.10. 1992
Suomen Kuvalehti 18.8. 1989

NATIONAL MINORITIES IN SOUTH JUTLAND/SCHLESWIG

Lorenz Rerup

The narrow part of the Jutland peninsula, demarcated to the North by the Kongeå and to the South by the Ejder, is called Sønderjylland (South Jutland) or Schleswig, and has an area of about 8,900 square km. Because of the importance of efficient border defense this area acquired a special position within the Danish realm as early as the 11th century, and in the 12th century it acquired the status of a duchy. Furthermore its history was closely linked with that of Holstein throughout the period between the 13th and the 19th centuries. This particular connection with both German-speaking Holstein and the Danish kingdom (which is defined as only including Denmark) resulted in a gradual penetration of the Low German language into Schleswig which went far beyond the limit of an earlier German (Saxon) immigration. German also established itself as the principle language of the higher-class city dwellers of Schleswig. The expansion of German into Denmark was connected with trade, and after the Reformation also with the church when liturgical language shifted from Latin to vernacular languages. National tensions did not emerge until the early 19th century and were not expressed overtly until around 1840. At this time both duchies were parts of the multi-ethnic Danish *"Helstat"* (a Danish term for the monarchy including the duchies and colonial possessions overseas). The King of Denmark was the duke of Schleswig, Holstein and Lauenburg. In 1815 the latter two duchies, without leaving the *Helstat*, joined the German Confederation, founded after the ending of the Napoleonic wars. Holstein and Lauenburg had been parts of the old German Empire which was dissolved in 1806. From 1848 until 1850 the

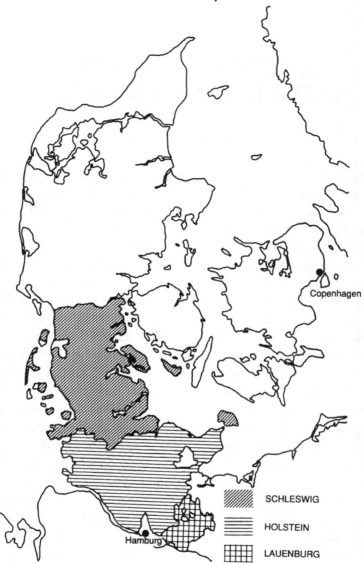

The Danish "Helstat", 1815–1864

Monarchy was shaken by a civil war (*Treårskrigen*, the "Three Years War"). The new national forces did not acquiesce in the ancient relation between the duchies and Denmark, and wished to destroy it. The Schleswig-Holstein movement demanded a border along the Kongeå, while the Danish National Liberals wanted one along the Ejder. However, the dominant European powers reestablished the *Helstat* after the civil war in order to preserve the "European Balance of Power" as outlined in the London treaty of 8 May 1852. The dominant European nations considered it undesirable that a single power should control the entrance to the Baltic sea. The reconstructed *Helstat* did not prove viable, and by 1864 the duchies had been conquered by Prussia and Austria. After Austria suffered defeat in the war of 1866, Schleswig and Holstein were incorporated as a Prussian province in 1867. After the First World War, Schleswig was divided between Denmark and Germany after two plebiscites in 1920. The Danish part (3,900 square km) is now the major part of the Sønderjylland County, whereas the German part (5,000 square km) has been a part of the Schleswig-Holstein *Land* since 1946. (See Map of Helstat)

Survey

A review of national minorities in Sønderjylland/Schleswig may adequately confine itself to the period after the expansion of mass-nationalism. This period can be subdivided into four parts, distinguishable by differing government policies towards the minorities.

Although national tensions emerged in this area between 1800 and 1850 no national policy of the Danish *Helstat* government towards Schleswig had yet emerged at that stage. Absolutist civil servants assessed the Schleswig-Holstein and the Danish movement as disturbing elements. However, the highest priority of the Danish king was the preservation of the *Helstat*, and all concessions and sanctions made by him to the conflicting parties should be seen in this perspective. Three major ethnic groups existed in Schleswig—

Danes, Germans and Frisians—which were not recognized by the government in terms of their emerging national identities.

During the period from 1851 until 1920 there were two groups, which although they were minorities could be distinguished as majorities at the local level: a geographically delimited group of pro-German Schleswigans in the reestablished *Helstat*, present from 1851 through 1863, and the Danish South Jutlanders in Prussia present from 1864 until 1920, including the time when Prussia was a part of the German Empire founded in 1871. These minorities obtained some political support and private assistance from their nations of identification, but in general they were not supported officially, and their host countries conducted an obvious and often crude assimilation policy towards them. These policies only applied to a restricted area within the restored *Helstat*, and in Prussia only after an extended transition period. In both cases minority relations were on either side of the border, first the Danish side and then the German.

From 1920 there were minorities on both sides of the new border. These minorities were supported by their nations of identification, in respect of their organisational and cultural activities. However, the German North Schleswigans received no such support until the curtailment of inflation in Germany in 1924. Both minorities were officially accepted, and to a certain degree supported, by their host countries, especially over education. Both host countries accepted the right of the minorities to receive education in their own language. However, the minorities still conceived of their relationship with the host country as antagonistic, overtly or covertly. The years between 1920 and 1955 can be divided into four distinct periods. The first is between 1920 and 1932, when Denmark and the Weimar Republic enjoyed a mutually tolerant relationship. The second is from 1933 until 1945, during which the Hitler regime, the Second World War and the German occupation of Denmark resulted in extreme antagonism. The third covers the period between 1945 and 1948, when the end of the hostilities resulted in the enormous growth of a pro-Danish movement in South Schleswig and, at the same time, in a judicial retribution of the German minority in North Schleswig. The last, between 1948 and 1955, is a period of consolidation of both minorities. During these periods the host countries did not give up their intention of assimilating the minorities, but the latter were granted the right to pursue cultural activities especially concerning the educational system. During the 20's and after the Second World War the policy of the host countries toward their respective minorities was to some extent reciprocal.

Denmark and the Federal Republic of Germany became allied when the FRG became a member of NATO in 1955. This represented the beginning of an era, which has continued to the present day, in which both minorities are sympathetically supported by their host countries and their nations of identification. Attempts by the host countries to assimilate their resident minorities have ceased. Conflicts between minorities and their host countries are now so restricted that the Danish German border region has become exemplary for the treatment of minorities.

Point of Departure

Around 1830 Southern Jutland was inhabited by three main ethnic groups distinguishable by languages: Firstly the German-speakers, who originally lived south of the line which extended from the towns of Schleswig and Husum, but before 1800 had expanded along the northern bank of the Sli inlet. Secondly the Frisian-speakers on the North Sea islands and along the west coast between Husum and Tønder; and finally the Danish-speaking inhabitants of North Schleswig. Danish-speaking were also the population of the ridge of land stretching down to the Husum-Schleswig line, but the Danish language had lost ground in Angel, between the Sli and the Inlet of Flensburg. This prosperous region was in a stage of transition between the use of Danish and German. Around 1850 it had changed entirely to German. The three main groups spoke Low

German and Danish dialects in addition to various Frisian vernacular languages. In 1803 the entire duchy, including the cities, had 276,300 inhabitants. In 1830 the population had risen to around 330,000, of which 122,000 spoke German, 23,000 used Frisian languages and 185,000 spoke Danish. Of the Danish-speakers, 109,000 lived in a cultural environment entirely dominated by the Danish language, whereas 76,000 used German as a church and school language. The latter group used Danish as a colloquial language only or in parallel with German. Of these 76,000 people, 30,000 lived in the North Schleswigan boroughs and Flensburg where German was used as the cultural language of the upper classes and the rest spoke the popular language of the agricultural environment. However, Flensburg and Tønder had a tradition of speaking Low German. (See map of language borders)

The institutional use of Danish and/or German did not correspond with the geographical distribution of both languages. The legal language of the duchy was German, which in 1840 was replaced by Danish in regions where it was spoken in churches and schools. These areas included the countryside in North Schleswig extending to a line corresponding roughly to the border as it exists today. However, exceptions did exist: German was used in all grammar schools and teacher training colleges, and was the predominant language of town churches and town schools.

In the towns the prevalent ideology in the upper strata concerning the state has been described as "Helstats-patriotism".[1] This patriotism was not connected with concepts of the "people" and the "mother tongue", but was rooted in loyalty towards a well-regulated country which generated a pride in citizenship. Indeed, until the war with England (1807–1814), the inhabitants of the Helstat, both Danish- and German-speaking, had a great sense of pride in their prolific country which, during almost 90 years of peace, had provided them with the opportunity for profitable trade under condi-

---

[1] Cf. Japsen: *Den nationale udvikling*, pp. 51–54.

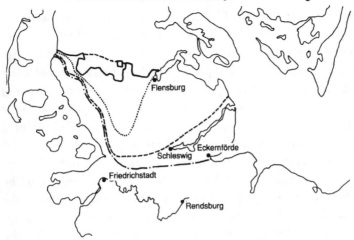

The Language borders

—— ca. 1950

······ ca. 1900

- - - - ca. 1800

—·—·— in the Middle Ages

Approximate Borders of Danish Language Spoken by the People

tions of neutrality while other major powers fought each other for most of the 18th century. The government of this country was also progressive and after 1784 introduced among other things major reforms in the agrarian sector and other areas. However, by 1830 the feelings of triumphant pride and joy in state citizenship had largely been dissipated. The war years had destroyed the finances of the *Helstat* and the strong creditor city of Hamburg which, although lying beyond the borders of the Monarchy, had become the economic capital of the duchies. Nevertheless, patriotism within the *Helstat* continued to play an important role in the policies of the Kingdom and the duchies until the dissolution of the *Helstat* in 1864. At this time patriotism had lost ground to new national ideologies, especially among the younger generation.

The patriotism of the *Helstat* was reconcilable with strong regional patriotism nourished by a variety of traditional legal and administrative policies including innumerable privileges and exemptions. The progress towards equality which had characterized Danish legal and administrative policies under the absolutist regime of the 1700s failed to penetrate the Duchies due to resistance from the local landed aristocracy *(ridderskab)*, who were worried about a possible diminution of their traditional privileges.

Although there were some feelings of particularism within the duchies, they remained fully loyal to the *Helstat,* and this could be paralleled with a strong sense of Danish identity which existed in the capital and upper classes of the other major cities within the kingdom also in full loyalty to the *Helstat.*[2] It should be noted that the peasants resident in both the duchies and the kingdom were deeply loyal to the King.

The Expansion of Nationalism

In the late 1830s opposing national ideologies gained ground in the loosely integrated societies that composed the *Helstat.* Support for these ideologies was boosted by the July Revolution of 1830. After the revolution the King was prompted to set up Consultative Estates Assemblies in the parts of his country which belonged to the German Confederation. This he had been obliged to do since 1815 according to the convention of the Confederation. The obligation obviously applied to Holstein, but in order not to treat one of his lands unfairly, the King also set up one Estates Assembly in Schleswig and two in the kingdom. It should be noted that the small Duchy of Lauenburg was not included in the *Helstat* until 1815 and that it already had an old-fashioned Diet. The Schleswigan Estates Assembly met for the first time in 1836, thereby

[2] Feldbæk: "Denmark", pp. 87–100; Feldbæk: "Fædrelandet og Indfødsret. 1700-tallets danske identitet", pp. 111–230.

allowing fairly free political expression. Between 1815 and 1836 nationalist ideologies were only of interest to small groups with few external contacts. After 1836 they were being disseminated by small but highly active groups to a much wider audience.[3] An essential part of this presentation was the combination of new political philosophy with contemporary political and economic problems. This is illustrated by the language question. As mentioned above, the administration and legal language in Northern Schleswig was German, whereas the peasants spoke Danish. This inconsistency prompted a North Schleswigan peasant spokesman to declare in the Schleswigan Estates Assembly that "my compatriots will be more at ease when the news arrives that from now on our mother tongue is also the language of civil servants."[4] An example from the German side was the so-called "Branch Bank case" *(Filialbanksagen)*. The finance of the duchies had been a controversial issue since the collapse of the state economy during the final phases of the war in 1813. After the emergence of nationalism the Danish National Branch Banks, which were projected in Rendsburg and Flensburg, were suddenly perceived as Trojan Horses for the promotion of Danish economic identity. According to one Schleswig-Holstein leader, the spirit of the public reacted *"wider Reichsbankgeld und die dänische Bank"* ("against Danish currency and the Danish bank").[5] The national leaders of Schleswig-Holstein and Denmark demonstrated great ingenuity in their attempts to mobilize the population in support of their cases. In addition to discussion of topical issues, their arsenal included petitions to the Estates, the founding of newspapers, the formation of associations

---

[3] Hroch: Social Preconditions, pp. 22–24, and his investigation in the Schleswigan case, "An Example of a Minority National Movement: The Danes in Schleswig", ibidem pp. 117–124; Rerup: "The Danes in Schleswig from the National Awakening to 1933", pp. 225–253.

[4] Rerup: *Slesvig og Holsten efter 1830*, p. 63.

[5] Cf. Jensen: *Nordfriesland*, p. 105.

and the organization of mass meetings, song festivals, libraries and folk high schools.[6]

At least two sorts of nationalism were discernable in the period before the Schleswigan wars. German nationalism in Schleswig-Holstein tended to be élitist and conservative, first because it included the cultured, and secondly because it was dependent on support from the powerful landed aristocracy. Support for Schleswig-Holstein nationalism was also provided by the very anti-liberal Duke of Augustenburg, head of the cadet branch of the Oldenburg dynasty, who would perhaps have a claim to the crown if there was no male successor in the royal branch.[7]

Danish nationalism took a more popular form partly due to the influence of the religious and cultural leader Grundtvig (1782–1872) and partly because it was firmly supported by the large homogeneous peasantry, originally a rather conservative class. The Danish nationalist movement in Southern Jutland, however, at first anti-liberal, found that it had to cooperate with the National Liberal opposition within the kingdom. This opposition in turn needed the support of the peasantry within the kingdom in their struggle for a more liberal constitution. Therefore the Danish nationalist movement tended to more popular and egalitarian policies.[8] In Copenhagen the idea of a united Scandinavia—especially shared by students and younger graduates—played an important role in counterbalancing Germany and the national movement for unity and freedom in the German countries.[9] The situation was complicated by a specific Schleswig-Holstein movement that enlisted some of the residents of the North Schleswigan towns. This kind of nationalism

---

[6] Cf. Carr: *Schleswig-Holstein*, pp. 181–198 and Rerup: *Slesvig og Holsten*, pp. 85–93; Rerup: "Channels of Communication", in: Kappeler, Adanir & O'Day (eds.): *Formation of National Elites*, pp. 309–326.

[7] Cf. Clausen: "Den augustenborgske politik", pp. 197–202 and 275–280.

[8] Rerup: "Elitärer und emanzipatorischer Nationalismus", p. 483.

[9] Cf. Becker-Christensen: *Skandinaviske drømme*, Chapters 4 & 5.

represented a development of the older Schleswig-Holstein identity within the *Helstat* rather than a kind of German nationalism. This was the case at least until the 1840s. Adherents of this movement took a stand for Denmark or for Schleswig-Holstein at a late point in time.[10] A similar case is found during the emergence of rural "Home-Germanism" *(Hjemmetyskhed)* in the county of Haderslev. This had its roots in a conservative protest against the political radicalization of the nationalist Danish Schleswigan Association (Den slesvigske Forening) in 1844. The majority of peasants who joined the protest movement, often people of a certain standing, spoke Danish just like their neighbours who chose to become Danes. However, they opted for the supremacy of the German language, since they regarded this as a prerequisite for the preservation of the special rights and privileges of Schleswig.[11] Also more recently the "Home German" peasants clung to a strong regional identity in addition to their German nationalism.

The reception of nationalist doctrines was determined by local preconditions. One factor could be social polarization, e.g. in Aabenraa between ship and shipyard owners, their employees and sailors;[12] another factor could be the intimate cooperation between urban trade groups and peasants, as was the case in Haderslev between artisans, merchants, innkeepers and peasants from the surrounding area.[13] Existing tensions between civil servants and peasants triggered political pressure from the peasants.[14] Corresponding tensions existed between the Duke of Augustenburg and the peasants in Als,[15] in addition to antagonism between areas with different

[10] Cf. Japsen: *Udviklingen i Aabenraa*, pp. 95 and 190–193.

[11] Cf. Pontoppidan Thyssen: *Vækkelse, kirkefornyelse og nationalitetskamp*, p. 315.

[12] Japsen: *Den nationale udvikling*, p. 260.

[13] Cf. Fangel: *Haderslev bys Historie*, pp. 403–408.

[14] Pontoppidan Thyssen: *Vækkelse, kirkefornyelse og nationalitetskamp*, p. 395.

[15] Cf. Clausen: "Dansk og Tysk på Als 1812–48", pp. 191–195.

legal status, e.g. the West Schleswigan Enclaves.[16] While Danish-educated clergymen were apparently indifferent to the spread of Danish nationalism in the County of Haderslev, German-educated clergymen and teachers were instrumental in spreading moderate Schleswig-Holstein doctrines.[17] A large majority of the Frisians joined the Schleswig-Holstein movement, but they were not strictly radical Schleswig-Holstein supporters. Loyalty to the King was deeply rooted in North Friesland, and the special geographic conditions of this area, governing trade, land-use and administration, promoted a strong feeling of uniqueness and pride.[18] As can be seen from the above, any scrutiny of nationalism in Schleswig reveals a surprising range of patterns of reception in a relatively small population.

The forceful endeavours of both national camps led to civil war in 1848, when the February Revolution shook the governments of the European nations. However, it must be emphasised that the nationalist mobilization of the population, despite the efforts of the activists, appealed only to a minority. The circulation of most newspapers was still very restricted, membership of associations was small, and even big popular events with many visitors attracted little more than a fraction of the population. In the cities, as well as in the countryside, large groups did not join in national unrest or only did so reluctantly. Many people, typically the elderly, did not sympathize with the new doctrines which had "sown the seeds of discord and strife, arousing hatred and animosity among the different nationalities within the country which previously walked hand in hand peacefully, mutually promoting prosperity and happiness."[19] The remaining majority could not afford to worry about anything but its

[16] Gregersen: "Nogle betragtninger", p. 26.—The Enclaves were small areas located mainly in Western Schleswig and on the Frisian Isles which belonged to the Kingdom from the Middle Ages until 1864.
[17] Pontoppidan Thyssen: *Vækkelse, kirkefornyelse og nationalitetskamp*, p. 314.
[18] Cf. Jensen: *Nordfriesland*, p. 130.
[19] Cf. Iversen: *Jens Wulffs dagbog*, p. 192.

day today survival. Nationalist mobilization of Danes and Germans, however, was profoundly affected by the three-year-long civil war and by the changing military fortunes of each side.

The Period between the Schleswigan Wars, 1850–1863

The Three Years War (1848–1850) ended with a Danish military victory, but conflicts still existed politically in the sense that the National Liberal program of the Ejder border, i.e. an incorporation of Southern Jutland/Schleswig in Denmark, could not be realized. The great European powers demanded that the multi-ethnic *Helstat* should be reconstructed in order to monitor the entrance to the Baltic Sea and the excellent harbour of Kiel. Prussia and Austria were additionally promised that all parts of the Danish monarchy should have equal status, thus giving Schleswig, Holstein and Lauenburg and the kingdom an equal position within the Danish Monarchy. These promises created insurmountable obstacles for fair constitutional development of the *Helstat* and were important preconditions for the war of 1864. After the Three Year War, Southern Jutland was ruled separately from Holstein for the first time since the Middle Ages. This situation provided a group of Danish public servants and politicians the opportunity to operate a national cultural policy within a well-defined area south of the old church and school language border. Danish was still spoken in this area but had lost ground to Low German in the decades after 1800. This had also been the case in the flourishing Angel region. In this mixed language belt the language ordinances of 1851 introduced Danish as the school language, leaving only four lessons a week for German, whereas the church language was either Danish or German on alternate Sundays. In addition the school language of the North Schleswigan towns became Danish, except in Christiansfeld, a community of Moravian brethren. In the churches of the towns the languages alternated every fortnight. A special policy was devised for Flensburg due to the loyalty of the inhabitants during the war. In this city German remained the administrative and teaching language, but Danish was used voluntarily in schools and churches. This policy was accepted without problems.[20]

The language policy in the Middle Schleswig area failed to achieve its stated goal "of wresting an unfinished conquest from Germanism",[21] and in fact proved harmful to Denmark's reputation abroad. Furthermore there was a popular reaction. For instance, in many areas church services in Danish were boycotted and the population accelerated the transition to German as a colloquial language. This was especially true for Angel. Only in entirely Danish-speaking areas were the language ordinances successful to some extent. The passive resistance of the people against the language ordinances did not lead to organised protest.

It is inaccurate to define the Middle Schleswig population as a national minority. The entire population of the duchy was subjected to a reactionary regime of public servants, who surveyed suspiciously any movement among German- and Danish-speaking people. German-speaking people were, obviously, after the civil war, more exposed to surveillance, but this was a political and not a national measure. Neither the Frisians nor the German-speaking regions outside the mixed language belt were pressured into absorbing any Danish culture. The pressure to adopt the Danish language was only exerted in the area defined by the historical language border.

The Danes in Prussia, 1864/67–1920

The war of 1864 was fought predominantly in Southern Jutland. The ramparts of Dybbøl were under siege by the Germans for more than two months. During this period the idea that the population of the duchy could be segregated according to nationality spread through a large proportion of the population. Schleswigans had con-

[20] Cf. Bracker: "Die dänische Sprachpolitik 1850–64".
[21] Jørgensen: *Breve*, p. 135.

Danish church and school language

the mixed area, in which Danish is introduced as school language and every fortnight as church language

German church and school language

The Language Ordinances of 1851

ceived of the duchy as an indivisible unit, obviously due to their traditional regionalism. The German wars of 1864 and 1866 resulted in the annexation in 1867 of the duchies of Schleswig and Holstein as a single Prussian province. When the Habsburg emperor entrusted his rights to the Prussian king at the Prague peace conference of 1866, Napoleon III proposed that a clause be added to the conveyance article of the peace treaty. The clause in Article 5 stated that " ...the populations in the Northern Districts of Schleswig shall be ceded to Denmark when by a free plebiscite they vote for reunification with Denmark." The clause was unspecific on the time limit for execution and the geographical area it covered. In 1867 and 1868 Prussia initiated negotiations with Denmark concerning the enactment of this clause, but withdrew when international relations changed in favour of Prussia. In 1878 Prussia induced Austria-Hungary to agree to a nullification of the clause in return for Prussian support of Austrian policy in the Balkans. However, the Southern Jutlanders considered Article 5 to be of the utmost importance because it encapsulated their hope for reunification even after its cancellation.[22]

Shortly after the annexation of Schleswig and Holstein, the result of elections for the North German Confederation parliament, held in February 1867 and again in August the same year, produced a Danish majority in North Schleswig down to a line north of Tønder and south of Flensburg. The Danish Southern Jutlanders had an overwhelming and cohesive majority in this area, especially in the north and west where it was more than 85%. Whereas the Prussian state had vigorously proceeded with the modernization of the entire provincial judicial and administrative system, the most drastic changes to economic and industrial policies took place in the southern part of the province close to Hamburg, Neumünster and Kiel. Moreover, the northern part of the country was a genuine agrarian peripheral area. Among the North Schleswigan towns only Flensburg grew rapidly, with its population tripling between the years 1860 and 1920. Other towns grew much more modestly, and the position of the agrarian sector of the country remained unchanged. Farming in North Schleswig followed the intensive Danish pattern and held a strong position with around 80% of the farms being owned by Danish-minded peasants. However, emigration from the northern half of Schleswig (roughly the area which was reunified with Denmark in 1920) was high, with around 60,000 people leaving between 1864 and 1920. This emigration was caused partly by resistance to changes, instigated by the Prussian authorities, e.g. the introduction of Prussian conscrip-

---

[22] Cf. Rerup: *Slesvig och Holsten,* p. 220.

tion, but the majority of emigrants left because of a static trade and agricultural structure which, despite good economic development, could not absorb the increase in population. For example, tradition prescribed that there would be no division of farms between brothers at a shift of generation. Whereas the population of Prussia grew by 63% and that of Denmark by 51% during the period between 1871 and 1910, the population of North Schleswig grew no more than 8% with a total of 165,000.

Prussia had great experience in converting annexed populations into loyal subjects. This subjugation was exercised within the framework of a society founded on the rule of law, even if it was costly in terms of money and time for the individual to sue the authorities. A compulsory three-year period of military service in the Prussian army was introduced immediately. Primary schools were gradually Germanized. In 1871 six lessons of German a week were introduced (except for the first grades) and in 1878 primary schools were made bilingual. In 1888 the schools became exclusively German except for six scripture lessons in Danish (however, in higher grades four lessons were in Danish and two in German). Danish private schools were closed after 1878. The Prussian policy towards the Danish minority followed the same pattern of coercion as that applied to the much bigger Polish minority in the Eastern Provinces, although with some delay.[23] Furthermore, a series of oppressive measures were enforced in order to restrict political representation and cultural activities of the Danish population, particularly in the press and associations. It was the policy after 1891 to buy Danish farms for immigrants—with little success, however. A similar "struggle about farmland" (*"jordkamp"*) also took place in the Polish areas of Prussia, although Prussian coercion policy was enforced with varying degrees. In general, Prussian repression paralleled the increase in organization

---

[23] Cf. Hauser: *Preussische Staatsräson*, pp. 62–73; Molik: "The Poles in the Grand Duchy of Poznan, 1840–1914", in: Kappeler et al.: *Formation of National Elites*, pp. 17 ff.

and solidarity of the Danish population. However, the current state of German-Danish relationships might influence repression; for example, Germany would seek to influence Danish foreign policy by stepping up the repression of North Schleswigans.

The Organizing of the Southern Jutlanders

In the period from 1850 to 1864, national associations from before 1848 declined, leaving the Danish part of the population disorganized and with few leaders when Schleswig and Holstein were annexed. However, an informal cooperation between urban and rural notabilities existed on several occasions, such as elections. Until around 1880 the leaders of the Danish population conducted a "policy of protest" rooted in hopes of a fulfilment of Article 5. Initially this expectation was based on the possibility of French intervention, and after the defeat of France in the war of 1870–1871, in the simple belief that justice would be done by any means. Protest policy resulted in the refusal of elected Danish representatives to take up their positions in the Prussian diet since they would be obliged to swear an oath of loyalty to the Prussian constitution. Further resistance was manifested in a mass emigration of young men to avoid military service. Moreover, inhabitants of the duchies could opt for Denmark until 1870 under the terms of the peace treaty of Vienna in 1864. In this case they became Danish subjects but could remain on native soil according to an agreement between Germany and Denmark reached in 1872. However, they were regarded as foreigners and would be subject to expulsion if they caused the slightest trouble.[24] The protest policy had the effect of weakening the Danish fraction of the population and was gradually changed to a long-term resistance. The highest priority became to strengthen the minority in order to secure its survival in German society until an opportunity for reunification emerged. It was conceivable that this opportunity could arise if Germany lost a

[24] Cf. Rerup: *Slesvig og Holsten*, p. 235 and 312.

war against other great powers or in the event of a democratization of German society. After 1899, the German Social Democratic Party, among others, supported self-determination.[25]

From 1888 on, a Voters' Union organized the political activities of the Danish minority. A North Schleswigan School Association was established in 1892, and provided funds to encourage adolescents over compulsory school age to attend a further education college or a folk high school in Denmark. Before this time, in 1880, a Language Association had already been established which administered book collections and distributed song books etc. Free church congregations and lecture societies were established which had to meet in private village halls, as public halls were closed for Danish activities. Sports clubs emerged after the turn of the century. The agricultural community had already been organized in many special associations after the Three Year War.

The emergence in the late 1880s of an organizational network reinforced Danish national consciousness in the population, bringing it closely in line with modern Denmark. However, in the slowly growing towns of North Schleswig a Danish majority could not be maintained. And the association network of North Schleswig did not gain ground in the Danish-speaking districts south of the present border. Flensburg, for instance, which had always previously sent a Danish representative to the German parliament, ceased to do so from 1884, when the city became industrialized. From 1887 workers in Flensburg, especially those employed in the shipyard, and including those speaking Danish, began to vote for the Social Democratic Party.

The prosperous agricultural community of North Schleswig provided a strong basis for Danish activity. An average farm had around 40 hectares, which allowed economic independence from both the towns and the Prussian authorities. At the same time other members of the rural population were dependent on the farm

[25] Cf. Callesen: *Die Schleswig-Frage*, p. 24.

owners.[26] As already mentioned, contact between the Southern Jutlanders and Denmark was intensified. Many originally conservative
peasants, like their peers in the kingdom, gradually switched loyalty
to "Venstre" ("the Left", the party of the peasants in Denmark),
and it became usual for them to be trained in Denmark, which by
the 1880s had achieved a leading position in agricultural development. Moreover the Southern Jutlanders were Danish-speaking
anyway, and numerous areas had such a large majority that German settlers could not get a foothold. For this reason any effort by
the Germans to buy land from the pro-Danish peasants would almost certainly be in vain.

The Referendum of 1920

After the defeat of Germany in the First World War two plebiscites
took place in Southern Jutland in 1920 in accordance with the
treaty of Versailles. The first one took place in North Schleswig, in
an area down to the present border. It was an *en bloc* plebiscite in
order to give the population of North Schleswig the opportunity to
sanction the cession to Denmark. The second plebiscite was arranged five weeks later in the adjacent area south of the border. The
purpose of this plebiscite—a plebiscite of definition—was to find
out if there were Danish majorities in that region. According to the
results from every municipality and the town of Flensburg, the border could be moved further south.[27] In North Schleswig (the First
Zone) 101,632 people voted, which represented 91.5% of the electorate. 75,431 (74.2 %) voted for Denmark, and 25,329 (24.9 %)
for Germany. In the Second Zone the turnout was 65,000 or 91.7
% of the electorate, and close to 52,000 voted German (or around

[26] Schultz Hansen: *Det Nordslesvigske landbrug,* p. 17.
[27] Rerup: "Den territoriale selvbestemmelsesret", p. 151; Rerup &
Doege: "The Schleswig-Holstein Question to 1933", in: Smith et al. (ed):
Ethnic groups in international relations.

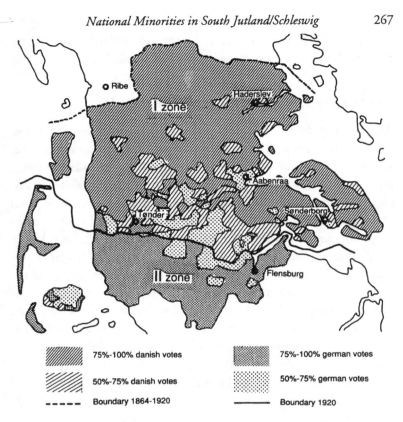

75%-100% danish votes

50%-75% danish votes

- - - - Boundary 1864-1920

75%-100% german votes

50%-75% german votes

———— Boundary 1920

Results of the Schleswig Plebiscites in 1920

80%), 13,000 (around 20%) Danish. Both plebiscites generated strong nationalist emotions, particularly in the Second Zone.

The new border created two minorities: a German one in North Schleswig (lowest number of votes: 7,505 in 1920, highest number: 15,016 in 1939, corresponding to 14.3 and 15.9 % of the total vote) and a smaller, Danish, minority in South Schleswig, mainly centered on Flensburg which represented 4,000 to 5,000 votes in the years before 1933. The Frisians found themselves divided by the plebiscite. A Schleswig-Frisian group emerged and campaigned for the development of Frisian culture following the patterns of Nordic cultural life. This group was pressured during the following years, especially under the Nazi regime when it was formally banned.[28]

The German Minority in Denmark, 1920–1945

The German minority rapidly established an organized social and political network and demanded not only cultural autonomy but also a revision of the border. Its members (which included in urban areas professional people and artisans, and in the countryside peasants who often had a little more than the average amount of land) often spoke colloquial Danish in the countryside and kept German as the language for meetings and cultural activities. The Danish government maintained the principle that members of the German minority should be treated in the same way as any other citizens of the country, and had no wish to treat the minority as a segregated community. Similarly, the government had no intention of setting up a bilateral treaty with Germany, since experience from the period between the two Schleswigan wars had demonstrated that such a treaty might give the more powerful partner in such a relationship the opportunity to interfere in the internal affairs of the weaker.[29] In fact, anybody was free to join the German minority. In the public schools of North Schleswig, German language sections were established and in addition the German minority, like all other citizens, were free to make use of the private education system. In comparison to other parts of Europe, this provided a generous opportunity, since the public sector paid the main part of the operating costs, with the remainder being paid by the parents. The private school system of the German minority gradually expanded, due to the preference of the minority for a private system with less supervision by Danish authorities. When Hitler came to power, the number of private German schools doubled.

---

[28] Steensen: *Die friesische Bewegung*, pp. 186–229 and 398–413.
[29] Becker-Christensen: *Dansk mindretalspolitik*, pp. 23 and 111.

In the 1920s, the main national conflict in North Schleswig was a revival of the land struggle. North Schleswigan agriculture had become accustomed to protection under German administration, but with the introduction of free trade it was confronted with the necessity of more intensive farming to supply the Danish export market. In addition it had to change from German to Danish currency. As a consequence, there were many difficulties and short-lived protest movements among factions of the North Schleswigan farming population, especially around 1925. The German minority sympathized with, and tried to profit from, these protests but without result. A credit institution, secretly supported by the German government, also attempted to increase the area of farmland owned by the German minority peasants, by offering cheap loans in return for signs of sympathy with German attitudes. Rumours about this got out and spoiled the attempt to expand the minority in this way.

The Nazis were slow to regiment the German minority organizations despite pre-existing conservative-nationalist attitudes which paved the way for the dissemination of certain aspects of National Socialist ideology.[30] However, due to their economic dependence on the German Reich, the fate of the minority was inevitable. The regimentation *(Gleichschaltung)* was completed in 1935 and led to an aggravation of national tension in the region. There had been a national antagonism between Germans and Danes earlier, which was aggravated after 1935 by a political antagonism between democrats and devotees of dictatorship. The continued demand by the German minority for a revision of the border was also reinforced, but these views were muffled by the leadership in the Reich in order to avoid upsetting the Scandinavian countries.[31] During the German occupation of Denmark between 1940 and 1945, nationalistic tensions escalated to open hatred. Young members of the minority joined the

---

[30] Cf. Japsen: *Den fejlslagne germanisering*, p. 241.

[31] Tägil: *Deutschland und die deutsche Minderheit*, pp. 32–39, 127–130 and 143.

German forces as volunteers, while others remained in North Schleswig and helped the occupation power as auxiliaries and guards. The German minority forced the appointment of a special school supervisor in 1942, and replaced the parliamentary representative, which it had won in the elections since 1920, with a German office attached to the Prime Minister's Department (1943). The minority leaders doubted that the seat could be held in the general election of 1943, due to widespread military service among the younger males of the minority.

The Danish Minority in Germany, 1920–1945

After 1920 the Danish minority in Germany, resident mainly in Flensburg and environs, was forced to consolidate and organize. The dense social network which the Danish North Schleswigans had developed in the Prussian period had only penetrated the Danish community in Flensburg to a limited extent. In contrast to the German minority in Denmark and to the Danish movement in North Schleswig, the Danes south of the new border consisted almost entirely of workers (60–80%), and low-paid wage earners (around 11%). The members often spoke colloquial German, and Danish was reserved for meetings in Danish associations. Close to one-fifth of the Danes in Flensburg had been born north of the new border.[32] The central leadership of this group was in the hands of Danish-speaking people in the liberal professions and executives from the ranks of the Danish movement itself. The Danish minority in South Schleswig found itself threatened during the first years of unrest in the Weimar Republic. For a number of years the relationship between the minority and successive governments in Denmark and individual Danish politicians was strained by a fierce campaign for the incorporation of Flensburg into Denmark, even after the demonstration of a German

---

[32] Cf. Noack: *Det danske mindretal,* on the composition of the minority, pp. 303–325.

majority in the Second Zone plebiscite of 1920. After the plebiscites this campaign resulted in a governmental and constitutional crisis in Denmark and was only resolved with difficulty. For this reason, some Danish politicians looked sceptically on the minority in South Schleswig and the organizations which continued to support it in Denmark after 1920. A broad consensus on whether pure cultural support should be given to the Danish South Schleswigans was not obtained until 1930, and only after the minority and its supporting organization in Denmark had been reconciled to the Danish parliamentary situation.[33]

Flensburg like North Schleswig established a double school system. The modest resources of the minority only permitted it to use Danish branches in public schools. Local authorities further restricted mass enrolment in these branches by testing the language capabilities of the children. Furthermore, although the constitution of the Weimar Republic had guaranteed "foreign language parts of population" a "free, nation-specific development" (Article 113), the majority of the children from the Danish minority were barred from the Danish branches because they were German-speaking. For these reasons a private school system had to be established which included both primary schools and a first grade of a secondary school *(Realskole)*. The local German attitude towards the Danish Southern Schleswigans had great repercussions on the national unrest during the plebiscite.[34] Finally in 1928, considering German-Polish negotiations, the principle of individual national self-determination was laid down by a Prussian school ordinance which stated: "The Danish Minority ... is defined as that part of the population within the

---

[33] The Easter Crisis of 1920 was a severe political conflict threatening the Danish King and dividing the parties and the population. Among other things the crisis was triggered by the Dannevirke Movement which would not give up hope of achieving territory south of the border in spite of the results of the second plebiscite; cf. Kaarsted: *Påskekrisen 1920*, passim.

[34] Noack: *Det danske mindretal*, p. 129 and pp. 174–190.

Reich which declare Danish nationality. This declaration shall
neither be tested nor contested."[35]

After 1933 the minority was allowed a narrow scope of activity,
e.g. by its press, which was censored, and by representatives in the city
council of Flensburg. Although a few new Danish private schools
were established, individuals in the minority were persecuted, and especially after 1936 many were exposed to severe social pressure, e.g.
unemployment and deprivation of social security support. During the
war the activity of the minority was almost completely paralysed.[36]

The South Schleswigan Movement, 1945–1955

The Danish minority, which had been reduced, little by little, to
around 2,500 members, became a focus for a pro-Danish mass
movement in South Schleswig after the disruption of state and society following the Second World War. The annual intake of new
members peaked in 1946, and overall membership was at its highest
in 1948, with 75,000. The number of votes in favour of the pro-
Danish movement reached a maximum at the general elections to
the Schleswig-Holstein parliament in April 1946. This was equivalent to 99,500 votes, or (about) 55% of the resident population in
the region, which had recently seen a large influx of refugees from
East Germany.[37] The pro-Danish mass movement was supported by
private groups in Denmark and by the Danish government. However, the desire among the South Schleswigans for an immediate
plebiscite was never shared by a majority in the Danish parliament.[38]
The movement was active all over South Schleswig down to the old
Ejder border but had a stronghold in Flensburg, Schleswig and the
northern border regions. It involved all levels of society.

[35] Noack: *Det danske mindretal* I, Chapter V and Broszat: "Außen- und
innenpolitische Aspekte", pp. 407–12.
[36] Mogensen: *Dansk i hagekorsets skygge*, pp. 282 ff.
[37] *Beiträge zur historischen Statistik*, p. 80 and *Lange Reihen*, p. 22.
[38] Rerup: *Grænsen*, p. 82.

This pro-Danish movement found itself being counteracted by the British occupation and domestic German authorities as the Allies gradually reestablished an ordered political environment within the new Schleswig-Holstein *Land.* The occupation authorities considered the pro-Danish movement a disturbing element against their vigorous efforts to reorganize political life in Schleswig-Holstein. Furthermore, politicians in Schleswig-Holstein conceived of the Danish movement as motivated by materialism and separatism while the country was in a state of emergency. The resident German population, in addition to the many East German refugees, could not accept that pro-Danish, German-speaking Schleswigans, with no prior cultural affiliation with Denmark, should demand the status of a national minority or claim to be unified with Denmark. Many of the new members of the minority reconciled this by enrolling their children in Danish schools. In 1945 nine Danish schools with around 450 children still existed. In 1948 the private Danish school system had increased to 60 schools with 14,500 pupils. A few public schools in Flensburg had a Danish branch, but this system disappeared shortly afterwards. The lending of Danish books in private Danish minority libraries increased enormously.

The European political situation in 1948, exacerbated by the beginning of the Cold War, led to negotiations between Denmark and Britain. They were accompanied by talks between the Danish minority and the government of Schleswig-Holstein. These activities resulted in the Kiel Statement in 1949. This Statement was intended to tone down the national tension in South Schleswig. In the Statement it was declared that the Danish and Frisian minorities enjoyed full civil rights, and the right of individual national self-determination was recognized as in the Prussian ordinance of 1928. Along with the reestablishment of German society after the currency reform and the foundation of the Federal Republic, the membership of the pro-Danish movement declined and so did the votes sympathetic with the movement. Nevertheless it still commanded a total of 71,864 votes in the general election of 1950. By 1957 this number was reduced by half to 34,136 and had stabilized at its present level by the 1960s. It should be noted that an overwhelming proportion of the Danish minority were, and still are, wage-earners.

The early Schleswig-Holstein governments which took office after 1950 resumed a pinprick policy towards the Danish minority, in part to reduce its membership down to a basic level, a "genuine core", and in part to achieve better conditions for the German minority in North Schleswig, but other aspects of German and Schleswig-Holstein domestic politics may have had a bearing on this harassment. The pinprick policy resulted in open scandal when repeated alterations of the Schleswig-Holstein election laws resulted in a failure of the Danish minority to provide a representative in the 1954 Kiel parliament inspite of commanding more than 42,000 votes, in comparison to the situation with the German North Schleswigans, who after a revision of the Danish constitution were granted a representative in parliament with 9,721 votes in 1953.[39]

North of the Border, 1945–1955

North of the border, the liberation of Denmark resulted in a judicial retribution against the German minority as a result of its behaviour during the occupation. Danish collaborators likewise suffered persecution in the whole of Denmark. The German minority found itself especially vulnerable. A fourth of its male members over 15 years of age (2,958) received minor sentences, most frequently for having served in the German military, but only around 90 prosecutions covered more severe crimes. Membership of the minority could be regarded as an extenuating circumstance, and all jail sentences were reduced on parole but without immediate return of voting rights.

---

[39] Before the 1954 election the Danish minority held 4 seats in the Kiel parliament. In Denmark, the German minority was represented in the Parliament *(Folketing)* in 1920–1943 and 1953–1964 when it failed to command a sufficient number of votes. In 1973–1979 the German minority regained a mandate in cooperation with a Danish party.

Anyway, the rehabilitation process was completed in 1955. The reckoning also affected the schools and institutions of the minority, which the German occupation power had forced the Danish National Bank to finance during the war. In November 1945, the German minority established a democratic association which acknowledged the 1920 border and declared its loyalty to the Danish state. In 1946 a new German private school system was founded, supported financially by the Danish authorities and the parents. Some years later it was also supported by German public and private sources. The psychological damage resulting from the occupation and the summer of liberation, nevertheless, remained for a long time.

In North Schleswig, independent peasants are still an important group in the German minority which is dominated by middle class people (1960, 35.90%; 1978, 27.65 %).[40] However, their influence is undermined by migration from rural districts.

The Bonn-Copenhagen Statements

In October 1954 the Danish Parliament expressed discontent with the minority policy applied by the *Land* of Schleswig-Holstein. At this time France had rejected earlier plans to establish an integrated Central European Army. Thus it was necessary to find another way to incorporate the future West German army into the Western European Defence system. This could be done by incorporating the Federal Republic into NATO. As a member of NATO, Denmark had to consent to the admission of new members. Therefore it was addressed in the Danish parliament. When the same issue was discussed at a NATO meeting in Paris, in October 1954, the Danish Foreign Minister, without going so far as to issue an ultimatum, raised the question of the position of the minority, and described the problem as a symbol of future cooperation in Europe. The German

[40] Toft: *Bäuerliche Struktur*, p. 16.

Federal Chancellor immediately declared his willingness to negotiate the issue, and after a rather complicated procedure negotiations resulted in the two so-called Bonn-Copenhagen statements of March 1955, in which Chancellor Konrad Adenauer and Prime Minister H.C. Hansen made a statement on the situation of the respective minorities within their own countries. A German desire for a mutual minority protection treaty had been rejected by Denmark.[41]

The statements removed the obstacles for the representation of Danish South Schleswigans in the parliament of Schleswig-Holstein and further entitled Home Germans to establish private secondary schools in North Schleswig. In fact the Danish and German governments and authorities, including the local government of Schleswig-Holstein, gradually changed their minority policies. Hoping for a final assimilation of the minorities into the host nations, the governments before this had been reluctant to grant rights and assist the minorities. After the statements the governments gradually accepted the minorities as valuable cultural assets in the border region deserving support. The governments in Copenhagen and Bonn had more important issues on the agenda than the continuation of a local antagonism. It also became clear that the minorities had an important role to play in mutual trade, and that competing cultural institutions in the same region provided a stimulating environment. In recent times, the threat against both minorities has changed from covert assimilation to the impact of modern lifestyle, which by migration and urban redevelopment has weakened the traditional strongholds of the minorities, e.g. parts of the countryside of North Schleswig and the backyards of the city of Flensburg. Increased public mobility and the impact of modern mass media, which has proved more invasive and intensive than the efforts of the old-fashioned media in the Prussian period, have contributed to this.

In our time the relative strength of the minorities is such that the German minority had 4,877 votes in South Jutland in the county

[41] Rerup: *Grænsen*, pp. 126—140.

elections in 1989, and ran 18 private schools with 1,184 pupils in 1990. The Danish population south of the border commanded 28,237 votes at the Schleswig-Holstein parliament election of 1992, and at the same time ran 53 schools with 5,270 children.

A major survey carried out in the 1970s, and concerning national affiliation in Northern Schleswig, showed that Germans could be clearly distinguished as individuals identifying themselves and behaving as Germans based on the coinciding critieria of colloquial language, selection of school, membership in associations, church affiliations, newspaper readership, voting patterns etc. Single criteria were considered insufficient to make this distinction.

The investigation concluded that the interviewees demonstrated a desire to maintain a minority with a national identity but at the same time to consider themselves economically, socially and politically as integrated parts of the adopted Danish society.[42] A corresponding investigation of the Danish minority within South Schleswig has not taken place, but it is likely that the same attitudes prevail.

Seen from a European point of view, the situation of the minorities might be considered ideal. This results from several interrelated criteria: Firstly, neither of the minorities challenge the border. Secondly, both are supported sufficiently by their host nation and their nation of identification for the maintenance of a cultural network. Lastly, at a local level the principle of individual national self-determination has been acknowledged; in other words the minorities are open to anybody who wishes to join them and the authorities are not allowed to interfere. Germany and Denmark cooperate well as neighbouring countries. This cooperation was reinforced in 1973 when Denmark joined the EC. And most important, there has been a parallel and convergent development of the German and Danish societies over the last few decades, after more than a hundred years of national rivalry. But of course, some historical factors have

---

[42] Elklit, Noack and Tonsgaard: *Nationalt tilhørsforhold,* p. 187.

facilitated the national co-existence in the border region: the antagonistic cultures are mutually related and, except for the wars in the 19th century, national tensions never resulted in violence.

LITERATURE

General use has been made of:

Fink, Troels: *Rids af Sønderjyllands historie* (A Survey of the History of Southern Jutland), København 1946

Gregersen, H.V.: *Slesvig og Holsten før 1830* (S. & H. before 1830), København 1981

Hoffmann, Erich: "The Germans in the Duchy of Schleswig before 1864: the German Minority in North Schleswig, 1920–33", in: Kappeler, A., F. Adanir & A. O'Day (eds.): *Formation of National Elites*, 1992

Rerup, Lorenz: *Slesvig og Holsten efter 1830* (S. & H. after 1830), København 1982

Rerup, Lorenz: "The Danes in Schleswig from the National Awakening to 1933", in: Kappeler, A., F. Adanir & A. O'Day (eds.): *Formation of National Elites*, 1992

Scharff, Alexander: *Geschichte Schleswig-Holsteins. Ein Überblick* (History of S.-H. A Survey), Neuausg. v. Manfred Jessen-Klingenberg, Freiburg/Würzburg 1991

Special use has been made of:

Becker-Christensen, Henrik: *Dansk mindretalspolitik i Nordslesvig, udformningen af den danske politik over for det tyske mindretal 1918–20* (Danish Minority Policy in Northern Schleswig. The Formation of Danish Policy towards the German Minority), Aabenraa 1984

Becker-Christensen, Henrik: *Skandinaviske drømme og politiske realiteter. Den politiske skandinavisme i Danmark 1830–1850* (Scandinavian Dreams and Political Reality. The Political Scandinavianism in Denmark ...), Aarhus 1981

Bracker A.: "Die dänische Sprachpolitik 1850–64 und die Bevölkerung Mittelschleswigs" (The Danish Language Policy ... and the Population of Middle Schleswig), in: *Zeitschrift für Schleswig-Holsteinische Geschichte* 97, 1972 & 98, 1973

Broszat, Martin: "Außen- und innenpolitische Aspekte in der preußischdeutschen Minderheitenpolitik in der Ära Stresemann" (Foreign and Domestic Political Aspects of the Prussian-German Minority Policy under the Era of Stresemann), in: K. Kluxen e.a. (eds.): *Politische Ideologie und nationalstaatliche Ordnung. Festschrift für Theodor Schieder* (Political Ideologies and Nation State Order. Homage for T.S.), München/Wien 1968

Callesen, G.: *Die Schleswig-Frage in den Beziehungen zwischen dänischer und deutscher Sozialdemokratie von 1912 bis 1924* (The Schleswig Problem in the Relations between Danish and German Social Democratic Parties from 1912 through 1924), Apenrade 1970

Carr W.: *Schleswig-Holstein 1815–48. A Study in National Conflict*, Manchester 1963

Clausen, H.P.: "Dansk og tysk på Als 1812–48" (Danish and German on Als 1812–48) in: *Sønderjyske årbøger* 1966

Clausen, H.P.: "Den augustenborgske politik og dens forlis " (The Augustenborg Policy and its Wreckage), in: Clausen, H.P. & Paulsen, Jørgen: *Augustenborgerne*, Sønderborg 1980

Elklit, J., J. P. Noack & O. Tonsgaard: *Nationalt tilhørsforhold i Nordslesvig* (Germans and Danes in North Schleswig), Aarhus 1978—The English summary in the book is identical with: Allemands et Danois dans le Schleswig du Nord, in: *Recherches sociologiques* VIII:1, 1977

Fangel, Henrik: *Haderslev bys historie 1800–1945*, vol. 1, Haderslev 1975

Feldbæk, Ole : "Denmark", in: Dann, Otto & Dinwiddy, John (eds.): *Nationalism in the Age of the French Revolution*, London 1988

Feldbæk, Ole: "Fædrelandet og Indfødsret. 1700-tallets danske identitet", in: Feldbæk, Ole (ed.): *Dansk identitetshistorie*, vol. 1, 1991

Gregersen, H.V.: "Nogle betragtninger over den historiske baggrund for hjemmetyskheden i Nordslesvig—specielt med henblik på Tønder og Højer" (Some Considerations about the Historical Background for The Home Germanism in North Schleswig—especially concerning Tønder and Højer), in: *Sønderjyske årbøger* 1986

Hauser, Oswald: *Preußische Staatsräson und nationaler Gedanke*, Neumünster 1960

Hroch, Miroslav: *Social Preconditions of National Revival in Europe*, Cambridge 1985

Iversen, Peter Kr. (ed.): *Kniplingskræmmer Jens Wulffs dagbog* (The Diary of the Lace Tradesman), Aabenraa 1955

Japsen, G.: *Den fejlslagne germanisering. Den tyske forening for det nordlige Slesvig—Bidrag til det tyske mindretals historie efter 1864* (The Unsuccessful Germanization. The German Union for Northern Schleswig. Studies in the History of the German Minority after 1864), Aabenraa 1983

Japsen, G.: *Den nationale udvikling i Åbenrå 1800–1850* (The National Development in Åbenrå), Aabenraa 1961

Jensen, Johannes: *Nordfriesland in den geistigen u. politischen Strömungen des 19. Jahrhunderts (1794–1864)* (Northern Friesland in the Spiritual and Political Trends of the 19th Century), Neumünster 1961

Jørgensen, Harald (ed.): *A.D. Jørgensens Breve* (The Letters of A.D. Jørgensen), København 1939

Kaarsted, Tage: *Påskekrisen 1920* (The Easter Crisis 1920), Aarhus 1968

Kappeler, A., F. Adanir & A. O'Day (eds): *The Formation of National Elites* (European Science Foundation: Comparative studies on governments and non-dominant ethnic groups in Europe, 1850–1940; Vol. VI) 1992

Mogensen, Carsten R.: *Dansk i hagekorsets skygge I-II* (Danish in the Shadow of the Swastika), Flensborg 1981

Noack, J.P.: *Det danske mindretal i Sydslesvig 1920–1945, I–II* (The Danish Minority in Southern Schleswig, ...), Aabenraa 1989

Pontoppidan Thyssen, A.: *Vækkelse, kirkefornyelse og nationalitetskamp i Sønderjylland 1815–1850* (Revival, Church Renewal and Struggle for Nationality in Southern Jutland), Aabenraa 1977

Rerup, L.: "Den territoriale selvbestemmelsesret" (The Right of Territorial Self-Determination), *Scandia* 1969

Rerup L.: "Elitärer u. emanzipatorischer Nationalismus", in: *XVIe Congres International des Sciences Historiques Stuttgart 1985, Rapports II*, Stuttgart 1985

Rerup, L.: *Grænsen, fra grænsekamp til sameksistens* (The Border, from Border Struggle to Co-existence), Albertslund 1969

Rerup, L.: *Slesvig og Holsten efter 1830* (S. and H. after 1830), København 1982

Schultz Hansen, Hans: "Den danske bevægelse i Sønderjylland ca. 1838–

50. National bevægelse, social forandring og modernisering" (The Danish Movement in Southern Jutland about 1838–50. National Movement, Social Change and Modernization), in: *Historie, Jyske Samlinger*, ny række, bd. 18, 1990

Schultz Hansen, Hans: *Det nordslesvigske landbrug og den danske bevægelse 1880–1914* (North Schleswigan Agriculture and the Danish Movement, 1880–1914), Åbenrå 1985

Smith, Paul, & K. Koufa & Arnold Suppan (eds): *Ethnic groups in international relations* (European Science Foundation: Comparative studies on governments and non-dominant ethnic groups in Europe, 1850–1940; Vol. V) 1991

Statistisches Landesamt Schleswig-Holstein (ed.): *Beiträge zur historischen Statistik Schleswig-Holsteins* (Contribution to Historical Statistics of S.-H.), Kiel 1967

Statistisches Landesamt Schleswig-Holstein (ed.): *Lange Reihen zur Bevölkerungs- und Wirtschaftsentwicklung Schleswig-Holsteins (1950–1975)* (Long Series of Population and Trade Statistics of S.-H.), Kiel 1977

Steensen, Thomas: *Die friesische Bewegung in Nordfriesland im 19. und 20. Jahrhundert (1879–1945)* (The Frisian Movement in Northern Friesland in the 19th and 20th Century), Neumünster 1986

Toft, Gösta: *Die bäuerliche Struktur der deutschen Volksgruppe in Nordschleswig* (The Agrarian Structure of the German Minority in N.S.), Flensburg 1982

Tägil, Sven: *Deutschland und die deutsche Minderheit in Nordschleswig. Eine Studie zur deutschen Grenzpolitik 1933–1939* (Germany and the German Minority in Northern Schleswig. A Study of the German Border Policy, 1933–1939), Lund 1970

PART FOUR

IMMIGRATION TO SCANDINAVIA AFTER WORLD WAR II

Harald Runblom

International migration has, indeed, served as a dynamic element in Nordic societies during the postwar period. Migration has altered the ethnic composition of population, added to the cultural and linguistic variety, and confronted individuals and local communities with a spectrum of new life styles. Immigration has also served as a challenge to traditional behaviour and policies in a variety of spheres: education, administration of justice, medical services, church life. The changes we are talking about here have taken place in varying degrees in the five Nordic countries. This process started at different times. For the Nordic area as a whole, the later war years (1943–1945) were important. One must not forget, though, that the Nordic area has always been a target of international migration. Hence, in all periods the countries have received small number of immigrants from the countries around the Baltic Sea and the North Sea as well as Central Europe. All countries have experienced Jewish immigration, Denmark as long ago as the seventeenth century. In contrast to earlier chapters in this volume which deal with territorial minorities, this chapter deals with immigration and immigrant groups.

The Problem

An historian normally has the ambition to analyse phenomena over time, as well as study causes and effects. There are, however, many difficulties in providing a comprehensive account and detailed answers on the effects of immigration, especially when it comes to issues of culture. One reason is that immigration has taken place parallel to several other internationalizing tendencies: new patterns of consumption, the globalization of media culture, "Americanization," mass tourism, the appearance of new religions and para-churches, and so on.

Another difficulty lies in the state of the art. Up till now, few historical studies have appeared which focus on the culture of immigrants to the Nordic region, and compared to the situation in the United States, an immigration country of some age, Nordic historians have devoted little attention to immigration phenomena, especially those of the 20th century. Since mass immigration to the Nordic countries is a recent phenomenon, the majority of immigrants are first-generation and no chronological perspective has developed to observe the more lasting effects of the new immigration.

Research on postwar European immigration has been dominated by social scientists. In the Nordic countries, most investigation has focused on immigration as a societal problem and has revolved around burning social, administrative and educational issues: immigrants' integration into the labour market, the flow of capital to the homeland, housing, immigrant children's language-training, etc. In Sweden at least, there has been a close link between immigration researchers and policy makers. This has many positive aspects, but one side-effect is the risk of narrowing the horizons and a tendency to study a "problem" mainly in the receiving communities' perspective. In the 1960s there was a concentration on the economic aspects of immigration, and in the 1970s on social and political issues. In the 1980s researchers' interest has tended to be linked more to the cultural aspects of the immigrants' long-term encounter with the host society. In the years around 1990 there has been a tendency to tackle the wider problems of creating a multicultural society.[1] Relatively few studies exist on immigrant cultures *per se*, and there is an obvious lack of studies that link observations from the country of emigration with investigations in the receiving country.[2] Too few studies take into account the wide cultural complexity of the total mass of immigrants, and too often data are given on citizenship categories instead of ethnic groups.[3] Immigrant research has, however, mushroomed, and one could easily list writers on immigration from some thirty or forty academic disciplines. Beside the many positive features of this fact, there is one negative aspect: fragmentation of knowledge.

Immigration has—as already indicated—received increasing attention from all segments of society in the Nordic countries, not least because the international refugee problem is seen as a potential burden and because immigrants from the Third World have been seen as a threat, at least indirectly, by serving as a possible trigger for racism. In this perspective, there is reason to stress that the rate of immigration to the Nordic countries has been low in comparison to continental countries (France, Germany, Switzerland). This also is true of Sweden, which during the period 1945–1970 received a considerably larger number of immigrants than Denmark and Norway. The percentages of foreign citizens give a rough picture:

[1] The exception here is Finland, where government supported migration research has had a strong focus on the causes and effects of emigration. A special centre for this purpose is the Institute of Migration in Turku.

[2] Notable exceptions are Schierup & Ålund: *Will they still be dancing?*; Magnusson: *Jugoslaver i Sverige*; Engelbrektsson: *The Force of Tradition: Turkish Migrants at Home and Abroad.*

[3] This point is strongly made by Svanberg: *Invandrare från Turkiet.*

Table 1. Foreign Citizens in Selected Countries 1986: Absolute and in Percent of the Total Population

Sweden	390,800	4.6%
West Germany	4,483,600	7.4%
Belgium	897,600	9.1%
France	3,680,000	6.8%
Netherlands	568,000	3.9%
Switzerland	956,000	14.7%
Denmark	116,949	2.4%
Finland	17,269	0.4%
Iceland	3,553	1.5%
Norway	109,286	2.6%

Source: Official statistics.

The goal in this chapter is 1) to place postwar Nordic immigration in a European and global perspective, 2) to analyse postwar population movements and immigration policies in a historical context and 3) to focus on the emergence of ethnic life and the tendencies to multiculturalism policies in the Nordic receiving countries. Comparison between the Nordic countries is essential. Greater attention is paid to Sweden, because of its much larger immigration.

Nordic Migration in a Global Perspective

It is obviously desirable to place the Nordic migration in a more global context. In Europe, World War II resulted in fewer changes of the political map than World War I. However, the demographic effects were greater of World War II because of greater losses in battle, the sufferings of the civilian populations, and genocide. Population movements in the wake of World War II resulted in considerable losses to certain countries. A combination of "precautionary" and other measures led to forced population movements and deportations in the Soviet Union. Crimean Tatars, Volga Germans and Don Cossacks were forced out of their areas of residence. The alterations to the western border of the Soviet Union were preceded and followed by population transfers. The Nordic countries were, of course, most affected by what happened in the eastern and southern Baltic region. In round figures, 40,000 Estonians, 100,000 Latvians and 80,000 Lithuanians were forced by Soviet authorities to move eastwards. During the final phase of the war, Balts fled *en masse* overseas, their ultimate goals being Sweden and Denmark. Some also sought refuge in Germany. For many Balts this became the first stage in a flight to countries outside Europe: the United States, Canada, Australia.

The adjustments of the borders between the Soviet Union, Poland and Germany caused domino effects in population movements, when masses of Russians, Belorussians, and Ukrainians moved into former Polish areas, while Poles were moved or fled to East Prussia and other areas which became Polish but had earlier been German. Germans (*Reichsdeutsche* as well as *Volksdeutsche*) on the other hand left these areas on their way west. In the Nordic countries, especially Sweden, migration in the wake of the war became quite marked.

The migration picture changed dramatically in another way during the early postwar period. Population losses due to the war and lower birth rates, in combination with economic reconstruction programs, created a demand for manpower in Western Europe which could not be supplied from within the countries themselves. Fairly soon after the war a pattern of migration from Southern Europe to Western Europe emerged.

Two of the European countries which had remained neutral during the war, Sweden and Switzerland, gained the lead. With strong economic potential, they were prepared for postwar production, and were the first to open their gates for foreign labour. Switzerland recruited migrants, foremost from Italy, and the proportion of foreigners rose from 5% (1940) to 15% (1970).

Within the framework of these systems, from the mid-1940s to the early 1970s there developed an area of immigration countries in Western Europe: France, Switzerland, West Germany, Belgium, the Netherlands, Luxembourg, Britain, Sweden and later Denmark and Norway. Pronounced countries of emigration were Finland, Portugal, Spain, Italy, Yugoslavia, France, and Turkey, as well as the former French colonies Algeria, Morocco and Tunisia. To complicate the picture, even emigration countries were targets of migration. Somewhat schematically, three zones may be recognized:

1. Centre (Western Europe)
2. Semi-periphery (parts of Southern Europe)
3. Periphery (rest of Southern Europe, bordering parts of North Africa and West Asia)

Parallel systems for migration recruitment also emerged in Europe: one in Eastern Europe, and one in Western and Southern Europe. With the building of the Berlin Wall in 1961, the flow between these systems almost stopped. Before this date, smaller migration streams reached Scandinavia from the Baltic area (1944–1945), Poland (the years around 1945) and Hungary (1956). Few immigrants arrived from East Germany after 1948. Yugoslavia, hanging between east and west, was early integrated in the Western system, and the regime in Belgrade not only permitted but even exhorted its citizens to seek employment abroad. Of the Nordic countries first Sweden, then Denmark, welcomed Yugoslav labour.

From the beginning of the 1970s there was a slackening, even a reversal of the labour migration streams to Western Europe. Several circumstances converged, most notably a deep economic recession, unemployment and the so-called oil crisis. Country after country in Western Europe embarked on a restricted immigration policy. Free migration, to the extent that it had existed, was stopped. Gradually many governments sought measures (including economic benefits) to encourage guest-workers and their families to return to their home countries.

While the chances to enter a West European country became almost nil, the possibilities for reunion of families increased. This pattern has been embraced by Denmark, Norway and Sweden. Thus, as immigration was choked off the effect has nonetheless been a continued immigration in the wake of labour migration. The early 1970s also saw another significant change: the increase of refugee migrations to the free countries of the world.

The migration in Europe has been largely channelled within the framework of regional labour market agreements. Most important was the establishment of a Nordic labour market in 1954, which led to an almost unrestricted flow of migrants among the Nordic countries. Until now only one Nordic country, Denmark in 1972, has joined the European Community, but the migration effect has been fairly limited.[4] While several European countries (France, Great Britain, The Netherlands) have received a flow of immigrants from former colonies, no Nordic country, for obvious reasons, has been confronted with any situation of that kind. Some Pakistani immigrants to Denmark were let into Great Britain as Commonwealth citizens before the rules of free movements in the EC were applied; then they headed for Denmark.

Intra-Nordic Migration

In sheer numbers, intra-Nordic migration dominated the population exchange in the Nordic countries for several decades after 1945. The flows westward from Finland were the largest, and the number of migrants who moved from Finland to Sweden during the years 1945–1980 was of the same magnitude as the emigration from Finland to America during the mass emigration period in the late 19th

---

[4] Ploug: "Population Migration in the Nordic and EC-area".

and the early 20th centuries, although re-migration and repetitive migration between Finland and Sweden reduced the net effect.[5] The emigration from Finland started at a modest level in 1945, but increased gradually and reached its climax around 1970. During the late 1980s Finland registered a net immigration in its exchange with Sweden.[6]

Because of its size the Finnish migration to Sweden deserves special treatment, not least because the Finns as an immigrant group have been instrumental in setting standards for immigrant groups generally in Swedish society. As noted above, Finnish immigration to Sweden during the first postwar years was fairly moderate, not least given the large demand for labour in Sweden, the serious economic problems in Finland and the differences in income levels between the two countries. Up to 1955 there was a surplus of females, and many women found household work.[7] Finnish male migrants to a large extent were blue collar workers; during the 1940s and 1950s they belonged primarily in the agricultural sector and forestry, but from the mid-1950s they were increasingly industrial workers. The share of intellectuals has been fairly low, since a major force behind migration was structural unemployment, which was most severe in rural areas far from industrial cities and expanding regions. Tradition is a strong factor in all migration between Finland and Sweden.[8] The postwar emigration to Sweden has had the same pattern and played the same role as the emigration to Russia in the 19th century and to America during the period of mass migration, 1880–1930: a movement from agriculture to industry, from rural to urban areas. Traditional areas of emigration are Ostrobothnia, southwestern Finland and the Åland Islands.

Re-migration is an important facet. After 1955 more men than

[5] On the role of remigration see Korkiassari: *Hem till Finland.*

[6] Söderling: "Efter de stora folkströmmarna till den multikulturella Norden".

[7] Majava: "Finns in Sweden: Characteristics and Living Conditions".

[8] De Geer: *Migration och influensfält.*

women migrated. Both before and after 1955 more males than females re-migrated, one reason being that men's migration is always
more sensitive to business fluctuations. Finnish men in particular
were attracted to industries which were extremely vulnerable in this
respect, especially the construction sector.[9]

From the point of view of the individual Finnish migrant, the
move to Sweden was also a step towards urbanization, since the
Swedish target areas were cities and industrial towns. The emigration to Sweden was strongest from Ostrobothnia, southwestern Finland and the Åland Islands, all Swedish-speaking areas. The majority
of the population in these areas has long been Swedish-speaking (the
Åland Islands totally), and by tradition all have had strong migration
contacts with Sweden.

As with the America emigration, language was a strong selection
factor. Among emigrants who came to Sweden during the postwar
period the Swedish speakers were strongly over-represented. One
should also note though, that Swedish-speaking areas were strongly
hit by unemployment and that Swedish speakers have been reluctant
to try to adjust in the large expanding centres of Helsinki and Tam-
pere where the Finnish language is dominant. In other words the
Sweden-directed migration has meant a reduction of the Swedish-
speaking minority in Finland, which has also diminished for other
reasons, mainly intermarriage, language-shift and low birth rates.[10]

The migration between the Nordic countries has taken place
within a framework of extensive political cooperation. As early as
1943 Sweden abolished the requirement for labour permits for
citizens of the other Nordic countries. Visa requirements were
abolished for Danes, Icelanders, and Norwegians in 1945 and for
Finnish citizens in 1949. This last measure opened the sluices for
large-scale migration from Finland to Sweden.[11] A full common

[9] Wadensjö: *Immigration och samhällsekonomi.*
[10] Finnäs: *Den finlandssvenska befolkningsutvecklingen 1950–1980.*
[11] Wadensjö: *Immigration och samhällsekonomi*, pp. 53–55.

Nordic labour market became a reality in 1954 when the same steps were taken in all Nordic countries. In 1955 another agreement improved the social security of Nordic immigrants. (Seen from a non-Nordic immigrant's perspective, a Nordic citizen in another Nordic country is the object of positive discrimination.)

The factors behind the large intra-Nordic movements were largely economic. The streams between Finland and Sweden have mainly followed the business cycles in the two countries. The intra-Nordic migration has been facilitated by the community of culture and language. As far as language is concerned, one exception is Finnish-speaking Finns; the language situation of this group has been one of the most discussed issues in Swedish-Finnish cooperation during recent decades. One should not, however, overestimate the ease of settling and adjusting in a neighbouring Nordic country. Some observers have pointed out that adjustment to a rather similar culture contains its special complex of problems. One may refer to the immigrant author Marianne Alopaeus, a Swedish-speaking Finn, who has written about decades of cultural surprises in her new homeland.[12]

Historically, movements between the Nordic areas are a very old phenomenon. Many regions have been linked by almost constant seasonal and permanent migration. There are also strong factors of tradition, and this is especially true of the migratory routes from Finland to Sweden. Traditionally, out-migration to the Stockholm area and the Mälardalen district has been strong from Swedish-speaking areas in Ostrobothnia, and it still is. Similarly, Copenhagen and Oslo have been strong magnets for certain regions in southern and southwestern Sweden, respectively.[13] As to assimilation of migrating Nordic populations, experience points in different directions. Swedes, Norwegians and Danes have assimilated quickly and

[12] Alopaeus: *Drabbad av Sverige.* Cf. Swedner: *Invandrare i Malmö,* pp. 40–44.

[13] Willerslev: *Den glemte indvandring,* passim.

almost totally within one generation or two in each other's countries. The traces of migration have been almost nonexistent in the grandchildren's generation. One scholar has even coined the expression "the forgotten emigration", when referring to the immigration of Swedes into the greater Copenhagen area in the 19th century.[14]

To understand the migration history after 1945—not least the large proportion of intra-Nordic migration—it is important to stress the strong tendencies to integration between the Nordic countries during the last half-century. Judging from feelings of solidarity, Denmark, Finland, Iceland, Norway and Sweden have become closer. The main basis for this integration is the sharing of language, culture and history. There has been steady progress in cooperation, although strong political tensions have existed for hundreds of years. Pan-Nordism has not been successful in the areas of defence policy or pure political integration, but rests rather on pragmatic solutions in day-to-day cooperation.

The Second World War brought a feeling of common destiny to the Nordic peoples. The many actions of loyalty—and the forms which this loyalty took may still be a bone of contention among historical interpreters from the various countries—testify to this feeling of togetherness. The balance sheet of Nordic cooperation contains several failures: for example, the attempts at a common Scandinavian defence agreement collapsed in 1949, and the plans for Nordic economic unity did not materialize in the 1970s. One may add that it has not been possible so far to formulate a common Nordic refugee policy, but the many small steps taken by governments, associations, professional organizations etc. have led to networks of cooperation that could hardly be matched by other groups of countries. One result is the long-range congruence of citizenship laws, with the effect that a Nordic citizen possesses extensive rights in other Nordic countries. Even the term "Nordic citizen", although it

---

[14] Willerslev, op.cit., pp. 7–9.

has no legal status, has been used to mark the many accomplishments in this sphere of legislative cooperation.[15]

Three Phases of Postwar Migration

One can distinguish three phases of immigration to the Nordic area after World War II. These phases overlap to some extent, and one may argue that the first of these phases should also include the later war years. The periods are:

1. 1943–1947, characterized by migrations that had their roots in war conditions.
2. 1946–1972, marked by labour migration.
3. The period after 1972, marked by gradual termination of relatively unregulated labour migration in Europe and constantly increasing refugee movements.

During the interwar period, all Nordic countries were restrictive in their attitude to refugees and immigrants. The gradual changes of the laws governing aliens reflected a desire to keep the countries free from foreign elements. In Sweden there was much talk about the unmixed race and the importance of preserving pure Swedish stock. One slogan was "Sweden for the Swedes".[16] Norway displayed much the same mentality: immigration was restricted, and political consensus existed concerning this policy. There was a widespread xenophobia, which was directed especially towards the Jews.[17] For many individuals and families who escaped the atrocities of Nazi Germany, the Scandinavian door was gradually closed, particularly to

[15] For a compilation of laws and regulations, see *Nordbors rättigheter i Norden*.

[16] Hammar: *Sverige åt svenskarna. Invandringspolitik, utlänningskontroll och asylrätt 1900–1932*; Lindberg: *Svensk flyktingpolitik under internationellt tryck 1936–1941*.

[17] Johansen: *Oss selv nærmest. Norge og jødene 1914–1943*.

Jews who fled Germany and other countries under Hitler's control. Jews were, by definition, not considered political refugees, and hence their chances of entering were minimal during the years 1938–1940.[18]

After the war the attitude was radically different, and the door was opened. This change began even during the war; one need only point to Raoul Wallenberg's activities in Budapest in 1944 and 1945. Why did the Swedish government support actions to rescue Jewish lives in Central Europe at the end of the war, when there had been so much reluctance to let in escaping Jews in 1938 and 1939? The fate of Wallenberg has helped to give Sweden a heroic reputation that may not be wholly deserved, if one considers its prewar refugee policy.

It is of interest to date the change of attitude in both governing circles and public opinion, which had already begun during the war. In Sweden, the only non-belligerent Nordic country, the latter part of 1943 seems to be the turning-point. In October of that year, the government, and obviously even large segments of the population, gave evidence of taking a new stand. One can point to a single episode which was of major importance in bringing about this change, namely the assistance given to approximately 6,000 Danish Jews who escaped from Denmark for Sweden over the straits of Öresund. The Israeli historian Leni Yahil has characterized this rescue action as a hope for mankind.[19]

This support for the escaping Danish Jews in 1943 is, however, a story with manifold psychological origins. The Danish Jews, who had begun to arrive in Denmark as early as the 17th century, were fairly well integrated in Danish society. They came to play a special role in the conflict between the occupiers and the Danes during World War II. As the war dragged on, relations between the occupiers and the Danes became more and more tense. With the situ-

[18] Petersen: "De nordiske lande og Hitler-flygtningene".
[19] Yahil: *The Rescue of Danish Jewry. Test of a Democracy.*

ation deteriorating, the plight of the Jews became critical, and in the fall of 1943 they were in danger of deportation. At this point the Danes carried out a disobedience campaign from which the Jews benefited: it became a patriotic deed to hide Jews and help them escape to Sweden.

The welcoming of the Danish Jews by the Swedes on the other side of the straits must not only be interpreted as an act of mercy. During the first three war years Sweden had carried out a "pro-German" neutrality policy. After the battles of El Alamein and Stalingrad, when it was evident that German successes were coming to an end, the Swedish government found an opportunity to do a "good deed" in the eyes of the world, and especially of the potential victors. Sweden's welcoming of the Danish Jews must also be seen as a need to demonstrate sympathy with the Danes and with Denmark in a precarious situation. The Swedish rescue action lowered the psychological pressure in a situation that was morally difficult for Sweden, and paved the way for a more positive stance towards the victims of war. After this, the Swedish government was accorded appreciation from all corners of the world.[20]

Immediate Wartime Effects on Migrations

Since the fate of the Nordic countries varied so much during the war, the patterns of war-time and postwar migration also diverged. Finland, involved in two wars with the Soviet Union (the Winter War of 1939–1940 and the War of Succession, 1941–1944), lost part of its territory along the eastern border and had to organize the resettlement of about 10% of its population, the Karelians.[21] The so-called War of Succession between the Soviet Union and Finland resulted in further population transfers during the 1941–1944, most notably the resettlement in Finland of 61,200 Ingrians, who arrived

[20] The Archive of the Foreign Office, National Archives, Stockholm.
[21] See the contribution by Engman in this volume.

in Finland by way of Estonia. They were Lutheran Finnish-speakers from the Leningrad region and north-eastern Estonia. The migration was organized with the goodwill of the German occupation forces; the understanding was that they should be allowed to reside permanently in Finland. However, the preconditions of this arrangement were altered in November 1944 by the so-called Finno-Soviet armistice treaty in Moscow. After the German-Finnish war coalition had collapsed and the Soviets had defeated the Finnish troops, the Finnish and Soviet governments made an agreement whereby the Ingrians would return to their places of origin in the Soviet Union. For various reasons around 4,000 were able to remain in Finland and about the same number fled to Sweden, where this refugee group has been a fairly invisible minority, sceptical of all kinds of authorities and with the ambition to preserve their cultural heritage. The fate of the Ingrians is typical of many small Finno-Ugric minorities in the Soviet Union with a weak population base and with cultural links to Finland.

Events during the war resulted in migrations with both temporary and more permanent repercussions. The two Nordic countries that were occupied by the Nazis, Denmark and Norway, experienced population movements which were more temporary but which nonetheless left their marks on history.

The population movements in the wake of the Second World War were different in the Nordic countries. Geopolitical position and the wartime effects on the economy were some of the most important factors that influenced the migration picture. When Denmark and Norway were liberated in May 1945 there were large contingents of occupation troops. In Denmark these amounted to a quarter of a million.[22] To this number were added some 225,000 refugees. Their presence on Danish soil was a result of the chaotic situation on the Eastern front: many had fled across the Baltic and landed in Copenhagen and other Danish ports. Others had arrived

---

[22] Østergaard: *Indvandrernes danmarkshistorie*, p. 210.

in Denmark over the southern border in the final phase of the war, for example, Soviet prisoners of war in German captivity. The Danish problem was to find a smooth way out of this confused state of affairs. Because of the Nazi occupation, 1940–1945, there was a general antipathy toward the many Germans who remained in the country. Strong measures were taken, and German ex-soldiers were sent off to German areas. Those who had been recruited to Denmark under constraint from the Nazis were, however, allowed to stay temporarily, and the Danish authorities improvised refugee camps. Physical separation between the Danes and Germans was a leading principle. To cite the chief of the refugee administration, Johs. Kjærbøl, the treatment was to be humane but the hospitality restricted. German Nazi victims, around 30,000, were held separately and had a freer situation. Danish authorities saw to it that refugees who were in the country were given the possibility to travel on to a third country. The refugee camps were closed in 1949.[23]

In relation to its own population, Norway housed a large number of foreigners during the war years, mostly German military personnel and civilians in the service of the Nazi occupation power. 350,000 troops in German service were estimated to be in the country. To this figure were added some 100,000 prisoners of war, mostly Russians and Central Europeans. Still other categories included some 13,000 forced labourers and 10,000 German workers. While these groups entered Norway, others left the country. During the war years Norway's Jewish population was deported or simply fled the country. The overwhelming majority of the foreigners, mostly Swedes, who had resided in Norway at the outbreak of war had left. Norwegians also left, and among the 100,000 of them abroad in May 1945, close to 45,000 had found temporary refuge in Sweden, where a Norwegian refugee community developed.[24] In all

---

[23] Havrehed: *De tyske flygtningene i Danmark 1945–1949*.

[24] Grimnes: *Et flyktingesamfunn vokser fram. Nordmenn i Sverige 1940–1945*; Thorud: *Norsk innvandringspolitikk 1860–1960*.

respects the population situation in Norway in 1945 was abnormal, but the invaders and the other involuntary "immigrants" who had come to the country during the war left when the war was over, with the exception of around 1,500 displaced persons, prisoners of war and forced labourers who wished to remain and were allowed to do so.[25]

In Sweden the number of foreigners (foreign citizens and stateless) was estimated at 194,000, somewhat more than half of whom were refugees. A majority of the refugees came from the neighbouring countries. The number of Norwegians who had crossed the border was calculated to be 43,300, and from Denmark it was estimated that 18,300 had crossed the straits of Öresund. The latter figure included the Danish Jews mentioned above. During the war Sweden had received about 65,000 Finnish children who had been evacuated.[26] Around 52,000 Finns arrived in Sweden over the border along Torne river, most of them in connection with conflicts between Finns and Germans when the German troops set fire to Finnish villages during their humiliating retreat from Finland.

The refugees in Sweden at the end of the war included 30,000 Balts, mainly Estonians. Most of the Balts had arrived in Sweden across the Baltic during the fall of 1944. Other refugees came from camps in Europe after the end of the war, primarily from Austria and Italy, but to a lesser extent also from Germany, Turkey, Greece, and Yugoslavia. East Europeans (Yugoslavs, Poles, Czechoslovaks) made up most of this category. Around 4,000 Sudeten Germans made their way to Sweden shortly before, during and immediately after the war.[27]

During the war and the first postwar years, immigration took

[25] The term "displaced" person has undergone a shift of meaning. In 1945 it referred to persons who had been forced to leave their countries, while nowadays it refers to persons who are "refugees" in their own countries.

[26] De Geer: *De finländska krigsbarnen i Sverige 1941–1948.*

[27] Svanberg: "Sudettyskar", p. 410.

place mainly from the Baltic Sea area and from the countries in Central Europe. However, after 1945 the Nordic countries' migration contacts with the rest of the world gradually widenend. This was mainly a result of Sweden's strong economic position. Since the Swedish production machinery remained intact during the war, Swedish industry had a flying start in 1945, and there was a strong demand for labour, especially in the manufacturing industry. At the same time as Sweden received refugees from the continent, Swedish enterprises and state authorities, notably the National Labour Market Board, recruited skilled labour abroad. Thus formal agreements were concluded in 1947 with the governments in Italy and Hungary. The same year the Swedish government and the British occupation authorities in Austria reached an agreement to transfer Sudeten Germans collectively to Sweden. Thus, large enterprises like Kockums, a shipbuilding enterprise in Malmö, The Swedish Ballbearing Industry (SKF) in Göteborg, and ASEA in Västerås received substantial cadres of Central and South European workers on the shop floor. In some cases there was a clash of interests between the employers and the trade unions on this point, and the Swedish workers argued that an influx of foreign labour would threaten their social welfare.[28]

During the 1960s Scandinavia also became the target for migrants from Greece and Turkey, and by the 1970s the sphere of attraction had grown almost global.

After Sweden had become a country of labour immigration in the mid-1940s, about two decades elapsed before the corresponding development took place in Denmark and Norway. It took an even longer time in Finland, if one considers the strong upswing in the Finnish economy in the 1980s and accepts that the return of Finnish labour from Sweden marked a new phase in Finland's migration history. In the 1980s the earlier income gap between Sweden and Finland had been considerably reduced.

In Denmark the start of labour immigration can be dated to

[28] Nelhans: *Utlänningen på arbetsmarknaden*, pp. 138–9.

1967, if one overlooks the relatively small stream of immigrants from the neighbouring Nordic countries and the United States. An economic recession caused foreign labourers in West Germany to seek their fortunes north of the border. Also in 1967, labourers arrived from Yugoslavia, Pakistan, and Morocco in search of work. They were allowed to enter the country provided they had been offered jobs and provided Danish manpower was not able to fill the vacancies.[29] However, between 1955 and 1970 Denmark had received about 5,000 refugees, primarily from Hungary in 1956 and Poland in 1969.

The Immigrants

Diversity and heterogeneity are two of the most noteworthy features of the immigrant populations in the Nordic countries. The large number of immigrant groups in Sweden and Denmark is striking: counted by citizenship Denmark (1989) had 23 citizenship groups exceeding 1,000 persons, while Sweden at the same time had some fifty groups with more than 1,000 registered per land of birth (not totally comparable with the Danish figure). The largest immigrant groups in each Nordic country are given in Table 2. There is no typical immigrant group, just as there is no typical immigrant. Since immigration has taken place under shifting political and economic conditions (from the perspective both of the sending areas and the receiving countries) the groups' demographic composition is extremely varied.

Immigrants can be grouped into a number of distinct categories:

1. *Re-migrants from overseas.* Every migration generates re-migration; hence the immigration statistics also include returning emigrants who have spent time abroad. Even up to the 1960s and 1970s, the Nordic immigration statistics contained first and second-generation emigrants to America who had left their home countries

---

[29] *Indvandrerforskning i Danmark*, pp. 21–36.

Table 2. Foreign Citizens in Nordic Countries: Largest Groups, 1988, 1989, 1990

Denmark 1990

Turkey	27,929
Norway	10,175
United Kingdom	9,983
Yugoslavia	9,535
Iran	8,362
German Federal Rep.	8,092
Sweden	8,047
Stateless	6,357
Pakistan	6,285
Poland	4,319
USA	4,126
VietNam	3,509
Iceland	3,045
France	1,951
Italy	1,938

Finland 1988

Sweden	5,422
USSR	2,071
German Federal Rep.	1,379
USA	1,211
United Kingdom	1,103
Stateless	454
Denmark	432
Norway	413
Poland	337
Italy	332
Canada	317
France	293
Switzerland	281
Netherlands	277
Spain	251
Japan	223

Iceland 1989

Denmark	1,079
USA	803
United Kingdom	501
Norway	342
German Federal Rep.	319
Sweden	199
Poland	133
France	100
Ireland	99
Netherlands	95

Norway 1990

Denmark	17,454
United Kingdom	12,510
Sweden	11,704
Pakistan	11,620
USA	9,640
Viet Nam	6,752
Chile	5,328
Turkey	5,267
Iran	5,248
German Federal Rep.	4,124
Yugoslavia	3,870
India	3,371
Finland	3,259
Poland	2,874
Netherlands	2,619

Sweden 1989

Finland	123,867
Yugoslavia	39,591
Iran	35,144
Norway	35,046
Denmark	28,081
Turkey	24,152
Chile	19,129
Poland	14,736
German Federal Rep.	12,020
United Kingdom	9,617
USA	7,501
Stateless	6,939
Greece	6,722
Iceland	4,490
Romania	4,446

before the end of the mass emigration period around 1930. A number of Danes, Finns, etc. who had set off for foreign countries after the war and returned home are also included in the statistics.

2. *Repatriated groups.* Repatriation here includes cases where the government has actively promoted the return of various groups. Under this heading there is reason to include at least two groups of immigrants in Sweden who have made their presence felt at the national level during the postwar period. The first is the Gammals-venskby Swedes, who arrived in Sweden in 1929 from the lower Dniepr area in the Ukraine. They were descendants of Swedes who settled in Estonia during the thirteenth century and were forced to move to the Ukraine as a result of a *ukase* issued by Catherine II. Their repatriation was partly a reflection of an attitude in Sweden, which grew stronger from the beginning of the century, to build bridges and unite Swedish population groups in various parts of the world. Although this group is Swedish-speaking, its re-integration was not without problems. The reception of this group also provided some experience for the reception of the much larger group of Swedish-speaking Estonians, also descendants of the 13th century emigration to Estonia. The idea of the migration of this group to Sweden arose after the signing of the mutual assistance treaty between Estonia and the Soviet Union in September 1939, which granted the latter the right to place military units in the central areas inhabited by the Swedish-speaking Estonians. The gradual Sovietization of the area was regarded as a threat to the group. A Swedish loyalty action followed, and the Swedish-speaking Estonians, numbering about 6,000, arrived in Sweden with the intent to stay.

3. *Nordic immigrants.* This group has been discussed above.

4. *Older non-Nordic immigrant groups.* Germans, Dutch, Englishmen and Scots have made their way to Scandinavia over the centuries; even Frenchmen and Russians might be included in this group. As craftsmen and professionals, many of them have brought specialized competence. The immigration of these groups during the

last half century is a sequel to earlier population movements. Although collectively invisible, Germans, for example, have made up one of the largest European immigrant groups in all Scandinavian countries. Jews may also be included in this group.

5. *European refugee groups.* The first extensive immigration to Denmark and Norway after 1954 consisted of refugees from Soviet-dominated Eastern Europe: Hungary (1956), Czechoslovakia (1968) and Poland (the years around 1970). All these groups were a blend of ethnic Hungarians, Slovaks, Czechs and Poles on the one hand and Jews on the other. Individuals, families and small groups have come from all East European countries to the Nordic area during the last five decades. Also, not all East Europeans have arrived as refugees; the immigration of individuals, mostly women who have come to marry or cohabit with Nordic citizens should also be noted.

6. *Labour migrants from Southern Europe and the rest of the world.* Southern Europeans came to the Nordic area in fairly restricted numbers before the Second World War. Already in the late 1940s, Southern Europe became a recruiting ground for Swedish industry. Italians, Greeks, Yugoslavs and Turks made up a large part of non-Nordic labour migrants in the 1950s, 1960s, and early 1970s.[30]

7. *Third World refugees.* This category started to arrive in the 1970s and the 1980s.

The Refugee Immigration during the 1980s

The late 1980s brought dramatic developments of the refugee situation in the Nordic countries. The pressure from refugees and asylum-seekers became heavier than at any time since the Second World War. The international solidarity of governments and

[30] One exception is Italians; see Catomeris: *Gipskattor och positiv. Italienare i Stockholm 1896–1910.*

peoples in the Nordic countries was put on trial. The chain of events took place against a background of many alarming developments on the global scene: tensions between North and South, the continued population explosions in several Third World countries (Iran, Kenya, Nicaragua),[31] acute supply problems in some parts of the world, above all Africa, internal conflicts in many Third World countries (Ethiopia/Eritrea, Iran, Lebanon, Central America), ecological catastrophes (Siberia, the Horn of Africa, various megalopolises), and international conflicts (Afghanistan, the war between Iraq and Iran). Also the gradual breakdown of Communist regimes added to uncertainty as to what numbers might seek refuge in Northern European countries. The last development resulted in one peak of population movements in 1989.[32] A small stream of asylum-seekers from the Communist satellite countries in Europe has reached Norway, Sweden and Denmark since 1945, but the prospects of a collapse of the Communist world led to rumours of an exodus in millions from East to West in 1989 and 1990. The growing numbers of asylum-seekers in the 1980s caused the Nordic governments and parliaments to evaluate and redesign their immigration policies and refugee reception procedures several times.

The issue of refugees developed into a field of Nordic cooperation in the 1980s. The Nordic countries have long had a tradition of tight cooperation in legislative and administrative matters. Considering the agreements in the field of migration and labour market initiatives, mutual Nordic actions were natural. These included political initiatives in international forums.

Because of their geographical position, the Nordic countries have played a relatively marginal role as targets for the population movements in Europe. Third World refugees had arrived in Denmark, Norway and Sweden as early as the 1970s. The increasing numbers

---

[31] Sadik (ed.): *Population Policies and Programmes.*
[32] Cf. Widgren: "International Migration and Regional Stability".

of refugees seeking asylum in the 1980s made it clear that the Nordic area's relative isolation from the global migration currents was a phenomenon of the past. The factors behind this development were complex, the most important being the international distress of poor and politically persecuted people in the Third World. An important precondition was the integration of Scandinavia into international airline networks with many direct flights between the Nordic capitals and Third World countries. The effect of this was felt in Nordic cities that house large international airports. The influx of refugees and asylum-seekers put the Nordic reception systems under strain, administratively and politically. The Swedish system for refugee reception built up at the beginning of the 1980s was not big enough to accommodate the large numbers that started to arrive toward the end of the decade. One endresult was the revision of the Aliens' Act. Denmark, which had liberalized its refugee policy in 1983 just before the increase of asylum-seekers throughout Europe, saw its newly introduced system sink, under the heavy pressure from increasing numbers of refugees. The ultimate consequence was a quick revision of the law in 1986, with new restrictions. The changes in Denmark resulted immediately in an increased number of asylum-seekers in Norway with similar consequences as in Denmark, i.e. a law revision and restrictions.

In Denmark, Norway and Sweden the reception systems were reorganized in the 1980s. In Sweden a new reception system was created, based on cooperation between the national government and (almost all) 273 municipalities. Denmark built further on an already elaborate system in which voluntary organizations (with extensive support from, and to some extent on behalf of, the government) took responsibility for the first 18 months of the refugees' time in Denmark. Norway built further on a system in which the municipalities took the responsibility for integration from the refugee's time of arrival in the country.

The refugee issue had a strong polarizing effect in the political life in Denmark and Norway. In both countries protest parties opposed the immigration of refugees from the Third World. Sweden has also experienced this tendency, and the New Democratic Party won seats in the parliament in 1991 with a party program in which restriction of refugee immigration was made an important issue.

Numbers and Settlement Patterns

Most immigrants who have arrived in the Nordic countries have sought their abode in urban areas. Only during the early postwar years could agriculture and forestry absorb new labour. For example, quite a few Estonians who arrived in Sweden in 1944 were directed to farms, and as late as 1947 there was a recruitment of agricultural labourers to Swedish farms from Hungary.

As long as immigration was nearly free and unregulated, that is, to the years around 1970, market factors and especially the demand for labour in industry and the service sector steered immigrants to cities and expansive industrial centres. Especially the capital regions and the larger industrial cities (Copenhagen, Århus, Oslo, Stockholm, Gothenburg, Malmö) attracted immigrants. During the years 1945–70 around 40% of the immigrants in Sweden settled in the Stockholm metropolitan area.

Border areas have their own patterns. For example, German immigrants have made up the largest immigrant group in Southern Jutland and some Danish islands. Danes in Sweden tend to settle in the southern provinces, and Finnish immigrants to Sweden in the central part of the country, with a concentration on a broad axis from Stockholm to Gothenburg. There are also other regional ethnic patterns among non-Nordic immigrants. Turks are primarily concentrated in the largest cities, among them Copenhagen. The same holds true for Pakistanis: in Norway and Denmark they are found mainly in the Oslo and Copenhagen metropolitan regions, respectively. Balts in Sweden tended to settle in the southeast, making up clusters in certain cities (Eskilstuna, Borås) while,

on the other hand, immigrants from the United States and Britain
tend to be spread throughout the countries.

In some cities certain neighbourhoods are more strongly flavoured
by immigrant culture than others, and immigrant districts exist in
some larger cities, such as Ishøj in Copenhagen, Rosengård in
Malmö, and Tensta and Rinkeby in Stockholm. In Oslo immigrants
have become concentrated in the older workers' districts such as Grü-
nerløkka. Many factors have lain behind the immigrants' choice:
economic standard, housing market, availability of apartments, housing policy, and the immigrants' own cultural strategies. When labour
immigration grew rapidly in the 1950s and early 1960s there was a
housing shortage that steered immigrants to old, unrenovated apartments in the older parts of the cities. In Sweden, the construction
boom during the so-called record years (*rekordåren*) of the 1960s resulted in many newly-built districts, to which much of the new immigration was directed. In the 1980s there has been a tendency in Denmark, Norway and Sweden to distribute refugees to a large number of
municipalities. This has been one aspect of refugee reception programmes, in which the ambition of the governments has been to
equalize the burdens of refugee reception.[33] Within the municipalities
the location of immigrants and refugees is largely a combined function of the public services and of housing policy. As opposed to many
world cities, where new arrivals cluster in slum areas in the city centres
or shanty-towns on the outskirts, the effect in the Nordic countries
during the 1970s and 1980s has been rather to place large numbers of
immigrants in newly built areas of a decent standard.[34]

In a few areas the strong concentration of immigrants from many
parts of the world has led to unique cultures and even ephemeral hy-
brid linguistic variations.[35] The clustering of immigrants in quarters

[33] Körmendi & Melchior: *Medgang og modgang. Overgangen fra Dansk
Flygtningehjælp til kommunerne;* Næss: "Refugees & National Policies: The
Norwegian Case".
[34] De Geer: *Göteborgs invandrargeografi.*
[35] Kotsinas: *Invandrare talar svenska.*

of a city or town has been observed and sometimes falsely branded as
an expression of discrimination and forced ghettoization. The settlement and housing patterns are partly a reflection of the infrastructure of immigrant groups as well as the need and ambition of individuals and families to support each other during the initial phase.
One factor which influences concentration is chain migration; especially striking are the links created by clustering immigrants from
Kulu, a rural area in Anatolia, and in certain districts of Gothenburg
and metropolitan Stockholm.[36]

Cultural Strategies and Patterns of Ethnicity

Space does not allow any in-depth discussion of aspects of ethnicity.
Here we will rather discuss expressions of collective strategies and efforts to preserve and develop cultural characteristics in the immigrant society. The various collectives of immigrants behave quite differently in these respects. A long series of factors decides the ambitions of both the individual and the group: the causes of migration,
time of arrival, the sex composition and social structure of the
group, level of education, basic values, and the existence or non-ex-
istence of an intention to return to the homeland. The collective
strategies fall between two extremes, one being to preserve as much
as possible of traditional culture in isolation from the host society,
and the other to integrate as fully as possible. In the Nordic societies
the former extreme is unusual. In reality the attitudes of ethnic
groups are a compromise between the host society's demands and
expectations, and the ethnic groups' ambitions. One condition for
the survival of ethnic groups as such is the control of primary sociali-
sation and the ability to keep together in religious and secular organisations. Certain immigrants are collectively anonymous. The

---

[36] Engelbrektsson: *The Force of Tradition*; Lundberg & Svanberg: *Kulu.
Utvandrarbygd i Turkiet.*

ambition to preserve the cultural heritage in modern westernized societies is different between labour migrants and refugees.[37]

Certain immigrant and ethnic groups have a low collective profile in the Nordic countries. This category includes Norwegians, Danes and Swedes in other Nordic societies: the migration is individual or based on single families; marriage migration is common; the geographical concentration in the immigrant societies is low; and the association spirit is weak. Language problems are minimal; hence the integration is quick. (The Finns were discussed above). As ethnic groups, French, Germans, Dutch, other West Europeans and North Americans have been fairly invisible during the postwar period, although some of them are among the most numerous immigrant groups. Baltic and Latin American groups in exile have had strong ambitions to preserve cultural traditions from their home countries. The political situations at home has preoccupied Latin American expatriates. The exile mentality has also characterized the second generation, which has been brought up in the Nordic countries. One effect, in Sweden at least, is that exiles from various countries in South and Central America have come together and built a Latin American community with an all-Latin American culture, and created an awareness of the continent that is not common in Latin America proper.[38]

The patterns of migration are also of vital importance for the cultural life of immigrant groups. Thus, the arrival of Jews from Poland around the end of the war and during the 1950s, 1960s and 1970s from Central Europe has vitalized the Jewish minorities in Denmark and Sweden. The birth of Israel also brought an injection of life into the Nordic Jewish minorities.[39]

[37] For different strategies of refugees and immigrants among the Chilean group in Sweden see Lindqvist: *Drömmar i vardag och exil.*

[38] Cf. Lundberg: *Flyktingskap. Latinamerikansk exil i Sverige och Västeuropa.*

[39] Broberg, Runblom & Tydén (ed.): *Judiskt liv i Norden.*

Religious Aspects

Postwar immigration has led to radical changes in the religious situation. New religious sects and churches have appeared. This has taken place against a background of uniform state-church relations in the Nordic countries. There is no separation between church and state, and all Nordic countries have state churches based on the concept of *folkkyrka* (a church for all people). In Sweden around 95% of the Swedish-born population are church members, although only a minority are active in a religious sense within the church. The Danish figure is somewhat lower. Varying numbers of immigrants from other countries become members, the highest figures being of immigrants from Western and Central Europe. The Swedish church has played an especially important role as the immigrant church for Finns and Estonians. Until recently, the majority of members of the Catholic church in all Nordic countries were people born of the country who had converted to Catholicism. The influx of people from countries with strong Catholic churches, such as Poland and Chile, has led to a situation where immigrants and their children make up the majority in some Catholic congregations.[40]

The greatest cultural challenge to the Nordic countries concerns Islam and the immigration from Muslim countries. Immigration of Muslims is a new phenomenon. Some single individuals came earlier, but a Swedish report on various religious groups from the beginning of the 1960s had nothing to report about Muslims.[41] The earliest Muslim groups arrived among the labour immigrants from Yugoslavia and Turkey during the 1960s. Among them were Bosnian Muslims and Albanians from Kosovo. Later on North Africans, Palestinians, Libanese, Muslim Indians (from Uganda), as well as smaller groups from other Asian and African countries have arrived. During the 1970s Iranian immigrants, escaping the regime of the

[40] Gustavsson: *Religionen i Sverige*, pp. 75–85.
[41] SOU 1963:39.

Shah, came to Sweden and Denmark. A second wave of Iranians, escaping military service in the Iran-Iraq war, followed during the 1980s. The Iranians have contributed to an increase in the number of Shia Muslims, but Iranians as a whole are religiously heterogeneous and far from all Iranians are Muslims.

The Muslim immigrants in Denmark have come mostly from Turkey and Pakistan. Since the cessation of labour immigration in the early 1970s their numbers have continued to increase, since Danish law admits family reunion. Finland has long had a Tatar minority, a group with a distinct cultural identity, which has not prevented it from being accepted in the labour market and integrated into the majority population.

In the Nordic countries there is a clear split in the attitudes toward Muslims. Above all, there is uncertainty as to how to interpret their cultural conduct and behaviour. The general level of knowledge about Islam in the Nordic societies is fairly low, and misgivings are felt concerning the immigrants' attitude to, and involvement with, the dominant political and religious movements in the Islamic world.

The Islamic immigrants in the Nordic societies do not make up a homogeneous group. Both *shia* and *sunni* are represented, but the antagonism between these movements is considerably less than in Islamic countries. They cooperate to a certain degree in Muslim associations and attend prayers together. Animosity between Muslim groups, however, is one reason why a mosque long planned in Stockholm has not been built.

The complications resulting from the encounter between the Muslims and the Nordic majority societies have only shallow roots in purely religious issues. All Nordic countries have an advanced law when it comes to religious freedom (the right to gather for religious purposes, freedom of expression etc.), and no formal obstacles exist to the exercise of religious rites. On the other hand, local reactions against plans to build mosques have been strong.

A study of religious minorities in the Swedish military services shows that the religious factor in some situations presents few problems. Religious variation is accepted by the military organization as such, and by the officers and the rank and file, even when Muslim believers are granted exceptional privileges in order to pray according to Koranic rules, and the requirements of Orthodox Jewish rules are recognized.[42] In line with this one can note the changing attitudes toward the deceased. Earlier, corpses were sent back to the homeland to be placed in holy soil, while they are now more often buried in the countries of immigration. Islamologist Jan Hjärpe's interpretation of this development suggests that this is rather a step in accommodation to the country of immigration and is part of a Swedization and Danization of Islam. This development reflects a change of Islam itself. The religion becomes spiritualized and the purely religious elements take a more central place, while Islam's secular role is diminished. It is therefore characteristic that Sufism, the religious variant of Islam, is on the increase.[43]

How should the Muslim ambition to build mosques in the Nordic countries and other non-Islamic countries be interpreted? Is this an expression of an Islamic offensive directed toward these societies? One interpretation is that this as an expression among Muslims of acceptance of the societies in which they live.

One central problem in the encounter between Muslims and Nordics is found in the secularization and privatization of religion in the Nordic societies. Collective religious worship is retreating and as a consequence open religious practice in public is often considered offensive.

Attempts at Creating Cultural Pluralism

In terms of ethnic composition, Denmark, Norway and Sweden have gone through a metamorphosis during the postwar period.

[42] Långström: "Invandrare i försvaret".
[43] Hjärpe: *Islams värld.*

Until 1940 these countries were linguistically and ethnically some of the most homogeneous countries in the world. The small autochthonous Sami (Lapp) and Finnish populations in Sweden and Norway hardly changed this picture, nor did the situation in South Jutland with "cohabiting" Danes and Germans. For example, the Swedish census of 1930 noted less than 1% of "foreign stock", and this category included Lapps and Finns.

Since then Denmark, Norway and Sweden have travelled a long way. Not only has there been a change in the ethnic composition as a consequence of immigration. There has also been a shift, at least in principle, towards acceptance of the right of immigrants to preserve their cultural traits. Sweden, and to some extent even Denmark and Norway, have embarked on an official policy of acceptance and even encouragement of cultural pluralism. Since this tendency has been most marked in Sweden—and also most complicated because of the large number of ethnic groups—it is natural to start by examining the Swedish experience.

It is a fact that the Swedish majority population never carried on any discourse on cultural issues with the Nordic and other European groups that arrived in the country in the 1940s and the 1950s. Only slowly did an understanding about the cultural ambitions of immigrant groups develop, and it took a long time before the consciousness matured into an understanding that the many refugees and economic migrants meant a cultural challenge to society. The established attitude was that immigrants should become Swedes, adopt Swedish manners and customs, and harmonize with Swedish society.

A statement by the Swedish Foreign Minister Östen Undén in 1945 serves to illustrate the official assimilationist stance towards the immigrant groups. In Parliament in January 1946, Undén commented on the arrival of approximately 30,000 Balts at the end of the war that it would be best if they returned to build up their home country, the Soviet Union. If they stayed in Sweden they were expected to become Swedish and behave as Swedes. It should be added that Undén's declaration was made at a time when the Soviet government was expressing a desire to gain control over the Baltic elements in Sweden.[44] Structurally, the Balts in Sweden were assimilated quickly, but they retained a strong collective identity and carried on traditions from their homeland. This was especially true of the Estonians who developed a rich and multifarious cultural and association life. So did the Latvians, although their much smaller number did not permit such a wide variety of ethnic institutions. For the Estonians the preservation of the language in exile was fundamental.[45]

How then could a society which had been so assimilationist and sceptical of making room for foreign cultures make a 180 degree turn and declare itself pluralistic? We can at least point to some important factors. First, there was a growing awareness that some groups that had arrived in Sweden during the late 1950s and the 1960s were not so easily integrated. While those immigrants who had come to the country during the 1940s and the 1950s were from a Central or West European background (industrialized and urbanized) which had at least some resemblance to Scandinavian lifestyles, those groups who started to arrive around 1960 and originated mainly from Turkey and Greece had rural backgrounds and substantially weaker educational backgrounds.

First, with these latter groups in mind, initiatives were taken in the mid-1960s within the government, and a task force, headed by Kjell Öberg, was appointed. Öberg's group reported directly to the National Labour Market Commission and the Ministry of Labour. They worked with unconventional methods, sought remedies and worked actively in contact with municipal boards and employers. They came up with and tested very concrete solutions (language training etc.).[46]

Secondly, in certain circles there gradually evolved a growing

[44] Runblom: "Baltutlämningen. Aktörer och beslutsfattare".
[45] Raag & Runblom (ed.): *Estländare i Sverige. Historia, språk, kultur.*
[46] Archive of the *Invandrarutredningen*, Riksarkivet, Stockholm.

awareness that the state had a moral responsibility for the well-being of people who had come to Sweden to work and who had decided to stay in the country. The very number of motions in the Swedish parliament in 1966, 1967 and 1968 testify to this new awareness. Many of these proposals were about educational and cultural support for ethnic groups, not least Balts.[47] Swedish authorities at last discovered and accepted the consequences of the fact that the population had a diverse cultural and linguistic composition.

Thirdly, there was international pressure on Sweden to exhibit a more flexible attitude to the linguistic and cultural maintenance of minorities. This pressure should perhaps not be over-emphasized, but there were clear signals from Finland. During the postwar years Finland had served as the main source of foreign labour for the Swedish labour market. In Finland there was fear what disastrous effects might follow from the large out-migration to Sweden. The emigration of Finnish men and women was perceived as a drain of blood and was regarded as parallel to the trans-Atlantic migration at the beginning of the century.

By the end of the 1960s the figures grew drastically, and the Finnish government felt the need to protect the country's economy. It became important to prepare Finns in Sweden for a return to Finland. This had deep cultural implications, and the language preservation of the Finnish speakers was a key issue. If the Finns in Sweden were able to preserve and strengthen their language, then the potential re-migration would be larger and the returning migrants' capacity to re-integrate in Finland greater. The Finns undertook measures both at home and abroad, and used the channels of the Nordic council to press for cooperation on certain regulations within the Nordic labour market.[48] Finland's demands on Sweden in

---

[47] Swedish Parliamentary Protocols and enclosures.

[48] One measure taken was the creation of the Institute of Migration (Siirtulaisinstitutti) in Turku, a research unit with one of its main tasks being to study the population movements between Finland and Sweden.

this question were important for the launching of the Swedish home language reform.

As a result of this change of direction immigrants were granted certain cultural rights. The cultural ambitions of immigrants were protected in the constitution. The Swedish Instrument of Government (*Regeringsformen*) of 1974 exhorts support for linguistic, religious and cultural groups who prefer to maintain their inherited characteristics.[49] A series of programs was designed, accepted and implemented. They included support for journals produced in immigrant languages and for instruction in home languages in the public school system, and even the right to participate in municipal elections.

The reforms designed to buttress the immigrants' ambitions to preserve their culture and give them greater elbow-room in Swedish society were accompanied by rhetoric. In Sweden the basis for this integration was summarized in the concepts "equality, freedom of choice, and cooperation" (*jämlikhet, valfrihet, samverkan*). Equality in this context was understood to mean parity between immigrants and Swedes in terms of rights, duties and opportunities. According to the freedom-of-choice goal, immigrants have the right to choose whether to retain their homeland culture, to "become Swedes", or to blend traits from the homeland and Swedish cultures. The cooperation goal aimed at concord between majority and minority populations. The three catchwords were repeated over and over again by Swedish members of government and officials on the state and local levels as the leading principles for the majority's relations to the immigrant minorities. However, these principles were decided on without much consideration by the legislature.[50] If time is taken to study the references to these principles, it is possible to notice shifting in-

[49] Regeringsformen 1974 (the Swedish Instrument of Government), Chapter 1, paragraph 2.

[50] David Schwarz has noted that immigration issues have been very little discussed in the Swedish parliament. Schwarz: *Svensk invandrar- och minoritetspolitik 1945–1968*.

terpretations. One clarification was given in 1986 when the main goals were repeated in a government proposition: immigrants were supposed to develop their cultural heritage "within the framework of the basic norms that are valid for human coexistence in our society."[51] It is hardly surprising that one could point at one arena after the other (court, school, public social assistance, etc.) where these principles have not been easy to apply.

In this context it may be of greater interest to mention briefly some of the reforms that have been effected in order to integrate immigrants into Swedish society. First, the National Aliens Commission (*Utlänningskommissionen*, 1944–1969) was replaced by a new Swedish Immigration Board. While the former had very much a supervisory role (residence and work permits, deportations, alien control), the new board was in addition supposed to take a more active role in promoting the welfare of immigrants and indeed did so. Its first general director, Kjell Öberg, set his mark on its first decade of existence and strongly advocated the immigrants' right to instruction in their home language and for their right to vote in Swedish elections.

During the late 1980s an ombudsman against ethnic discrimination (*Diskrimineringsombudsmannen*) was appointed. However, working in the traditional manner of the Swedish ombudsman institutions, he lacked, however, the authority to bring prosecutions or to act through the courts.

Nordic Immigration in Perspective

After having been emigration countries until the late 1920s, three of the five Nordic countries—namely Denmark, Norway and Sweden—developed into countries characterized by immigration in the postwar period. Of the other two, after the Second World War Finland sent many of her sons and daughters abroad in large numbers. Iceland too,

---

[51] Tydén: "Pluralismens gränser".

even after the war must be called a country of emigration, but the numbers were considerably smaller than during the mass emigration period in the 19th century. Thus, about 9,000 Icelandic citizens were living in the other Nordic countries in the late 1980s, while the total number of foreign citizens residing in Iceland in 1988 was 4,829.[52]

It is striking that the Scandinavian legacy of large-scale emigration has been almost entirely absent in the discussion of how societies should adjust to large bodies of newcomers. Finland, on the other hand, has pursued the policy of making its role permanent in terms of migration, namely by dispatching its surplus population overseas; the postwar experience is seen merely as another phase in a constant outflow that has earlier gone to Sweden, Russia and America. Finland's task during the last half century has been mainly to guard its own national interests: to find measures to control the outflow, to protect the emigrants' cultural interests abroad, and to prepare potential returnees for a new life in the homeland. Finland's ambitions to build bridges and maintain common ground with its overseas populations resembles corresponding actions from many mass-emigration countries after the turn of the century. President Urho Kekkonen, for example, took great pains to remind Finns abroad about their adherence to Suomi.

Since Sweden was the main target of the Finnish postwar exodus, migration issues have frequently been on the agenda in the official and semi-official relations between the two countries. Thus Finland has acted in much the same way as other countries that have felt (sometimes combined with relief) the burden of emigration. In Finland's case this has been all the easier, because a single country and moreover a neighbour, has taken the lion's share, and because the Nordic Council and other cooperation agencies have provided channels for communication and negotiation. In all Nordic postwar migration, the flow of Finns to Sweden was by far the largest single current. Moreover, the case of the Finnish-speaking Finn in Sweden,

[52] *Yearbook of Nordic Statistics* 1989/90 (NORD 1990:5), pp. 40–41.

has served as a precedent for other groups in their efforts to find a place in the new society.

The Finland-Sweden case underlines the relationship between foreign policy, immigration and immigrant policy, and this aspect is perhaps even more crucial when it comes to the treatment of refugees. Lack of research, at least up to this point, precludes an exhaustive answer to this question. Let it suffice here to dwell on some of the observations made above. Finland's delicate relations with Moscow inhibited the country from welcoming refugees from the east. Official Swedish attitudes towards the Baltic immigrants were long marked by a healthy respect for the Soviet Union. For example, in 1946 the Swedish Social Democrat government extradited some 160 Balts who had arrived in Sweden from the eastern front in German uniform before the armistice in May 1945. It did so despite strong protests from groups in parliament and vociferous criticism in the press.

Historians from Lund University have underscored that the postwar refugee concept was wrought in the genesis of the Cold War.[53] The immigration from Europe behind the Iron Curtain to the West must be seen in this context, and this circumstance brought to the fore the relatively eagerness in Scandinavia to receive East Europeans. A Norwegian researcher has hinted that not only humanitarian but also political motives were behind the Norwegian eagerness to receive Hungarians after the 1956 revolt. (Norway has been a member of NATO since 1949).[54] This assessment of refugees may even have made it more difficult for Asians or Africans to achieve refugee status since East Europeans (and Latin Americans for rather different reasons) had the status of "most-favoured nations."[55]

There is probably a connection between the development of soli-

[53] See e.g. Johansson: "The Refugee Experience in Europe after World War II: Some Theoretical and Empirical Considerations", and other Lund contributions to the volume.

[54] Thorud: *Norsk innvandringspolitikk 1860–1960*, pp. 118–119.

[55] Lundberg: *Flyktingskap. Latinamerikansk exil i Sverige och Västeuropa*, pp. 98–99.

darity with immigrants in Sweden and the country's global commit-
ment, perhaps most of all during Olof Palme's governments. One of
Palme's historic accomplishments was to open Sweden to the Third
World and support the struggle for liberation in Africa and Latin
America. Sweden was active in Santiago after the Chilean coup in
1973, and the Swedish embassy there became a haven for fugitives at
odds with the regime. It is difficult to say to what extent Swedish
support for democratic Chile influenced feelings towards Sweden in
Latin America. However, in the years after 1973, something like a
chain migration started from South America to Sweden. Immigrants
arrived not only from Chile, but from Bolivia, Brazil, Argentina and
elsewhere. Refugees who had already arrived in Sweden encouraged
others to join them. Thus, numerous Argentines made their way to
Sweden instead of to Latin countries where they would have found a
greater cultural affinity, but where they would have been forced into
a vicious circle of illegal jobs and unemployment.[56]

Glasnost, perestroika, and the wide-ranging political and social
changes in Eastern Europe 1989–1991 have brought new prospects
for the ethnic and cultural situation in the Nordic countries, too.
Scandinavia's geopolitical situation has changed, and within the new
framework of regionalism in Europe there are tendencies to re-estab-
lish old links and create new combinations. This has reverberations
for the ethnic minorities in the Nordic countries. New identities are
being shaped, and even the concept of *Norden* is undergoing a change.
This is not least the result of ambitions in Estonia, Latvia, Lithuania
to gain a foothold in Nordic cooperation, something they have to
some extent achieved already through occasional observer status at
Nordic Council meetings. It is likely that the Baltic countries, when
their recently acquired independence becomes more established, will
achieve a more permanent status in Nordic organizations. This would
have an effect on the identity-building around the Baltic Sea.

The lack of a history of colonialism in the Third World had un-

---

[56] María Luján Leiva: "Argentinare", pp. 493–95.

doubtedly affected the Nordic countries' relations to immigrant groups and the creation of multicultural societies. It is, however, interesting to see how old historical combinations around the Baltic influence immigration policy and the conditions of ethnic groups. The role of Denmark and Sweden as former regional great powers are reflected in attitudes to the Baltic groups. Estonians, especially, refer to the good old days of the late 16th and the 17th centuries, when Estonia was a Swedish province. Swedish rule is contrasted to the German, Tsarist, and Soviet regimes, sometimes with a romantic colouring.

Perestroika has led to a reactivation of support for the home countries by the Baltic immigrant groups in Sweden. The linguistic competence of exiles and their children has been used by the Swedish government and by Swedish firms in their contacts with the countries on the other side of the Baltic. Andres Küng, a Swedish-born Estonian writer, has even assumed the responsibility of serving as a member of the Estonian national assembly; other Baltic-Scandinavians have joined him in taking on roles to promote cooperation between the Baltic and Nordic countries.

The most dramatic consequence of postwar immigration is the change in the ethnic composition of Denmark, Norway and Sweden, the most conspicuous aspect of which is the presence of tens of thousands of immigrants from non-European countries. Their presence has brought to the fore issues of homeland identities and cultures.

LITERATURE

Ahlberg, Nora: *New Challenges, Old Strategies. Themes of Variation and Conflict among Pakistani Muslims in Norway,* Transactions of the Finnish Anthropological Society nr. 25, Helsinki 1990

Alopaeus, Marianne: *Drabbad av Sverige,* Stockholm 1983

Broberg, Gunnar, Runblom, Harald & Tydén, Mattias (eds.): *Judiskt liv i Norden,* Studia Multiethnica Upsaliensia, Uppsala 1988

Catomeris, Christian: *Gipskattor och positiv. Italienare i Stockholm 1896–1910*, Stockholm 1988

De Geer, Eric: *De finländska krigsbarnen i Sverige 1941–1948*, Föreningen Norden & Kulturfonden för Sverige och Finland, Stockholm 1986

De Geer, Eric: *Göteborgs invandrargeografi. De utländska medborgarnas regionala fördelning*, Uppsala Multiethnic Papers 16, Uppsala 1989

De Geer, Eric: *Migration och influensfält. Studier av emigration och intern migration i Finland och Sverige 1816–1972*, Uppsala 1977

Engelbrektsson, Ulla-Britt: *The Force of Tradition: Turkish Migrants at Home and Abroad*, Gothenburg Studies in Social Anthropology 1, Göteborg 1978

Finnäs, Fjalar: *Den finlandssvenska befolkningsutvecklingen 1950–1980. En analys av en språkgrupps demografiska utveckling och effekten av blandäktenskap*, Svenska litteratursällskapet i Finland, Helsingfors 1986

Grimnes, Ole Kristian: *Et flyktingesamfunn vokser fram. Nordmenn i Sverige 1940–1945*, Oslo 1969

Gustavsson, Göran: *Religionen i Sverige. Ett sociologiskt perspektiv*, Stockholm 1981

Hammar, Tomas: *Sverige åt svenskarna. Invandringspolitik, utlänningskontroll och asylrätt 1900–1932*, Stockholm 1964

Havrehed, Henrik: *De tyske flygtningene i Danmark 1945–1949*, Odense University Studies in History and the Social Sciences 107, Odense 1987

Hjärpe, Jan: *Islams värld*, Stockholm 1987

Indvandrerforskning i Danmark. Rapport fra udvalget vedrørende indvandrerforskning, Copenhagen 1983

Johansen, Per Ole: *Oss selv nærmest. Norge og jødene 1914–1943*, Oslo 1984

Johansson, Rune: "The Refugee Experience in Europe after World War II. Some Theoretical and Empirical Considerations", in Rystad, Göran (ed.): *The Uprooted: Forced Migration as an International Problem in the Post-War Era*, Lund 1990

Johansson, Rune & Persson, Hans-Åke (eds.): *Nordisk flyktingpolitik i världskrigens epok*, Lund 1989

Korkiassari, Jouni: *Hem till Finland. Sverige-finländarnas återflyttning*, Delegationen för invandrarforskning, Stockholm 1986

Kotsinas, Ulla-Britt: *Invandrare talar svenska*. Malmö 1985

Körmendi, Eszter & Melchior, Marianne: *Medgang og modgang. Overgangen fra Dansk Flygtningehjælp til kommunerne*, Socialforskningsinstitutet, Copenhagen 1987

Långström, Carl-Einar: "Invandrare i försvaret" (preliminary paper), Department of Theology, Uppsala University, Uppsala 1990

Leiva, María Luján: "Argentinare", in Svanberg, Ingvar & Runblom, Harald (eds.): *Det mångkulturella Sverige*, Second edition 1990

Lindberg, Hans: *Svensk flyktingpolitik under internationellt tryck 1936–1941*, Stockholm 1973

Lindqvist, Beatriz: *Drömmar i vardag och exil. Om chilenska flyktingars kulturella strategier*, Stockholm 1991

Lundberg, Ingrid & Svanberg, Ingvar: *Kulu. Utvandrarbygd i Turkiet.* Uppsala Multiethnic Papers, Uppsala 1992

Lundberg, Svante: *Flyktingskap. Latinamerikansk exil i Sverige och Västeuropa*, Stockholm 1989

Magnusson, Kjell: *Jugoslaver i Sverige. Invandrare och identitet i ett kultursociologiskt perspektiv*, Uppsala Multiethnic Papers 17, Uppsala 1989

Majava, Altti: "Finns in Sweden: Characteristics and Living Conditions", in Karni, Michael G. (ed.): *Finnish Diaspora I: Canada, South America, Africa, Australia and Sweden*, Toronto 1981

Næss, Ragnar: "Refugees & National Policies: The Norwegian Case", in Joly, Danièle & Cohen, Robin (ed): *Reluctant Hosts: Europe and its Refugees*, Aldershot 1989

Nelhans, Joachim: *Utlänningen på arbetsmarknaden*, Lund 1973

Nordbors rättigheter i Norden, Nordisk Ministerråd, Oslo 1986

Østergaard, Bent: *Indvandrernes danmarkshistorie*, Copenhagen 1983

Petersen, Hans-Uwe: "De nordiske lande og Hitler-flygtningene", in Johansson, Rune & Persson, Hans-Åke (ed): *Nordisk flyktingpolitik i världskrigens epok*, Lund 1989

Ploug, Niels: "Population Migration in the Nordic and EC-area", Socialforskningsinstitutet, Copenhagen, Working Paper 1991:2

Raag, Raimo & Runblom, Harald (eds.): *Estländare i Sverige. Historia, språk, kultur*, Uppsala Multiethnic Papers, Uppsala 1988

Runblom, Harald: "Baltutlämningen. Aktörer och beslutsfattare", in Raag, Raimo & Runblom, Harald (ed): *Estländare i Sverige. Historia, språk, kultur*, Uppsala Multiethnic Papers, Uppsala 1988

Rystad, Göran (ed.): *The Uprooted: Forced Migration as an International Problem in the Post-War Era*, Lund 1990

Sadik, Nafis (ed.): *Population Policies and Programmes. Lessons Learned from Two Decades of Experience*, New York & London 1991

Schierup, Carl-Ulrik & Ålund, Aleksandra: *Will they still be dancing? Integration and Ethnic Transformation among Yugoslav Immigrants in Scandinavia*, Stockholm 1987

Schwarz, David: *Svensk invandrar- och minoritetspolitik 1945–1968*, Stockholm 1971

Söderling, Ismo: "Efter de stora folkströmmarna till den multikulturella Norden", in *Den glemte Indvandring. Rapport från ett symposium om Nordisk migration 1989–09–27/2*, sine loco et anno

SOU [Sveriges Offentliga Utredningar] 1963:39

Svanberg, Ingvar: *Invandrare från Turkiet. Etnisk och sociokulturell variation*, Uppsala Multiethnic Papers 4, Uppsala 1988 (second edition)

Svanberg, Ingvar: "Sudettyskar", in Svanberg & Runblom (eds.): *Det mångkulturella Sverige*, Second edition 1990

Svanberg, Ingvar & Runblom, Harald (eds.): *Det mångkulturella Sverige. En handbok om etniska grupper och minoriteter*, Stockholm 1989. Second edition 1990

Swedner, Harald: *Invandrare i Malmö*. Forskningsrapport från invandrarutredningen. Ds In 1973:11. Stockholm 1973

Thorud, Espen, *Norsk innvandringspolitikk 1860–1960*, Institutt for rettssosiologi (Stencilskrift Nr. 48), Oslo 1989

Tydén, Mattias: "Pluralismens gränser", *Invandrare & Minoriteter* 6, 1990

Wadensjö, Eskil: *Immigration och samhällsekonomi*, Lund 1973

Widgren, Jonas: "International Migration and Regional Stability", *International Affairs* 66:4, 1990

Willerslev, Richard: *Den glemte indvandring: Den svenske indvandring til Danmark 1850–1914*, Copenhagen 1982

Yahil, Leni: *The Rescue of Danish Jewry. Test of a Democracy*, The Jewish Publication Society of America, Philadelphia 1969

Yearbook of Nordic Statistics 1989/90 (NORD 1990:5)

INDEX